The Complete Guide to
PLUMBING

Expanded Fourth Edition

Modern Materials and Current Codes

Creative Publishing international

MINNEAPOLIS, MINNESOTA
www.creativepub.com

Creative Publishing international

Copyright © 2008
Creative Publishing international, Inc.
400 First Avenue North, Suite 300
Minneapolis, Minnesota 55401
1-800-328-3895
www.creativepub.com

Printed in China

20 19 18 17 16 15

Library of Congress Cataloging-in-Publication Data

The complete guide to home plumbing : modern materials and current codes all new guide to working with gas pipe. -- Expanded 4th ed.
    p. cm.
  Summary: "Expanded 4th edition includes all standard plumbing projects, as well as new information on outdoor plumbing, PEX, and gas line hook ups"--Provided by publisher.
  At head of title: Black & Decker.
  ISBN-13: 978-1-58923-378-2 (soft cover)
  ISBN-10: 1-58923-378-6 (soft cover)
  1. Plumbing--Amateurs' manuals. 2. Dwellings--Remodeling--Amateurs' manuals. I. Title: Home plumbing. II. Title: Black & Decker, the complete guide to plumbing.

TH6124.C66 2008
696'.1--dc22

2008008636

The Complete Guide to Plumbing
Created by: The editors of Creative Publishing international, Inc., in cooperation with Black & Decker.
Black & Decker® is a trademark of The Black & Decker Corporation and is used under license.

President/CEO: Ken Fund

Home Improvement Group

Publisher: Bryan Trandem
Managing Editor: Tracy Stanley
Senior Editor: Mark Johanson
Editor: Jennifer Gehlhar

Creative Director: Michele Lanci-Altomare
Senior Design Managers: Jon Simpson, Brad Springer
Design Manager: James Kegley

Lead Photographer: Steve Galvin
Photo Coordinator: Joanne Wawra
Shop Manager: Bryan McLain
Shop Assistant: Cesar Fernandez Rodriguez
Technical Consultant: Joe Robillard

Production Managers: Linda Halls, Laura Hokkanen

Page Layout Artists: Laura Rades, Danielle Smith
Copy Editor: Ruth Strother
Photographers: Andrea Rugg, Joel Schnell
Shop Help: Scott Boyd, David Hartley

NOTICE TO READERS

For safety, use caution, care, and good judgment when following the procedures described in this book. The publisher and Black & Decker cannot assume responsibility for any damage to property or injury to persons as a result of misuse of the information provided.

The techniques shown in this book are general techniques for various applications. In some instances, additional techniques not shown in this book may be required. Always follow manufacturers' instructions included with products, since deviating from the directions may void warranties. The projects in this book vary widely as to skill levels required: some may not be appropriate for all do-it-yourselfers, and some may require professional help.

Consult your local building department for information on building permits, codes, and other laws as they apply to your project.

Contents

The Complete Guide to Plumbing

Introduction

Since first hitting bookstore shelves in 1998, *The Complete Guide to Home Plumbing* has established itself as the best-selling and most authoritative do-it-yourself home plumbing manual available. Now in its 4th edition, *The Complete Guide to Plumbing* is bigger and better than ever, and completely current with the current National Plumbing Code. In this comprehensive new volume, you will find all the practical information and know-how you need to understand, install, repair, replace, and maintain your home plumbing system safely and with confidence.

For this new edition, we have freshened up some of the meat-and-potatoes projects to reflect newer products and refinements to the methods. If you have ever installed a toilet before, read through the very first project in the book, "Replace a Toilet." You'll find a couple of new helpful hints that you haven't seen in the past. And if you are a follower of bathroom design trends, you won't want to miss our all-new sequences on installing urinals and bidets. These two fixtures are growing quickly in popularity for home usage. You won't find step-by-step information on either of these projects in any other home plumbing book.

Another unique feature of this 4th edition is the inclusion of some basic information on working with gas pipe, including a couple of gas projects. Working with gas pipe is not for everyone. It has the potential for danger and in some areas, homeowners are simply not allowed to install or service gas pipe or connections. But if you have the inclination and the approval to install a new branch line in your natural gas system or just to hook up a gas water heater, you'll find all the information you need right here.

For your convenience, you will find all of the step-by-step projects in the front of this book where they're easy to find. We've even ranked them more or less in order of popularity, according to the plumbing service pros we've spoken to. The indispensable information on tools, materials, and techniques is included in the back of the book for easy reference.

In preparing *The Complete Guide to Plumbing* we have tried to anticipate your situation and needs as accurately as possible. If at any time you find yourself stuck or a question arises that is not covered in this book, do not hesitate to contact a plumber or your local plumbing inspector.

The Home Plumbing System

Because most of a plumbing system is hidden inside walls and floors, it may seem to be a complex maze of pipes and fittings. In fact, home plumbing is simple and straightforward. Understanding how home plumbing works is an important first step toward doing routine maintenance and money-saving repairs.

A typical home plumbing system includes three basic parts: a water supply system, a fixture and appliance set, and a drain system. These three parts can be seen clearly in the photograph of the cut-away house on the opposite page.

Fresh water enters a home through a main supply line (1). This fresh water source is provided by either a municipal water company or a private underground well. If the source is a municipal supplier, the water passes through a meter (2) that registers the amount of water used. A family of four uses about 400 gallons of water each day.

Immediately after the main supply enters the house, a branch line splits off (3) and is joined to a water heater (4). From the water heater, a hot water line runs parallel to the cold water line to bring the water supply to fixtures and appliances throughout the house. Fixtures include sinks, bathtubs, showers, and laundry tubs. Appliances include water heaters,

dishwashers, clothes washers, and water softeners. Toilets and exterior sillcocks are examples of fixtures that require only a cold water line.

The water supply to fixtures and appliances is controlled with faucets and valves. Faucets and valves have moving parts and seals that eventually may wear out or break, but they are easily repaired or replaced.

Waste water then enters the drain system. It first must flow past a drain trap (5), a U-shaped piece of pipe that holds standing water and prevents sewer gases from entering the home. Every fixture must have a drain trap.

The drain system works entirely by gravity, allowing waste water to flow downhill through a series of large-diameter pipes. These drain pipes are attached to a system of vent pipes. Vent pipes (6) bring fresh air to the drain system, preventing suction that would slow or stop drain water from flowing freely. Vent pipes usually exit the house at a roof vent (7).

All waste water eventually reaches a main waste and vent stack (8). The main stack curves to become a sewer line (9) that exits the house near the foundation. In a municipal system, this sewer line joins a main sewer line located near the street. Where sewer service is not available, waste water empties into a septic system.

Water meters and main shutoff valves are located where the main water supply pipe enters the house. The water meter is the property of your local municipal water company. If the water meter leaks, or if you suspect it is not functioning properly, call your water company for repairs.

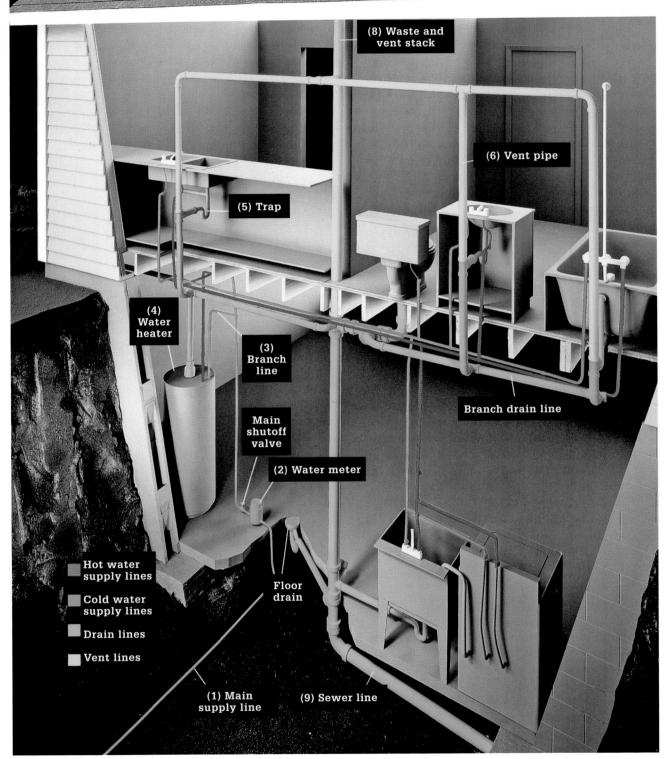

(7) Roof vent

(8) Waste and vent stack

(6) Vent pipe

(5) Trap

(4) Water heater

(3) Branch line

Main shutoff valve

(2) Water meter

Branch drain line

Hot water supply lines

Cold water supply lines

Drain lines

Vent lines

Floor drain

(1) Main supply line

(9) Sewer line

Water Supply System

Water supply pipes carry hot and cold water throughout a house. In homes built before 1960, the original supply pipes were usually made of galvanized iron. Newer homes have supply pipes made of copper. In most areas of the country, supply pipes made of rigid plastic or PEX are accepted by local plumbing codes.

Water supply pipes are made to withstand the high pressures of the water supply system. They have small diameters, usually ½" to 1", and are joined with strong, watertight fittings. The hot and cold lines run in tandem to all parts of the house. Usually, the supply pipes run inside wall cavities or are strapped to the undersides of floor joists.

Hot and cold water supply pipes are connected to fixtures or appliances. Fixtures include sinks, tubs, and showers. Some fixtures, such as toilets or hose bibs, are supplied only by cold water. Appliances include dishwashers and clothes washers. A refrigerator icemaker uses only cold water. Tradition says that hot water supply pipes and faucet handles are found on the left-hand side of a fixture, with cold water on the right.

Because it is pressurized, the water supply system is prone to leaks. This is especially true of galvanized iron pipe, which has limited resistance to corrosion.

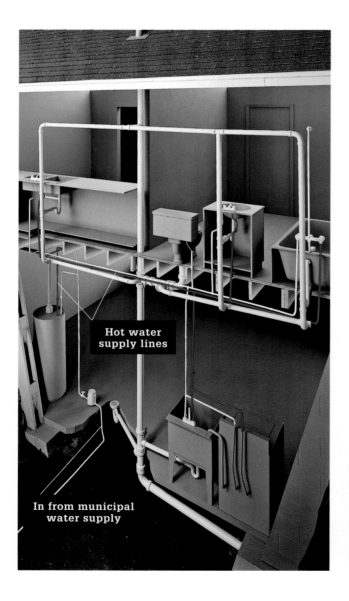

Hot water supply lines

In from municipal water supply

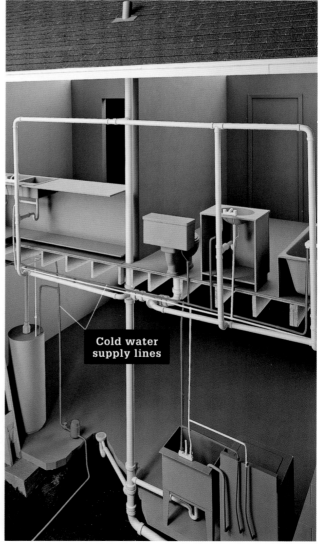

Cold water supply lines

Drain-Waste-Vent System

Drain pipes use gravity to carry waste water away from fixtures, appliances, and other drains. This waste water is carried out of the house to a municipal sewer system or septic tank.

Drain pipes are usually plastic or cast iron. In some older homes, drain pipes may be made of copper or lead. Because they are not part of the supply system, lead drain pipes pose no health hazard. However, lead pipes are no longer manufactured for home plumbing systems.

Drain pipes have diameters ranging from 1¼" to 4". These large diameters allow waste to pass through easily.

Traps are an important part of the drain system. These curved sections of drain pipe hold standing water, and they are usually found near any drain opening. The standing water of a trap prevents sewer gases from backing up into the home. Each time a drain is used, the standing trap water is flushed away and is replaced by new water.

In order to work properly, the drain system requires air. Air allows waste water to flow freely down drain pipes.

To allow air into the drain system, drain pipes are connected to vent pipes. All drain systems must include vents, and the entire system is called the drain-waste-vent (DWV) system. One or more vent stacks, located on the roof, provide the air needed for the DWV system to work.

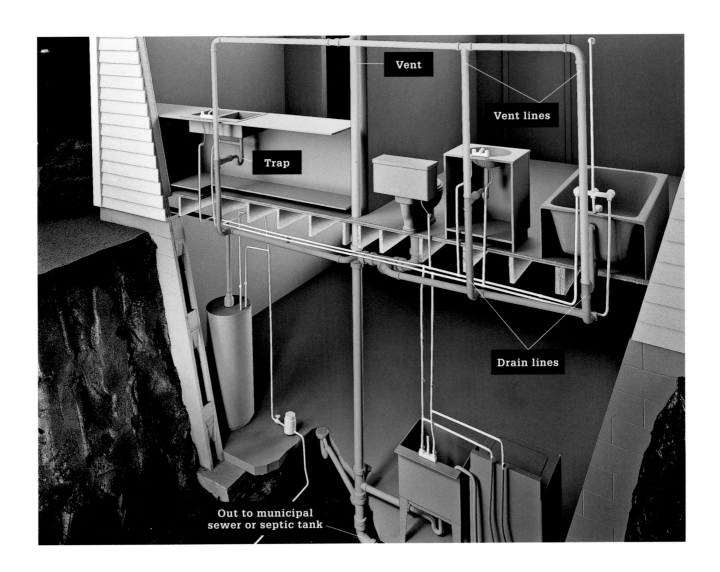

Vent

Vent lines

Trap

Drain lines

Out to municipal sewer or septic tank

Plumbing Fixtures

Although it might be a bit of a stretch to refer to any aspect of plumbing as glamorous or fun, installing fixtures like sinks and showers is the heart of the plumbing pursuit. It is the aspect of plumbing we naturally think of first, and in many cases the payoff is almost instantaneous.

In this section you will find photos and step-by-step instructions for the 27 plumbing fixture installations you, as a do-it-yourselfer, are most likely to attempt. The section with the most common fixture project by far is Toilets. From removal of the old unit to wrangling the new one into place, making all the hookups and even installing the seat, the entire project is laid out for you in full color photos. From there, you'll find a series of projects that move from kitchen to bath to laundry and back again, all shown in full detail.

In this chapter:

- Toilets
- Kitchen Faucets
- Kitchen Drains & Traps
- Dishwashers
- Food Disposers
- Water Heaters
- Bathroom Faucets
- Shower Kits
- Custom Shower Bases
- Alcove Tubs
- 3-Piece Tub Surrounds
- Sliding Tub Doors
- Bidets
- Urinals
- Water Softners
- Hot Water Dispensers
- Icemakers
- Pot Fillers
- Reverse-Osmosis Water Filters
- Freezeproof Sillcocks
- Pedestal Sinks
- Wall-Hung Vanities
- Vessel Sinks
- Integral Vanity Tops
- Kitchen Sinks
- Undermount Sinks
- Standpipe Drains

Toilets

You can replace a poorly functioning or inefficient toilet with a high-efficiency, high-quality new toilet in just a single afternoon. All toilets made since 1996 have been required to use 1.6 gallons or less per flush, which has been a huge challenge for the industry. Today, the most evolved 1.6-gallon toilets have wide passages behind the bowl and wide (3") flush valve openings—features that facilitate short, powerful flushes. This means fewer second flushes and fewer clogged toilets. These problems were common complaints of the first generation of 1.6-gallon toilets and continue to beleaguer inferior models today. See what toilets are available at your local home center in your price range, then go online and see what other consumers' experiences with those models have been. New toilets often go through a "de-bugging" stage when problems with leaks and malfunctioning parts are more common. Your criteria should include ease of installation,

good flush performance, and reliability. With a little research, you should be able to purchase and install a high-functioning economical gravity-flush toilet that will serve you well for years to come.

Tools & Materials ▸

Adjustable wrench	Supply tube
Bucket and sponge	Teflon tape
Channel-type pliers	Toilet seat bolts
Hacksaw	Toilet seat
Penetrating oil	Towels
Pliers	Utility knife
Putty knife	Wax ring
Rubber gloves	without flange
Screwdriver	Wax ring with flange

Replacing a toilet is simple, and the latest generation of 1.6-gallon water-saving toilets has overcome the performance problems of earlier models.

Choosing a New Toilet

Toilets have changed in recent years. There's a toilet to fit every style. You can even buy a square or stainless steel toilet, among many other new options. The new designs are efficient, durable, and less susceptible to clogs.

A toilet's style is partly affected by the way it's built. You have a number of options from which to choose:

Two-piece toilets have a separate water tank and bowl.

One-piece toilets have a tank and bowl made of one seamless unit.

Elongated bowls are roughly 2" longer than regular bowls.

Elevated toilets have higher seats, generally 18", rather than the standard 15".

You have a choice of two basic types of flush mechanisms: gravity- and pressure-assisted.

Gravity-assisted toilets allow water to rush down from an elevated tank into the toilet bowl. Federal law mandates that new toilets consume no more than 1.6 gallons of water per flush, less than half the volume used by older styles.

Pressure-assisted toilets rely on either compressed air or water pumps to boost flushing power.

Dual-flush systems feature two flush buttons on the top of the tank, allowing you to select either an 8-ounce flush for liquids or a 1.6-gallon flush for solids.

Toilets are available in a variety of styles and colors to suit almost any decor. Two-piece toilets are generally cheaper and come in a great assortment of styles and colors. Many high end models have a matching bidet available.

Gravity-assisted toilets are now designed with taller tanks and steeper bowl walls to increase the effects of gravity.

Pressure-assisted toilets are more expensive than standard toilets, but they can reduce your water usage significantly. The flush mechanism of a pressure-assisted toilet boosts the flushing power by using either compressed air or water pumps.

How to Remove a Toilet

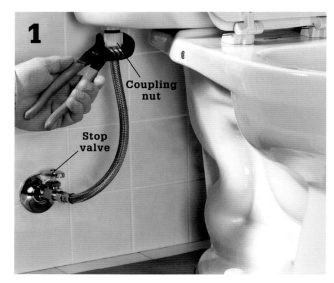

Coupling nut

Stop valve

Remove the old supply tube. First, turn off the water at the stop valve. Flush the toilet, holding the handle down for a long flush, and sponge out the tank. Unthread the coupling nut for the water supply below the tank using channel-type pliers. Use a wet/dry vac to clear any remaining water out of the tank and bowl.

Grip each tank bolt nut with a box wrench or pliers and loosen it as you stabilize each tank bolt from inside the tank with a large slotted screwdriver. If the nuts are stuck, apply penetrating oil to the nut and let it sit before trying to remove them again. You may also cut the tank bolts between the tank and the bowl with an open-ended hacksaw. Remove and discard the tank.

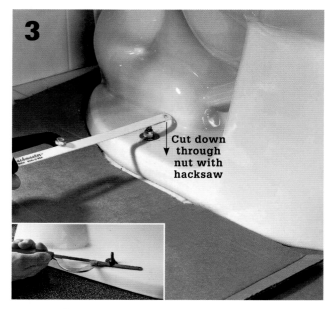

Cut down through nut with hacksaw

Remove the nuts that hold the bowl to the floor. First, pry off the bolt covers with a screwdriver. Use a socket wrench, locking pliers, or your channel-type pliers to loosen the nuts on the tank bolts. Apply penetrating oil and let it sit if the nuts are stuck, then take them off. As a last resort, cut the bolts off with a hacksaw by first cutting down through one side of the nut. Tilt the toilet bowl over and remove it.

Tip ▸

Removing an old wax ring is one of the more disgusting jobs you'll encounter in the plumbing universe (the one you see here is actually in relatively good condition). Work a stiff putty knife underneath the plastic flange of the ring (if you can) and start scraping. In many cases the wax ring will come off in chunks. Discard each chunk right away—they stick to everything. If you're left with a lot of residue, scrub with mineral spirits. Once clean, stuff a rag in a bag in the drain opening to block sewer gas.

How to Install a Toilet

Clean and inspect the old closet flange. Look for breaks or wear. Also inspect the flooring around the flange. If either the flange or floor is worn or damaged, repair the damage. Use a rag and mineral spirits to completely remove residue from the old wax ring. Place a rag-in-a-bag into the opening to block odors.

Tip ▸

If you will be replacing your toilet flange or if your existing flange can be unscrewed and moved, orient the new flange so the slots are parallel to the wall. This allows you to insert bolts under the slotted areas, which are much stronger than the areas at the ends of the curved grooves.

Insert new tank bolts (don't reuse old ones) into the openings in the closet flange. Make sure the heads of the bolts are oriented to catch the maximum amount of flange material.

Remove the wax ring and apply it to the underside of the bowl, around the horn. Remove the protective covering. Do not touch the wax ring. It is very sticky. Remove the rag-in-a-bag.

(continued)

4

Lower the bowl onto the flange, taking care not to disturb the wax ring. The holes in the bowl base should align perfectly with the tank bolts. Add a washer and tighten a nut on each bolt. Hand tighten each nut and then use channel-type pliers to further tighten the nuts. Alternate back and forth between nuts until the bowl is secure. *Do not overtighten.*

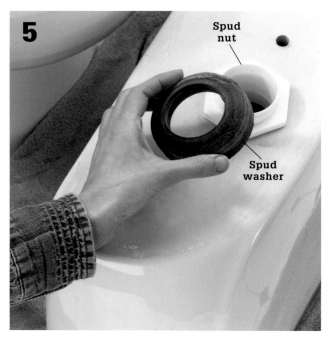

5

Spud nut

Spud washer

Attach the toilet tank. Some tanks come with a flush valve and a fill valve preinstalled. For models that do not have this, insert the flush valve through the tank opening and tighten a spud nut over the threaded end of the valve. Place a foam spud washer on top of the spud nut.

6

Threaded fill valve shank

Adjust the fill valve as directed by the manufacturer to set the correct tank water level height and install the valve inside the tank. Hand tighten the nylon lock nut that secures the valve to the tank (inset photo) and then tighten it further with channel-type pliers.

7

Intermediate nut goes between tank and bowl

With the tank lying on its back, thread a rubber washer onto each tank bolt and insert it into the bolt holes from inside the tank. Then, thread a brass washer and hex nut onto the tank bolts from below and tighten them to a quarter turn past hand tight. Do not overtighten.

8

Intermediate nut

Position the tank on the bowl, spud washer on opening, bolts through bolt holes. Put a rubber washer, followed by a brass washer and a wing nut, on each bolt and tighten these up evenly.

9

You may stabilize the bolts with a large slotted screwdriver from inside the tank, but tighten the nuts, not the bolts. You may press down a little on a side, the front, or the rear of the tank to level it as you tighten the nuts by hand. Do not overtighten and crack the tank. The tank should be level and stable when you're done. Do not overtighten.

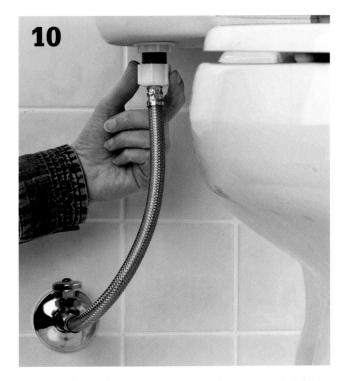

10

Hook up the water supply by connecting the supply tube to the threaded fill valve with the coupling nut provided. Turn on the water and test for leaks. Do not overtighten.

11

Attach the toilet seat by threading the plastic or brass bolts provided with the seat through the openings on the back of the rim and attaching nuts.

Kitchen Faucets

Most new kitchen faucets feature single-handle control levers and washerless designs that rarely require maintenance. Additional features include brushed metallic finishes, detachable spray nozzles, or even push-button controls.

Connect the faucet to hot and cold water lines with easy-to-install flexible supply tubes made from vinyl or braided steel. If your faucet has a separate sprayer, install the sprayer first. Pull the sprayer hose through the sink opening and attach to the faucet body before installing the faucet.

Where local codes allow, use plastic tubes for drain hookups. A wide selection of extensions and angle fittings lets you easily plumb any sink configuration. Manufacturers offer kits that contain all the fittings needed for attaching a food disposer or dishwasher to the sink drain system.

Tools & Materials ▸

Adjustable wrench	Scouring pad
Basin wrench or channel-type pliers	Scouring cleaner
	Plumber's putty
Hacksaw	Flexible vinyl or
Faucet	braided steel
Putty knife	supply tubes
Screwdriver	Drain components
Silicone caulk	Penetrating oil

Modern kitchen faucets tend to be single-handle models, often with useful features such as a pull-out head that functions as a sprayer. This Price Pfister™ model comes with an optional mounting plate that conceals sink holes when mounted on a predrilled sink flange.

Choosing a New Kitchen Faucet

You'll find many options when choosing a new kitchen faucet. The best place to start the process is with your sink. In the past, most faucets were mounted directly to the sink deck, which had three or four predrilled holes to accommodate the faucets, spout, sprayer, and perhaps a liquid soap dispenser or an air gap for your dishwasher. Modern kitchen faucets don't always conform to this setup, with many of them designed to be installed in a single hole in the sink deck or in the countertop. If you plan to keep your old sink, look for a faucet that won't leave empty holes in the deck. Generally, it's best to replace like for like, but unfilled stainless sink holes can be filled with snap-in plugs or a soap dispenser.

The two most basic kitchen faucet categories are single-handle and two-handle. Single-handle models are much more popular now because you can adjust the water temperature easily with just one hand.

Another difference is in the faucet body. Some faucets have the taps and the spout mounted onto a faucet body so the spacing between the tailpieces is preset. Others, called widespread faucets, have independent taps and spouts that can be configured however you please, as long as the tubes connecting the taps to the spouts reach. This type is best if you are installing the faucet in the countertop (a common way to go about it with new countertops such as solid surface, quartz, or granite).

In the past, kitchen faucets almost always had a remote pull-out sprayer. The sprayer was attached to the faucet body with a hose directly below the mixing valve. While this type of sprayer is still fairly common, many faucets today have an integral pull-out spout that is very convenient and less prone to failure than the old-style sprayers.

A single-handle, high arc faucet with traditional remote sprayer. The mounting plate is decorative and optional.

Single-handle faucets may require four holes, as does this model with its side sprayer and matching soap/lotion dispenser.

Two-handled faucets are less common, but remain popular choices for traditional kitchens. The gooseneck spout also has a certain elegance, but avoid this type if you have a shallow sink that's less than 8" deep.

A single-handle faucet with pull-out spray head requires only one hole in your sink deck or countertop—a real benefit if your sink is not predrilled or if it is an undermount model.

How to Remove an Old Faucet

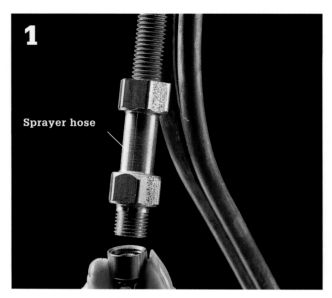

Sprayer hose

To remove the old faucet, start by clearing out the cabinet under the sink and laying down towels. Turn off the hot and cold stop valves and open the faucet to make sure the water is off. Detach the sprayer hose from the faucet sprayer nipple and unscrew the retaining nut that secures the sprayer base to the sink deck. Pull the sprayer hose out through the sink deck opening.

Mounting nut

Spray the mounting nuts that hold the faucet or faucet handles (on the underside of the sink deck) with penetrating oil for easier removal. Let the oil soak in for a few minutes.

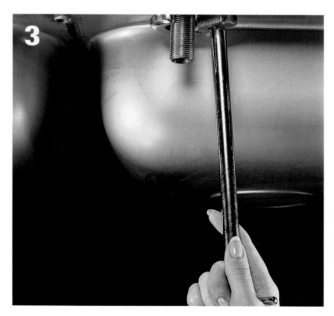

Unhook the supply tubes at the stop valves. Don't reuse old chrome supply tubes. If the stops are missing or unworkable, replace them. Then remove the coupling nuts and the mounting nuts on the tailpieces of the faucet with a basin wrench or channel-type pliers.

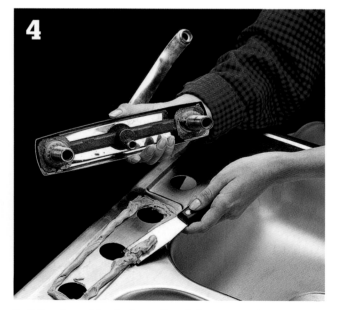

Pull the faucet body from the sink. Remove the sprayer base if you wish to replace it. Scrape off old putty or caulk with a putty knife and clean off the sink with a scouring pad and an acidic scouring cleaner like Bar Keeper's Friend®. *Tip: Scour stainless steel with a back and forth motion to avoid leaving unsightly circular markings.*

How to Install a Kitchen Sink Faucet

Shut off hot and cold water at the faucet stop valves. Assemble the parts of the deck plate that cover the outer mounting holes in your sink deck (unless you are installing a two-handle faucet, or mounting the faucet directly to the countertop, as in an undermount sink situation). Add a ring of plumber's putty in the groove on the underside of the base plate.

Set the base plate onto the sink flange so it is correctly aligned with the predrilled holes in the flange. From below, tighten the wing nuts that secure the deck plate to the sink deck.

Retract the pullout hose by drawing it out through the faucet body until the fitting at the end of the hose is flush with the bottom of the threaded faucet shank. Insert the shank and the supply tubes down through the top of the deck plate.

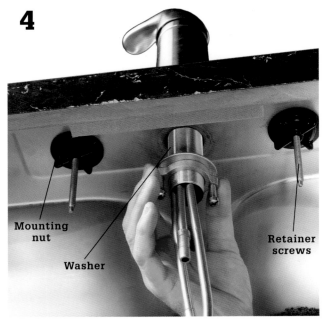

Slip the mounting nut and washer over the free ends of the supply tubes and pullout hose, then thread the nut onto the threaded faucet shank. Hand tighten. Tighten the retainer screws with a screwdriver to secure the faucet.

(continued)

Slide the hose weight onto the pullout hose (the weight helps keep the hose from tangling and it makes it easier to retract).

Connect the end of the pullout tube to the outlet port on the faucet body using a quick connector fitting.

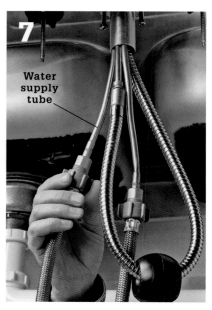

Water supply tube

Hook up the water supply tubes to the faucet inlets. Make sure the lines are long enough to reach the supply risers without stretching or kinking.

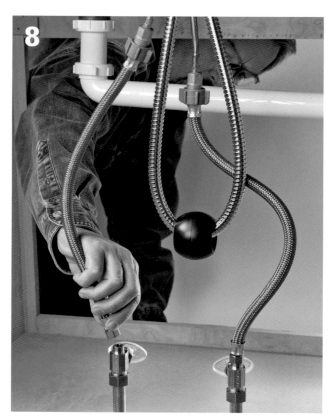

Connect the supply lines to the supply risers at the stop valves. Make sure to get the hot lines and cold lines attached correctly.

Attach the spray head to the end of the pullout hose and turn the fitting to secure the connection. Turn on water supply and test. *Tip: Remove the aerator in the tip of the spray head and run hot and cold water to flush out any debris.*

Variation: One-Piece Faucet with Sprayer ▶

Apply a thick bead of silicone caulk to the underside of the faucet base and then insert the tailpieces of the faucet through the appropriate holes in the sink deck. Press down lightly on the faucet to set it in the caulk.

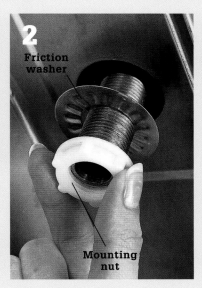

Friction washer
Mounting nut

Slip a friction washer onto each tailpiece and then hand tighten a mounting nut. Tighten the mounting nut with channel-type pliers or a basin wrench. Wipe up any silicone squeeze-out on the sink deck with a wet rag before it sets up.

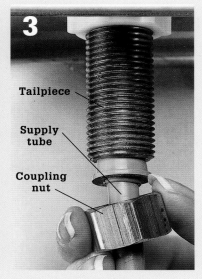

Tailpiece
Supply tube
Coupling nut

Connect supply tubes to the faucet tailpieces. Make sure the tubes you buy are long enough to reach the stop valves and that the coupling nuts will fit the tubes and tailpieces.

Sprayer tailpiece

Apply a ¼" bead of plumber's putty or silicone caulk to the underside of the sprayer base. With the base threaded onto the sprayer hose, insert the tailpiece of the sprayer through the opening in the sink deck.

Plumber's putty
Friction washer
Mounting nut

From beneath, slip the friction washer over the sprayer tailpiece and then screw the mounting nut onto the tailpiece. Tighten with channel-type pliers or a basin wrench. Wipe any excess putty or caulk on the sink deck from around the base.

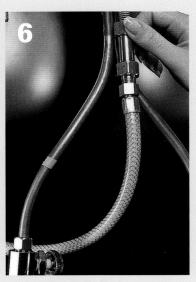

Screw the sprayer hose onto the hose nipple on the bottom of the faucet. Hand tighten and then give the nut one quarter turn with channel-type pliers or a basin wrench. Turn on the water supply at the shutoff, remove the aerator, and flush debris from the faucet.

Kitchen Drains & Traps

Kitchen sink drains don't last forever, but on the plus side, they're very easy and inexpensive to replace. The most common models today are made of PVC plastic pipe and fittings held together with slip fittings. In addition to making the installation fairly forgiving, the slip fitting makes the drain easy to disassemble if you get a clog. The project shown here is a bit unusual by today's standards, in that it does not include either a dishwasher drain or a garbage disposer. But you will see how to add each of these drain systems to your kitchen sink in the following two chapters.

You can buy the parts for the kitchen drain individually (you can usually get better quality materials this way) or in a kit (see photo, next page). Because most kitchen sinks have two bowls, the kits include parts for plumbing both drains into a shared trap, often with a baffle in the T-fitting where the outlet line joins with the tailpiece from the other bowl. If you are installing a disposer, consider installing individual traps to eliminate the baffle, which reduces the flow capacity by half (see page 34).

Tools & Materials ▸

Flat screwdriver
Spud wrench
Trap arm
Mineral spirits
Cloth
Strainer kit
Plumber's putty

Teflon tape
Washers
Waste-T fitting
S- or P-trap

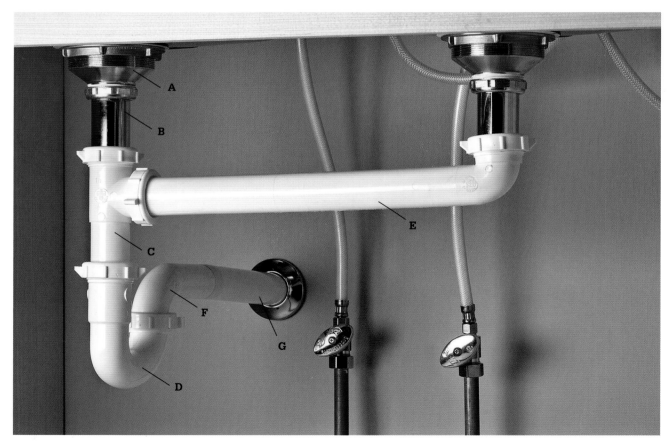

Kitchen sink drains include a strainer basket (A), tailpiece (B), continuous waste T (C), P- or S-trap (D), outlet drain lines (E), trap arm (F), and wall stubout (G).

Drain Kits ▸

Kits for installing a new sink drain include all the pipes, slip fittings, and washers you'll need to get from the sink tailpieces (most kits are equipped for a double bowl kitchen sink) to the trap arm that enters the wall or floor. For wall trap arms, you'll need a kit with a P-trap. For floor drains. you'll need an S-trap. Both drains normally are plumbed to share a trap. Chromed brass or PVC with slip fittings let you adjust the drain more easily and pull it apart and then reassemble if there is a clog. Kitchen sink drains and traps should be 1½" o.d. pipe—the 1¼" pipe is for lavatories and doesn't have enough capacity for a kitchen sink.

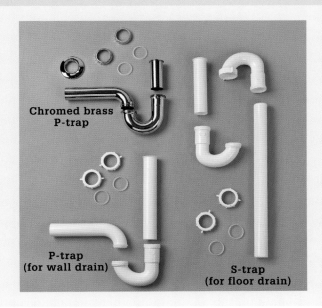

Chromed brass P-trap

P-trap (for wall drain)

S-trap (for floor drain)

Tips for Choosing Drains ▸

Wall thickness varies in sink drain pipes. The thinner plastic material is cheaper and more difficult to obtain a good seal with the thicker, more expensive tubing. The thin product is best reserved for lavatory drains, which are far less demanding.

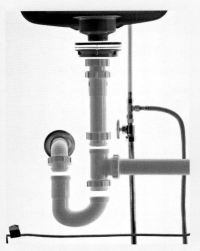

Slip joints are formed by tightening a male-threaded slip nut over a female-threaded fitting, trapping and compressing a beveled nylon washer to seal the joint.

Use a spud wrench to tighten the strainer body against the underside of the sink bowl. Normally, the strainer flange has a layer of plumber's putty to seal beneath it above the sink drain, and a pair of washers (one rubber, one fibrous) to seal below.

How to Hook Up a Kitchen Sink Drain

If you are replacing the sink strainer body, remove the old one and clean the top and bottom of the sink deck around the drain opening with mineral spirits. Attach the drain tailpiece to the threaded outlet of the strainer body, inserting a nonbeveled washer between the parts if your strainer kits include one. Lubricate the threads or apply Teflon tape so you can get a good, snug fit.

Apply plumber's putty around the perimeter of the drain opening and seat the strainer assembly into it. Add washers below as directed and tighten the strainer locknut with a spud wrench (see photo, previous page) or by striking the mounting nubs at the top of the body with a flat screwdriver.

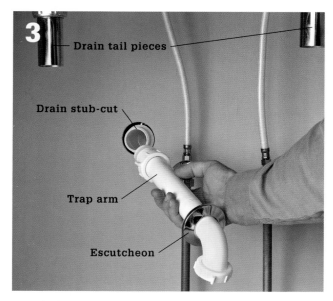

Attach the trap arm to the male-threaded drain stubout in the wall, using a slip nut and beveled compression washer. The outlet for the trap arm should point downward. *Note: The trap arm must be higher on the wall than any of the horizontal lines in the set-up, including lines to dishwasher, disposer, or the outlet line to the second sink bowl.*

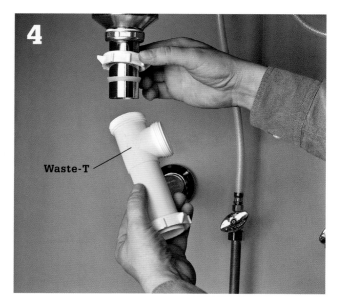

Attach a waste-T-fitting to the drain tailpiece, orienting the opening in the fitting side so it will accept the outlet drain line from the other sink bowl. If the waste-T is higher than the top of the trap arm, remove it and trim the drain tailpiece.

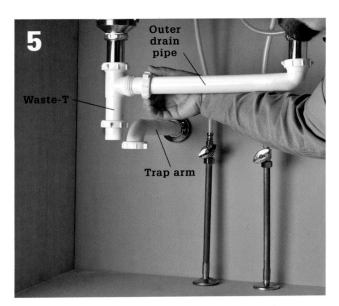

5

Outer drain pipe

Waste-T

Trap arm

Joint the short end of the outlet drain pipe to the tailpiece for the other sink bowl and then attach the end of the long run to the opening in the waste-T. The outlet tube should extend into the T ½" or so—make sure it does not extend in far enough to block water flow from above.

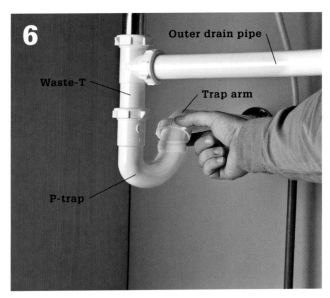

6

Outer drain pipe

Waste-T

Trap arm

P-trap

Attach the long leg of a P-trap to the waste-T and attach the shorter leg to the downward-facing opening of the trap arm. Adjust as necessary and test all joints to make sure they are still tight, and then test the system.

Variation: Drain in Floor ▸

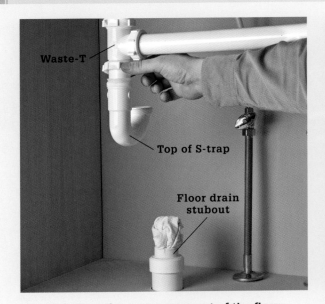

Waste-T

Top of S-trap

Floor drain stubout

If your drain stubout comes up out of the floor instead of the wall, you'll need an S-trap to tie into it instead of a P-trap. Attach one half of the S-trap to the threaded bottom of the waste-T.

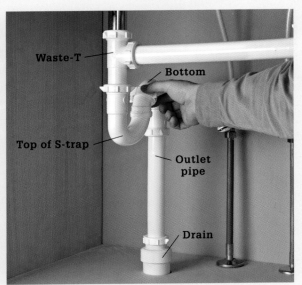

Waste-T

Bottom

Top of S-trap

Outlet pipe

Drain

Attach the other half of the S-trap to the stubout with a slip fitting. This should result in the new fitting facing downward. Join the halves of the S-trap together with a slip nut, trimming the unthreaded end if necessary.

Dishwashers

A dishwasher that's past its prime may be inefficient in more ways than one. If it's an old model, it probably wasn't designed to be very efficient to begin with. But more significantly, if it no longer cleans effectively, you're probably spending a lot of time and hot water pre-rinsing the dishes. This alone can consume more energy and water than a complete wash cycle on a newer machine. So even if your old dishwasher still runs, replacing it with an efficient new model can be a good green upgrade.

In terms of sizing and utility hookups, dishwashers are generally quite standard. If your old machine is a built-in and your countertops and cabinets are standard sizes, most full-size dishwashers will fit right in. Of course, you should always measure the dimensions of the old unit before shopping for a new one to avoid an unpleasant surprise at installation time. Also be sure to review the manufacturer's instructions before starting any work.

Tools & Materials ▸

Screwdrivers
Adjustable wrench
2-ft. level
⅝" automotive heater hose
Automotive heater hose
4"-length of ½" copper tubing

Cable connector
Teflon tape
Hose clamps
Wire connectors
Carpet scrap
Bowl

Replacing an old, inefficient dishwasher is a straightforward project that usually takes just a few hours. The energy savings begin with the first load of dishes and continue with every load thereafter.

Efficient Loading ▸

To get the best circulation of water for effective wash action, follow these tips when loading dishes:

- Make sure dishes are loaded so water can reach all of the soiled surfaces.
- Be sure that larger items are not blocking smaller items from the wash action.
- Place all items in both racks so that they are separated and face the center of the dishwasher. This will help to ensure that water reaches all soiled surfaces.
- Place glasses with the open end facing downward to allow proper washing action.
- Do not place glasses over the tines, but between them. This will allow the glasses to lean toward the spray arm and will improve washing. It also promotes drying by reducing the amount of water remaining on the top of the glass after the wash cycle is complete.
- Do not allow flatware to "nest." This prevents proper water distribution between the surfaces.
- Load flatware, except knives, with some handles up and some down to prevent nesting. For safety, knives should always be loaded handles up.

How to Replace an Inefficient Dishwasher

Start by shutting off the electrical power to the dishwasher circuit at the service panel. Also, turn off the water supply at the shutoff valve, usually located directly under the floor.

Disconnect old plumbing connections. First unscrew the front access panel. Once the access panel is removed, disconnect the water supply line from the L-fitting on the bottom of the unit. This is usually a brass compression fitting, so just turning the compression nut counterclockwise with an adjustable wrench should do the trick. Use a bowl to catch any water that might leak out when the nut is removed.

Disconnect old wiring connections. The dishwasher has an integral electrical box at the front of the unit where the power cable is attached to the dishwasher's fixture wires. Take off the box cover and remove the wire connectors that join the wires together.

Disconnect the discharge hose, which is usually connected to the dishwasher port on the side of the garbage disposer. To remove it, just loosen the screw on the hose clamp and pull it off. You may need to push this hose back through a hole in the cabinet wall and into the dishwasher compartment so it won't get caught when you pull the dishwasher out.

Detach the unit surrounding cabinets before you pull out the unit. Remove the screws that hold the brackets to the underside of the countertop. Then put a piece of cardboard or old carpet under the front legs to protect the floor from getting scratched, and pull the dishwasher out.

First, prepare the new dishwasher. Tip it on its back and attach the new L-fitting into the threaded port on the solenoid. Apply some Teflon tape or pipe sealant to the fitting threads before tightening it in place to prevent possible leaks.

Attach a length of new automotive heater hose, usually ⅝" diameter, to the end of the dishwasher's discharge hose nipple with a hose clamp. The new hose you are adding should be long enough to reach from the discharge nipple to the port on the side of the kitchen sink garbage disposer.

Prepare for the wiring connections. Like the old dishwasher, the new one will have an integral electrical box for making the wiring connections. To gain access to the box, just remove the box cover. Then install a cable connector on the back of the box and bring the power cable from the service panel through this connector. Power should be shut off at the main service panel at all times.

(continued)

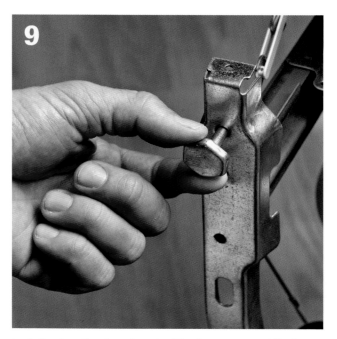

9

Install a leveling leg at each of the four corners while the new dishwasher is still on its back. Just turn the legs into the threaded holes designed for them. Leave about ½" of each leg projecting from the bottom of the unit. These will have to be adjusted later to level the appliance. Tip the appliance up onto the feet and slide it into the opening. Check for level in both directions and adjust the feet as required.

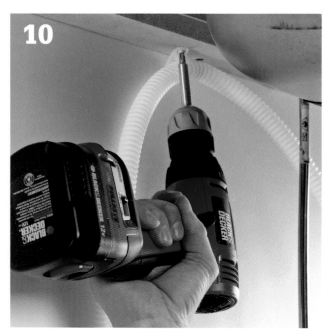

10

Once the dishwasher is level, attach the brackets to the underside of the countertop to keep the appliance from moving. Then pull the discharge hose into the sink cabinet and install it so there's a loop that is attached with a bracket to the underside of the countertop. This loop prevents waste water from flowing from the disposer back into the dishwasher.

Lengthening a Discharge Hose ▸

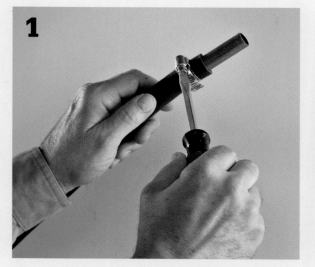

1

If the discharge hose has to be modified to fit onto the disposer port, first insert a 4"-long piece of ½" copper tubing into the hose and hold it in place with a hose clamp. This provides a nipple for the rubber adapter that fits onto the disposer.

2

Clamp the rubber disposer adapter to the end of the copper tubing nipple. Then tighten the hose clamp securely.

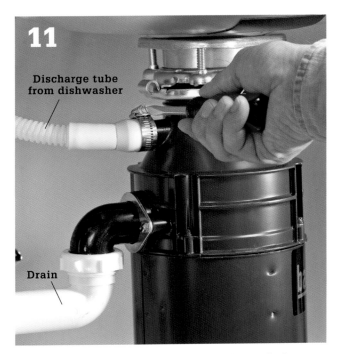

11

Discharge tube from dishwasher

Drain

Push the adapter over the disposer's discharge nipple and tighten it in place with a hose clamp. If you don't have a disposer, this discharge hose can be clamped directly to a modified sink tailpiece that's installed below a standard sink strainer.

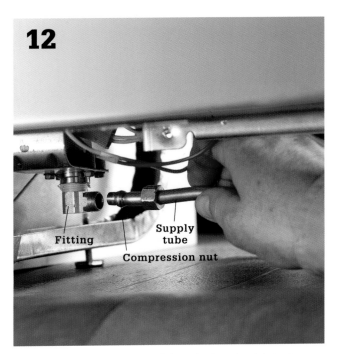

12

Fitting

Supply tube

Compression nut

Adjust the L-fitting on the dishwasher's water inlet valve until it points directly toward the water supply tubing. Then lubricate the threads slightly with a drop of dishwashing liquid and tighten the tubing's compression nut onto the fitting. Use an adjustable wrench and turn the nut clockwise.

13

Complete the electrical connections by tightening the connector's clamp on the cable and then join the power wires to the fixture wires with wire connectors. Attach the ground wire (or wires) to the grounding screw on the box, and replace the cover.

14

Install the access panel, usually by hooking it on a couple of prongs just below the dishwasher's door. Install the screws (if any) that hold it in place, and turn on the water and power supplies. Replace the toe-kick panel at the bottom of the dishwasher.

Food Disposers

Food disposers are standard equipment in the modern home, and most of us have come to depend on them to macerate our plate leavings and crumbs so they can exit the house along with waste water from the sink drain. If your existing disposer needs replacing, you'll find that the job is relatively simple, especially if you select a replacement appliance that is the same model as the old one. In that case, you can probably reuse the existing mounting assembly, drain sleeve, and drain plumbing.

Most food disposers are classified as "continuous feed" because they can only operate when an ON/OFF switch on the wall is being actively held down. Let go of the switch, and the disposer stops. Each appliance has a power rating between 1/3 and 1 HP (horsepower). More powerful models bog down less under load and the motors last longer because they don't have to work as hard. They are also costlier.

Disposers are hardwired to a switch mounted in an electrical box in the wall above the countertop. If your kitchen is not equipped for this, consult a wiring guide or hire an electrician. The actual electrical hookup of the appliance is quite simple (you only have to join two wires) but do hire an electrician if you are not comfortable with the job.

Tools & Materials ▸

Screwdriver
Channel-type pliers
Spud wrench (optional)
Hammer
Hacksaw or tubing cutter
Kitchen drain supplies
Drain auger

Putty knife
Mineral spirits
Plumber's putty
Wire caps
Hose clamps
Threaded Y-fitting
Electrical tape

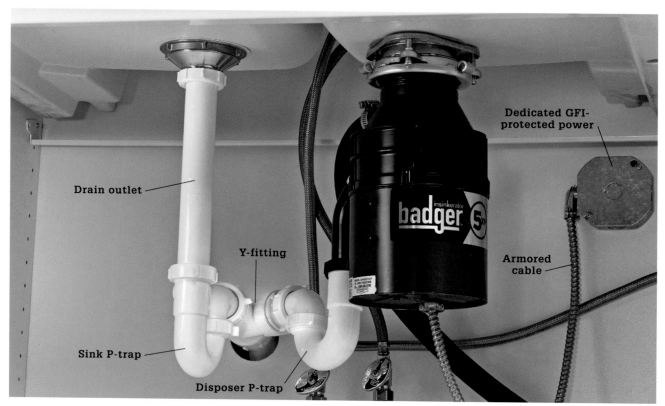

Drain outlet

Y-fitting

Sink P-trap

Disposer P-trap

Dedicated GFI-protected power

Armored cable

A properly functioning food disposer that's used correctly can actually help reduce clogs by ensuring that large bits of organic matter don't get into the drain system by accident. Many plumbers suggest using separate P-traps for the disposer and the drain outlet tube as shown here.

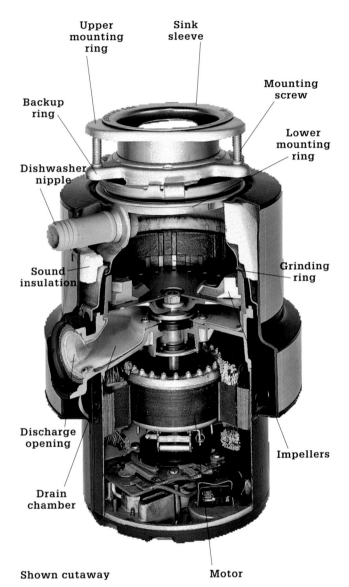

Upper mounting ring
Sink sleeve
Mounting screw
Backup ring
Lower mounting ring
Dishwasher nipple
Sound insulation
Grinding ring
Discharge opening
Impellers
Drain chamber
Motor

Shown cutaway

A food disposer grinds food waste so it can be flushed away through the sink drain system. A quality disposer has a ½–horsepower, self-reversing motor that will not jam. Other features to look for include foam sound insulation, a grinding ring, and overload protection that allow the motor to be reset if it overheats. Better food disposers have a 5-year manufacturer's warranty.

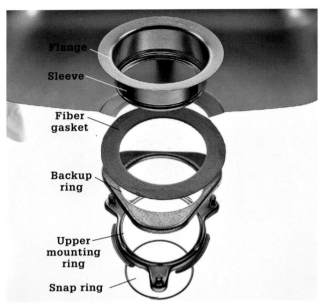

Flange
Sleeve
Fiber gasket
Backup ring
Upper mounting ring
Snap ring

The disposer is attached directly to the sink sleeve, which comes with the disposer and replaces the standard sink strainer. A snap ring fits into a groove around the sleeve of the strainer body to prevent the upper mounting ring and backup ring from sliding down while the upper mounting ring is tightened against the backup ring with mounting screws. A fiber gasket seals the connection from beneath the sink.

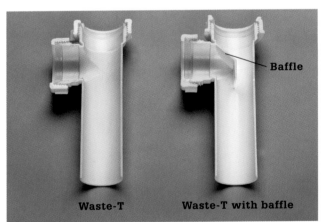

Baffle

Waste-T   **Waste-T with baffle**

Kitchen and drain tees are required to have a baffle if the tee is connected to a dishwasher or disposer. The baffle is intended to prevent discharge from finding its way up the drain and into the sink. However, the baffle also reduces the drain flow capacity by half, which can cause the dishwasher or disposer to back up. You cannot, by most codes, simply replace the tee with another that has no baffle. The safest way to get around the problem is to run separate drains and traps to a Y-fitting at the trap arm (as shown on previous page).

How to Install a Food Disposer

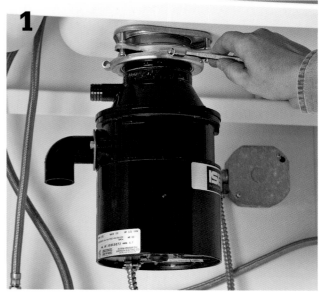

Remove the old disposer if you have one. You'll need to disconnect the drain pipes and traps first. If your old disposer has a special wrench for the mounting lugs, use it to loosen the lugs. Otherwise, use a screwdriver. If you do not have a helper, place a solid object directly beneath the disposer to support it before you begin removal. *Important: Shut off electrical power at the main service panel before you begin removal. Disconnect the wire leads, cap them, and stuff them into the electrical box.*

Tip ▶

Alternate: If you are installing a disposer in a sink that did not previously have one, remove the old sink strainer and drain tailpiece. Scrape up any old plumbers putty and clean the sink thoroughly around the drain opening with mineral spirits.

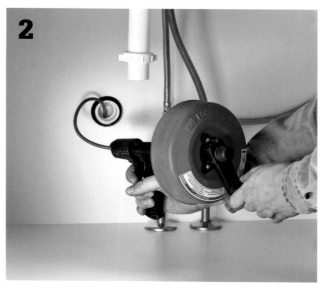

Clear the drain lines all the way to the branch drain before you begin the new installation. Remove the trap and trap arm first.

Upper mounting ring

Lower mounting ring

Snap ring

Disassemble the mounting assembly and then separate the upper and lower mounting rings and the backup ring. Also remove the snap ring from the sink sleeve. See photo, previous page.

4

Press the flange of the sink sleeve for your new disposer into a thin coil of plumber's putty that you have laid around the perimeter of the drain opening. The sleeve should be well-seated in the coil.

Sink sleeve

5

Fiber gasket

Sink sleeve

Backup ring

Slip the fiber gasket and then the backup ring onto the sink sleeve, working from inside the sink base cabinet. Make sure the backup ring is oriented the same way it was before you disassembled the mounting assembly.

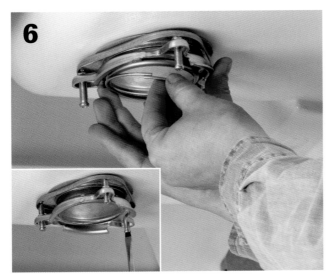

6

Insert the upper mounting ring onto the sleeve with the slotted ends of the screws facing away from the backup ring so you can access them. Then, holding all three parts at the top of the sleeve, slide the snap ring onto the sleeve until it snaps into the groove. Tighten the three mounting screws on the upper mounting ring until the tips press firmly against the backup ring (inset photo). It is the tension created by these screws that keeps the disposer steady and minimizes vibrating.

7

Make electrical connections before you mount the disposer unit on the mounting assembly. Shut off the power at the service panel if you have turned it back on. Remove the access plate from the disposer. Attach the white and black feeder wires from the electrical box to the white and black wires (respectively) inside the disposer. Twist a small wire cap onto each connection and wrap it with electrical tape for good measure. Also attach the green ground wire from the box to the grounding terminal on your disposer.

(continued)

Knock out the plug in the disposer port if you will be connecting your dishwasher to the disposer. If you have no dishwasher, leave the plug in. Insert a large flathead screwdriver into the port opening and rap it with a mallet. Retrieve the knock plug from inside the disposer canister.

Hang the disposer from the mounting ring attached to the sink sleeve. To hang it, simply lift it up and position the unit so the three mounting ears are underneath the three mounting screws and then spin the unit so all three ears fit into the mounting assembly. Wait until after the plumbing hookups have been made to lock the unit in place.

Attach the discharge tube to the disposer according to the manufacturer's instructions. It is important to get a very good seal here, or the disposer will leak. Go ahead and spin the disposer if it helps you access the discharge port.

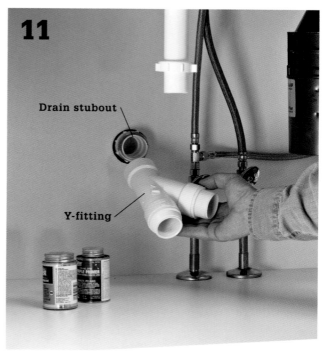

Attach a Y-fitting at the drain stubout. The Y-fitting should be sized to accept a drain line from the disposer and another from the sink. Adjust the sink drain plumbing as needed to get from the sink P-trap to one opening of the Y.

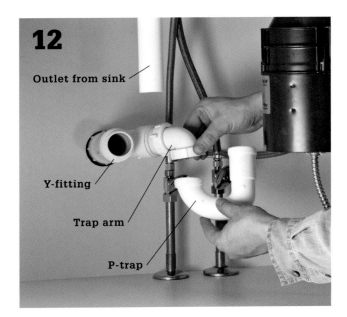

Install a trap arm for the disposer in the open port of the Y-fitting at the wall stubout. Then, attach a P-trap or a combination of a tube extension and a P-trap so the low end of the trap will align with the bottom of the disposer discharge tube.

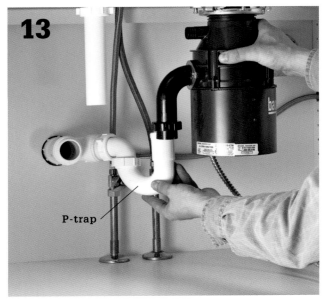

Spin the disposer so the end of the discharge tube is lined up over the open end of the P-trap and confirm that they will fit together correctly. If the discharge tube extends down too far, mark a line on it at the top of the P-trap and cut through the line with a hacksaw. If the tube is too short, attach an extension with a slip joint. You may need to further shorten the discharge tube first to create enough room for the slip joint on the extension. Slide a slip nut and beveled compression washer onto the discharge tube and attach the tube to the P-trap.

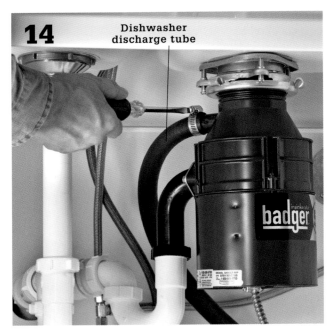

Connect the dishwasher discharge tube to the inlet port located at the top of the disposer unit. This may require a dishwasher hookup kit (see page 30).

Lock the disposer into position on the mounting ring assembly once you have tested to make sure it is functioning correctly and without leaks. Lock it by turning one of the mounting lugs with a screwdriver until it makes contact with the locking notch.

Water Heaters

Replacing a water heater is a relatively easy DIY plumbing task as long as it is a like-for-like replacement. In an ideal situation, you'd replace the old unit with one of the exact same size and make, and thereby avoid having to move any gas, water, or electrical lines. But if you choose to upgrade or downgrade in size, or perhaps replace an old electric water heater with a gas water heater that costs less to run, you'll find that relocating the necessary lines isn't that difficult.

It is a commonly held belief that a water heater should last around 10 years. The longevity depends on many factors, including initial quality, usage levels, maintenance diligence, and other miscellaneous factors such as hardness of water. While it is everyone's goal to get as much use out of our major appliances as possible, it is also undeniable that the best time to replace a water heater is before it leaks and fills your basement with water. It's a bit of a gamble, but once your old heater starts showing signs of wear and perhaps even acting up a bit, go ahead and make the change.

Water heaters for primary duty in residences range in size from 30 gallons to 65 gallons. For a family of four, a 40- or 50-gallon model should be adequate. While you don't want to run out of hot water every morning, you also don't want to pay to heat more water than you use. Base your choice on how well your current water heater is meeting your demand.

Water heaters typically last for at least 10 years, but once they start to show signs of aging, it's a good idea to replace them with a new, more efficient appliance.

Tools & Materials ▸

Tubing cutter
Hacksaw
Pipe wrenches (2)
Adjustable wrench
Channel-type pliers
Screwdriver
MAPP torch kit
Appliance dolly
Water heater
T & P relief valve
Discharge tube

Garden hose
Drain pan
Pipe thread lubricant
Vent pipe elbow
Gas supply pipe
    and fittings
Copper
    soldering supplies
Leak detector solution
Ball-type water
    shutoff valve

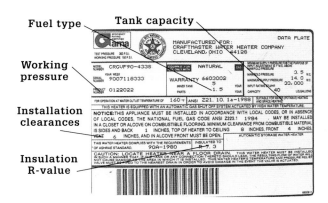

Fuel type

Tank capacity

Working pressure

Installation clearances

Insulation R-value

The nameplate on the side of a water heater lists tank capacity, insulation R-value, and working pressure (pounds per square inch). More efficient water heaters have an insulation R-value of 7 or higher. The nameplate for an electric water heater includes the voltage and the wattage capacity of the heating elements and thermostats. Water heaters also have a yellow energy guide label that lists typical yearly operating costs.

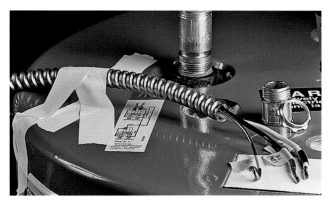

Use armored cable or wires housed in metal conduit to bring electrical power to electric water heaters. The armored cable or conduit should enter the top of the unit through a conduit clamp.

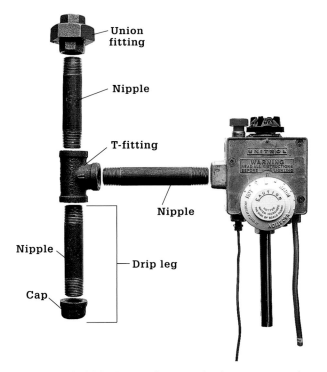

Union fitting

Nipple

T-fitting

Nipple

Nipple

Drip leg

Cap

Use threaded black gas pipe to make the gas connection at the water heater. Other connectors, including flexible copper or stainless steel connectors, are not allowed by some codes and are not as sturdy. The black pipe may be supplied by other pipe materials, such as soft copper. The basic construction involves three 6" threaded nipples, a T-fitting, a cap, and a union to connect to the supply line.

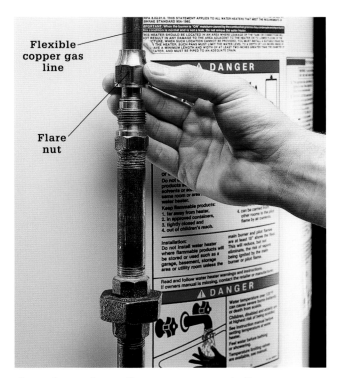

Flexible copper gas line

Flare nut

If your house has soft copper gas supply lines, use a flare fitting to connect an additional threaded nipple from the black pipe assembly that connects to the water heater regulator. If you have black pipe supply lines, use a union fitting like the one in the previous photo.

Gas Water Heater

Gas water heater parts include:
(A) Flue
(B) Hot water outlet
(C) Tank
(D) Anode rod
(E) Gas burner
(F) Cold water inlet pipe
(G) Pressure-relief valve
(H) Dip tube
(I) Thermostat
(J) Thermocouple

Electric Water Heater

Electric water heater parts can include:
(A) Cold water inlet pipe
(B) Cold water inlet valve
(C) Insulation
(D) Draincock
(E) Hot water outlet pipe
(F) Pressure-relief valve
(G) Power cable
(H) High temperature thermostat
(I) Upper heating element
(J) Bracket
(K) Lower heating thermostat
(L) Lower heating element
(M) Gasket

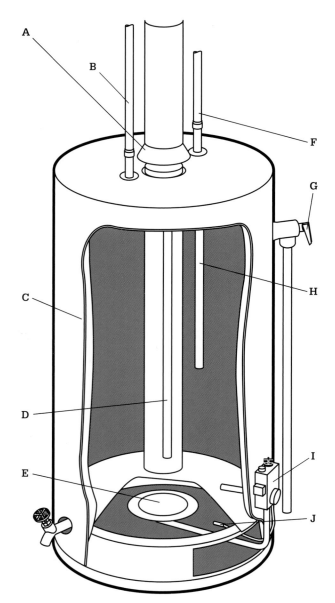

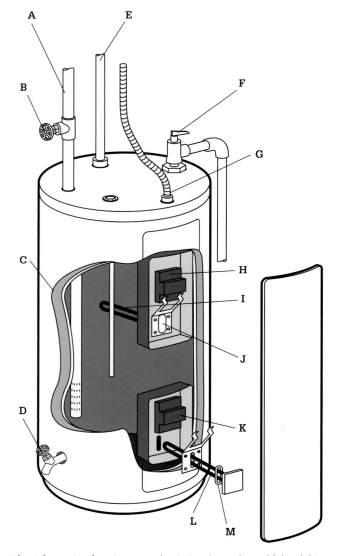

Gas water heaters operate on either propane or natural gas and are generally very economical to run. They do cost a bit more than electric heaters up front. The following installation features a gas water heater. Check with your local building department to find out if homeowners are allowed to install gas appliances in your municipality.

Electric water heaters require 240-volt service, which might overload your service panel if you are replacing a gas heater with an electric model. Their primary advantage is that they are cheaper to purchase (but not to operate) and they do not require that you make gas connections.

How to Install a Gas Water Heater

Shut off the gas supply at the stopcock installed in the gas line closest to the water heater. The handle of the stopcock should be perpendicular to the gas supply pipe.

Drain the water from the old heater by hooking a garden hose up to the sillcock drain and running it to a floor drain. If you don't have a floor drain, drain the water into buckets. For your personal safety, wait until the water heater has been shut off for a couple of hours before draining it.

Disconnect the gas supply from the water heater. To do so, loosen the flare fitting with two wrenches or pliers in a soft copper supply line or loosen the union fitting with two pipe wrenches for black pipe supply lines (inset photo).

Disconnect the vent pipe from the draft hood by withdrawing the sheet metal screws connecting the parts. Also remove vent pipes up to and including the elbow so you may inspect them for corrosion buildup and replace if needed.

(continued)

5

Cut the water supply lines. Prior to cutting, shut off the cold water supply either at the stop valve near the heater or at the water meter. Inspect the shutoff valve. If it is not a ball-type valve in new condition, replace it with a ball valve.

Tip ▸

Prepare the new water heater for installation. Before you put the water heater in place, add a T & P relief valve at the valve opening. Make sure to read the manufacturer's instructions and purchase the recommended valve type. Lubricate the threads and tighten the valve into the valve opening with a pipe wrench. *Note: The water heater shown in this sequence came with a T & P relief valve that's preinstalled.*

6

Remove the old water heater and dispose of it properly. Most trash collection companies will haul it away for $20 or $30. Don't simply leave it out at the curb unless you know that is allowed by your municipal waste collection department. A two-wheel truck or appliance dolly is a big help here. Water heaters usually weigh around 150 pounds.

7

Drip pan

Hose bib

Position the unit in the installation area. If you have flooring you wish to protect from leaks, set the unit on a drip pan (available where water heater accessories are sold). The shallow pans feature a hose bib so you can run a drain line from the pan to a floor drain. If the water heater is not level, level it by shimming under the bottom with a metal or composite shim. Note that you'll need to shift the unit around a bit to have clearance for installing the water supply connectors (step 13).

Attach a discharge tube to the T & P relief valve. You may use either copper pipe or CPVC drain pipe. Cut the tube so the free end is 6" above the floor. If you have floorcoverings you wish to protect, add a 90-degree elbow and a copper drain tube that leads from the discharge tube to a floor drain.

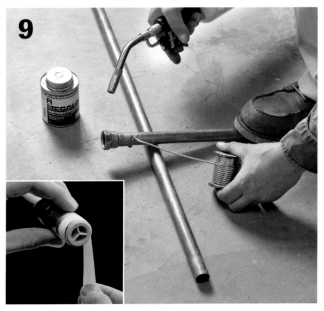

Fabricate water connectors from lengths of copper tubing, threaded copper adaptors, and plastic-lined galvanized threaded nipples. Plastic-lined nipples (inset photo) reduce the corrosion that can occur when you join two dissimilar metals. Size the connector assemblies so they will end up just short of the cut copper supply tubing when the connectors are inserted into the water heater ports.

Install the connectors in the cold water inlet port (make sure you use the blue-coded lined nipple) and the hot outlet port (red-coded nipple) on top of the water heater. Lubricate the nipple threads and tighten with channel-type pliers. Slip a copper tubing repair coupling over each connector and reposition the unit so the supply pipes and connector tops align.

Join the connectors to the supply tubes with slip-fitting copper repair couplings. Be sure to clean and prime the parts first.

(continued)

Reassemble the vent with a new elbow fitting (if your old one needed replacement, see step 4, page 43). Cut the duct that drops down from the elbow so it will fit neatly over the top flange of the draft hood.

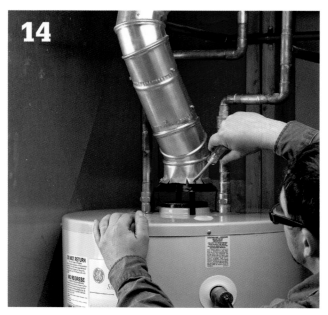

Attach the vertical leg of the vent line to the draft hood with ⅜" sheet metal screws.

Install the parts for the black pipe gas connector assembly (see photo page 41). Use pipe dope to lubricate all joints. Attach a T-fitting to one end of a 3" nipple first and attach the other end of the nipple into the female-threaded regulator port. Attach a cap to another 6" nipple and then thread the other end into the bottom opening of the T-fitting to form a drip leg. Install a third nipple in the top opening of the T-fitting.

Connect the gas supply line to the open end of the gas connector. Use a union fitting for black gas pipe connections and a flare fitting for copper supply connections. See pages 41 to 43 for more information on making these connections.

Test the connections. Turn on the gas supply and test the gas connections with testing solution (see page 315). Before turning on the water supply, make sure the tank drain valve is closed. Allow the tank to fill with water and then turn on a hot water faucet until water comes out (the water won't be hot yet, of course). Visually check all plumbing joints for leaks.

Light the pilot. This is usually a multi-step process that varies among manufacturers, but all new water heaters will have pilot-lighting instructions printed on a label near the water heater controls. Adjust the water temperature setting.

Tip: Hooking Up Electric Water Heaters ▸

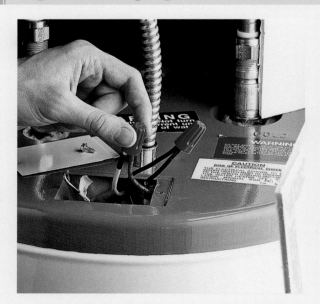

The fuel supply connection is the only part of installing an electric water heater that differs from installing a gas heater, except that electric heaters do not require a vent. The feeder wires (240 volts) are twisted together with mating wires in the access panel located at the top of the unit.

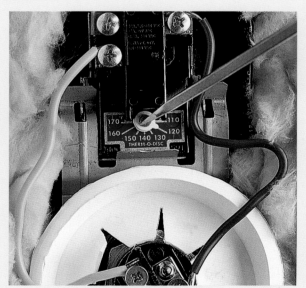

Temperature adjustments on electric water heaters are made by tightening or loosening a thermostat adjustment screw located near the heating element. Always shut off power to the unit before making adjustment. In this photo you can see how close the live terminals for the heating element are to the thermostat.

Bathroom Faucets

One-piece faucets, with either one or two handles, are the most popular fixtures for bathroom installations.

"Widespread" faucets with separate spout and handles are being installed with increasing frequency, however. Because the handles are connected to the spout with flex tubes that can be 18" or longer, widespread faucets can be arranged in many ways.

Tools & Materials ▶

Hacksaw or tin snips	Teflon tape
Channel-type pliers	Faucet kit
Pliers	Pipe joint compound
Basin wrench	Flexible supply tubes
Adjustable wrench	Heat-proof grease
Screwdriver	Loctite basin
Plumber's putty	

Bathroom sink faucets come in two basic styles: the widespread with independent handles and spout (top); and the single-body, deck-mounted version (bottom).

Bathroom Faucet & Drain Hookups

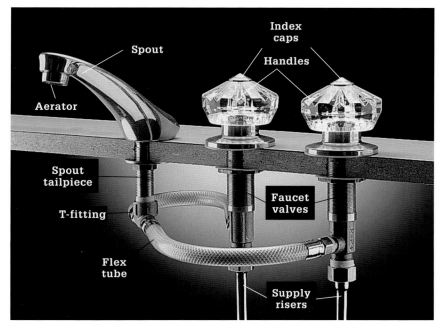

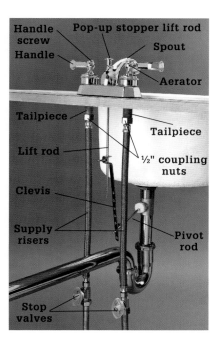

Widespread lavatory faucets have valves that are independent from the spout so they can be configured however you choose, provided that your flex tube connectors are long enough to span the distance.

Single-body lavatory faucets have both valves and the spout permanently affixed to the faucet body. They do not offer flexibility in configurations, but they are very simple to install.

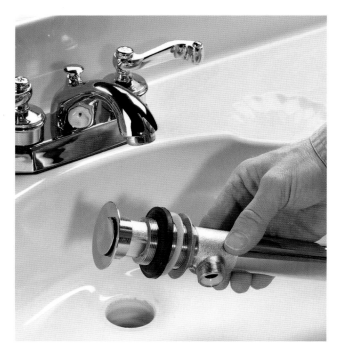

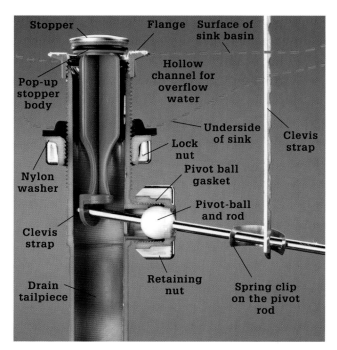

The pop-up stopper fits into the drain opening so the stopper will close tightly against the drain flange when the pop-up handle is lifted up.

The linkage that connects the pop-up stopper to the pop-up handle fits into a male-threaded port in the drain tailpiece. Occasionally the linkage will require adjustment or replacement.

How to Install a Widespread Faucet

Insert the shank of the faucet spout through one of the holes in the sink deck (usually the center hole but you can offset it in one of the end holes if you prefer). If the faucet is not equipped with seals or O-rings for the spout and handles, pack plumber's putty on the undersides before inserting the valves into the deck. *Note: If you are installing the widespread faucet in a new sink deck, drill three holes of the size suggested by the faucet manufacturer.*

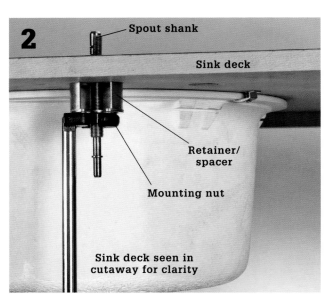

In addition to mounting nuts, many spout valves for widespread faucets have an open-retainer fitting that goes between the underside of the deck and the mounting nut. Others have only a mounting nut. In either case, tighten the mounting nut with pliers or a basin wrench to secure the spout valve. You may need a helper to keep the spout centered and facing forward.

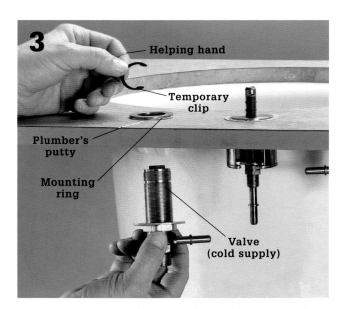

Mount the valves to the deck using whichever method the manufacturer specifies (it varies quite a bit). In the model seen here, a mounting ring is positioned over the deck hole (with plumber's putty seal) and the valve is inserted from below. A clip snaps onto the valve from above to hold it in place temporarily (you'll want a helper for this).

From below, thread the mounting nuts that secure the valves to the sink deck. Make sure the cold water valve (usually has a blue cartridge inside) is in the right-side hole (from the front) and the hot water valve (red cartridge) is in the left hole. Install both valves.

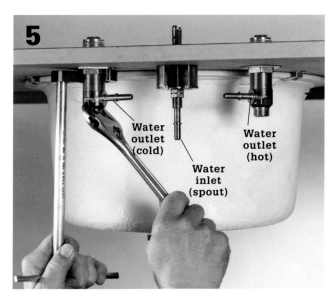

Once you've started the nut on the threaded valve shank, secure the valve with a basin wrench, squeezing the lugs where the valve fits against the deck. Use an adjustable wrench to finish tightening the lock nut onto the valve. The valves should be oriented so the water outlets are aimed at the inlet on the spout shank.

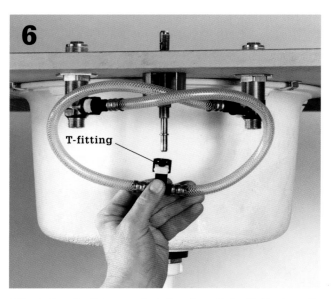

Attach the flexible supply tubes (supplied with the faucet) to the water outlets on the valves. Some twist onto the outlets, but others (like the ones above) click into place. The supply hoses meet in a T-fitting that is attached to the water inlet on the spout.

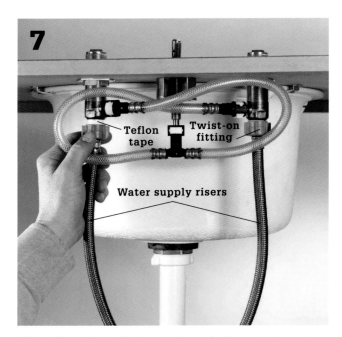

Attach flexible braided-metal supply risers to the water stop valves and then attach the tubes to the inlet port on each valve (usually with Teflon tape and a twist-on fitting at the valve end of the supply riser).

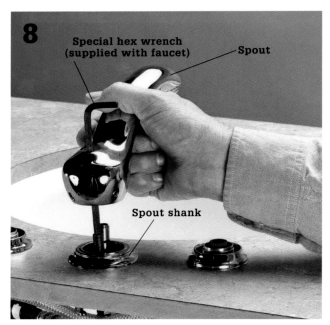

Attach the spout. The model shown here comes with a special hex wrench that is threaded through the hole in the spout where the lift rod for the pop-up drain will be located. Once the spout is seated cleanly on the spout shank, you tighten the hex wrench to secure the spout. Different faucets will use other methods to secure the spout to the shank.

(continued)

9

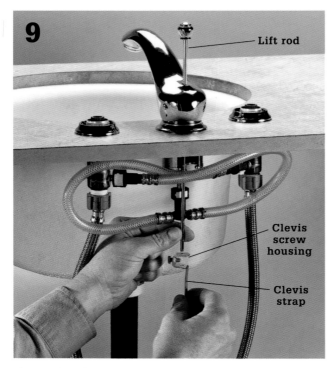

Lift rod

Clevis
screw
housing

Clevis
strap

If your sink did not have a pop-up stopper, you'll need to replace the sink drain tailpiece with a pop-up stopper body (often supplied with the faucet). See page 243. Insert the lift rod through the hole in the back of the spout and, from below, thread the pivot rod through the housing for the clevis screw.

10

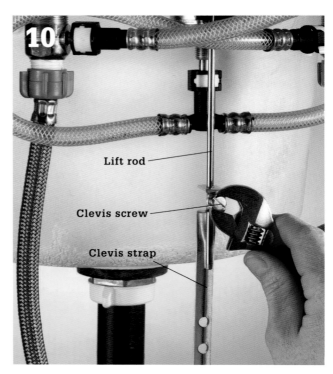

Lift rod

Clevis screw

Clevis strap

Attach the clevis strap to the pivot rod that enters the pop-up drain body, and adjust the position of the strap so it raises and lowers properly when the lift rod is pulled up. Tighten the clevis screw at this point. It's hard to fit a screwdriver in here, so you may need to use a wrench or pliers.

11

Attach the faucet handles to the valves using whichever method is required by the faucet manufacturer. Most faucets are designed with registration methods to ensure that the handles are symmetrical and oriented in an ergonomic way once you secure them to the valves.

12

Turn on the water supply and test the faucet. Remove the faucet aerator so any debris in the lines can clear the spout.

Most faucets come with a plastic or foam gasket to seal the bottom of the faucet to the sink deck. These gaskets will not always form a watertight seal. If you want to ensure no splash water gets below the sink, discard the seal and press a ring of plumber's putty into the sealant groove built into the underside of the faucet body.

Insert the faucet tailpieces through the holes in the sink. From below, thread washers and mounting nuts over the tailpieces, then tighten the mounting nuts with a basin wrench until snug. Put a dab of pipe joint compound on the threads of the stop valves and thread the metal nuts of the flexible supply risers to these. Wrench tighten about a half-turn past hand tight. Overtightening these nuts will strip the threads. Now tighten the coupling nuts to the faucet tailpieces with a basin wrench.

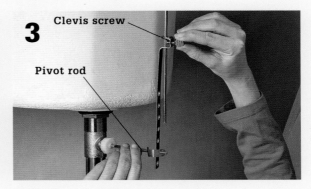

Slide the lift rod of the new faucet into its hole behind the spout. Thread it into the clevis past the clevis screw. Push the pivot rod all the way down so the stopper is open. With the lift rod also all the way down, tighten the clevis to the lift rod.

Grease the fluted valve stems with heatproof grease, then put the handles in place. Put a drop of Loctite on each handle screw before tightening it on. (This will keep your handles from coming loose.) Cover each handle screw with the appropriate index cap—Hot or Cold.

Unscrew the aerator from the end of the spout. Turn the hot and cold water taps on full. Turn the water back on at the stop valves and flush out the faucet for a couple of minutes before turning off the water at the faucet. Check the riser connections for drips. Tighten a compression nut only until the drip stops.

How to Install a Pop-up Drain

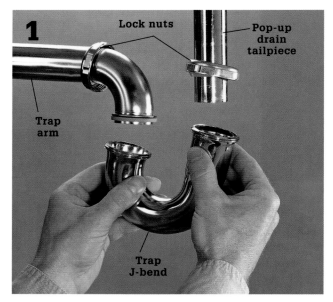

1

Lock nuts

Pop-up drain tailpiece

Trap arm

Trap J-bend

Put a basin under the trap to catch water. Loosen the nuts at the outlet and inlet to the trap J-bend by hand or with channel-type pliers and remove the bend. The trap will slide off the pop-up body tailpiece when the nuts are loose. Keep track of washers and nuts and their up/down orientation by leaving them on the tubes.

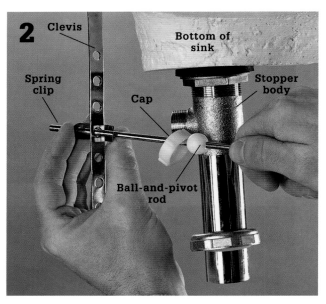

2

Clevis

Bottom of sink

Spring clip

Cap

Stopper body

Ball-and-pivot rod

Unscrew the cap holding the ball-and-pivot rod in the pop-up body and withdraw the ball. Compress the spring clip on the clevis and withdraw the pivot rod from the clevis.

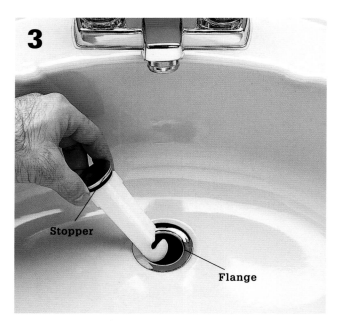

3

Stopper

Flange

Remove the pop-up stopper. Then, from below, remove the lock nut on the stopper body. If needed, keep the flange from turning by inserting a large screwdriver in the drain from the top. Thrust the stopper body up through the hole to free the flange from the basin, and then remove the flange and the stopper body.

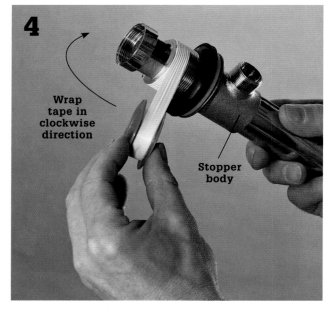

4

Wrap tape in clockwise direction

Stopper body

Clean the drain opening above and below, and then thread the locknut all the way down the new pop-up body, followed by the flat washer and the rubber gasket (beveled side up). Wrap three layers of Teflon tape clockwise onto the top of the threaded body. Make a ½"-dia. snake from plumber's putty, form it into a ring, and stick the ring underneath the drain flange.

5

Plumber's putty

From below, face the pivot rod opening directly back toward the middle of the faucet and pull the body straight down to seat the flange. Thread the locknut/washer assembly up under the sink, then fully tighten the locknut with channel-type pliers. Do not twist the flange in the process, as this can break the putty seal. Clean off the squeezeout of plumber's putty from around the flange.

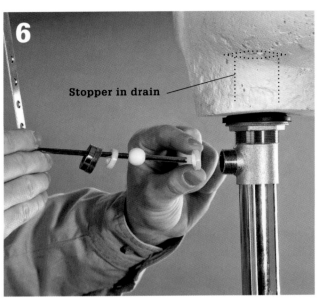

6

Stopper in drain

Drop the pop-up stopper into the drain hole so the hole at the bottom of its post is closest to the back of the sink. Put the beveled nylon washer into the opening in the back of the pop-up body with the bevel facing back.

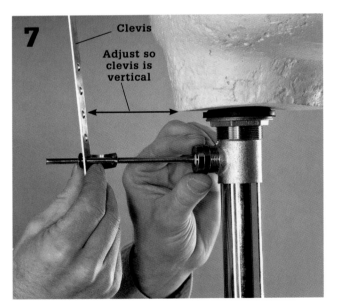

7

Clevis

Adjust so clevis is vertical

Put the cap behind the ball on the pivot rod as shown. Sandwich a hole in the clevis with the spring clip and thread the long end of the pivot rod through the clip and clevis. Put the ball end of the pivot rod into the pop-up body opening and into the hole in the the stopper stem. Screw the cap on to the pop-up body over the ball.

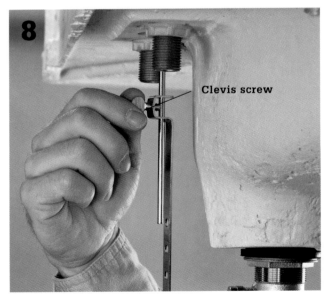

8

Clevis screw

Loosen the clevis screw holding the clevis to the lift rod. Push the pivot rod all the way down (which fully opens the pop-up stopper). With the lift rod also all the way down, tighten the clevis screw to the rod. If the clevis runs into the top of the trap, cut it short with your hacksaw or tin snips. Reassemble the J-bend trap.

Shower Kits

The fastest and easiest way to create a new shower in your bathroom is to frame in the stall area with lumber and wallboard and then install a shower enclosure kit. Typically consisting of three fiberglass or plastic walls, these enclosure kits snap together at the corners and nestle inside the flanges of the shower pan to create nearly foolproof mechanical seals. Often, the walls are formed with shelves, soap holders, and other conveniences.

If you are on a tight budget, you can find extremely inexpensive enclosure kits to keep costs down. You can even create your own custom enclosure using waterproof beadboard panels and snap-together connectors. Or, you can invest in a higher grade kit made from thicker material that will last much longer. Some kits are sold with the receptor (and perhaps even the door) included. The kit shown here is designed to be attached directly to wall studs, but others require a backer wall for support. The panels are attached to the backer with high-tack panel adhesive.

Tools & Materials ▸

Tape measure
Pencil
Hammer
Carpenter's square
Screwdrivers
Pipe wrench
Level
Strap wrench
Adjustable wrench
Pliers
Drill/driver
Center punch
File
Utility knife
Hacksaw

Masking tape
Slicone caulk
  and caulk gun
Shower enclosure kit
Shower door
Showerhead
Faucet
Plumbing supplies
Panel adhesive
Spud wrench
Large-head roofing nails
Jigsaw
Duct tape
Miter box

A paneled shower surround is inexpensive and easy to install. Designed for alcove installations, they often are sold with matching shower pans (called receptors).

How to Install a Shower Enclosure

Mark out the location of the shower, including any new walls, on the floor and walls. Most kits can be installed over wallboard, but you can usually achieve a more professional looking wall finish if you remove the wallcovering and floor covering in the installation area. Dispose of the materials immediately and thoroughly clean the area.

Sill plate

If you are adding a wall to create the alcove, lay out the locations for the studs and plumbing on the new wood sill plate. Also lay out the stud locations on the cap plate that will be attached to the ceiling. Refer to the enclosure kit instructions for exact locations and dimensions of studs. Attach the sill plate to the floor with deck screws and panel adhesive, making sure it is square to the back wall and the correct distance from the side wall.

Align a straight 2 × 4 right next to the sill plate and make a mark on the ceiling. Use a level to extend that line directly above the sill plate. Attach the cap plate at that point.

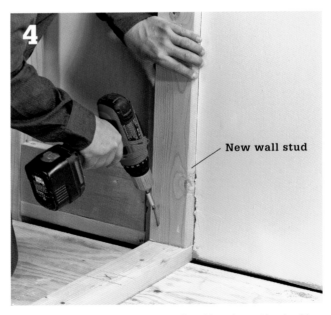

New wall stud

Install the 2 × 4 studs at the outlined locations. Check with a level to make sure each stud is plumb, and then attach them by driving deck screws toenail style into the sill plate and cap plate.

(continued)

5

Drain location

Cut an access hole in the floor for the drain, according to the installation manual instructions. Drill openings in the sill plate of the wet wall (the new wall in this project) for the supply pipes, also according to the instructions.

6

Install a drain pipe and branch line and then trim the drain pipe flush with the floor. If you are not experienced with plumbing, hire a plumber to install the new drain line.

7

Faucet body

Cross brace

Bull valves

Supply riser

Install new supply risers as directed in the instruction manual (again, have a plumber do this if necessary). Also install cross braces between the studs in the wet wall for mounting the faucet body and shower arm.

8

If the supply plumbing is located in a wall (old or new) that is accessible from the non-shower side, install framing for a removable access panel.

9

Attach the drain tailpiece that came with your receptor to the underside of the unit, following the manufacturer's instructions precisely. Here, an adjustable spud wrench is being used to tighten the tailpiece.

Option: To stabilize the receptor, especially if the floor is uneven, pour or trowel a layer of thinset mortar into the installation area, taking care to keep the mortar out of the drain access hole. Do not apply mortar in areas where the receptor has feet that are intended to make full contact with the floor.

10

Set the receptor in place, check to make sure it is level, and shim it if necessary. Secure the receptor with large-head roofing nails driven into the wall stud so the heads pin the flange against the stud. Do not overdrive the nails.

11

Lay out the locations for the valve hole or holes in the end wall panel that will be installed on the wet wall. Check your installation instructions. Some kits come with a template marked on the packaging carton. Cut the access hole with a hole saw and drill or with a jigsaw and fine-tooth blade. If using a jigsaw, orient the panel so the good surface is facing down.

(continued)

Position the back wall so there is a slight gap (about ½₂") between the bottom of the panel and the rim of the receptor—set a few small spacers on the rim if need be. Tack a pair of roofing nails above the top of the back panel to hold it in place (or, use duct tape). Position both end walls and test the fits. Make clip connections between panels (inset) if your kit uses them.

Remove the end wall so you can prepare the installation area for them. If your kit recommends panel adhesive, apply it to the wall or studs. In the kit shown here, only a small bead of silicone sealant on the receptor flange is required.

Reinstall the end panels, permanently clipping them to the back panel according to the kit manufacturer's instructions. Make sure the front edges of the end panels are flush with the front of the receptor.

Once the panels are positioned correctly and snapped together, fasten them to the wall studs. If the panels have predrilled nail holes, drive roofing nails through them at each stud at the panel tops and every 4" to 6" along vertical surfaces.

16

Install wallcovering material above the enclosure panels and anywhere else it is needed. Use moisture-resistant materials, and maintain a gap of ¼" between the shoulders of the top panel flanges and the wallcovering.

17

Finish the walls and then caulk between the enclosure panels and the wallcoverings with silicone caulk.

18

Install the faucet handles and escutcheon and caulk around the escutcheon plate. Install the shower arm escutcheon and showerhead.

19

Access panel

Make an access panel and attach it at the framed opening created in step 8. A piece of ¼" plywood framed with mitered case molding and painted to match the wall is one idea for access panel covers.

How to Install a Hinged Shower Door

Measure the width of the shower opening. If the walls of the shower slope inward slightly before meeting the base, take your measurement from a higher point at the full width of the opening so you don't cut the door base too short. Cut the base piece to fit using a hacksaw and a miter box. File the cut ends if necessary to deburr them.

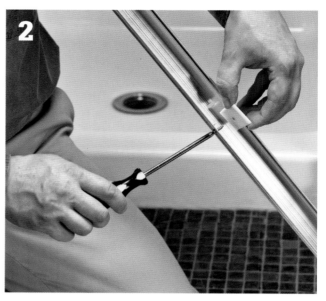

Identify which side jamb will be the hinge jamb and which will be the strike jamb according to the direction you want your hinged door to swing—an outward swing is preferred. Prepare the jambs for installation as directed in your instructions.

Place the base jamb on the curb of the shower base. If the joint where the wall meets the curb is sloped, you'll need to trim the corners of the base piece to follow the profile. Place a jamb carefully onto the base and plumb it with a level. Then, mark a drilling point by tapping a centerpunch in the middle of each nail hole in each jamb. Remove the jambs, drill pilot holes, and then attach the jambs with the provided screws.

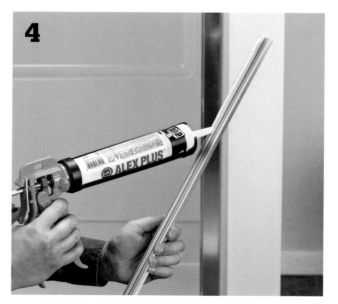

Remove the bottom track and prepare the shower base curb for installation of the base track, following the manufacturer's directions. Permanently install the bottom track. Bottom tracks (not all doors have them) are usually attached to the side jambs or held in place with adhesive. Never use fasteners to secure them to curb.

Working on the floor or another flat surface, attach the door hinge to the hinge jamb, if required. In most systems, the hinge is fitted over the hinge jamb after you attach it to the wall.

Attach the hinge to the door panel, according to the manufacturer's instructions. Attach any cap fitting that keeps water out of the jamb.

Fit the hinge jamb over the side jamb and adjust it as directed in your instruction manual. Once the clearances are correct, fasten the jambs to hang the door.

Install the magnetic strike plate and any remaining caps or accessories such as towel rods. Also attach the sweep that seals the passage, if provided.

Custom Shower Bases

Building a custom-tiled shower base lets you choose the shape and size of your shower rather than having its dimensions dictated by available products. Building the base is quite simple, though it does require time and some knowledge of basic masonry techniques because the base is formed primarily using concrete or mortar. What you get for your time and trouble can be spectacular.

Before designing a shower base, contact your local building department regarding code restrictions and to secure the necessary permits. Most codes require water controls to be accessible from outside the shower and describe acceptable door positions and operation. Requirements like these influence the size and position of the base.

Choosing the tile before finalizing the design lets you size the base to require mostly or only full tiles. Consider using small tile and gradate the color from top to bottom or in a sweep across the walls. Or, use trim tile and listellos on the walls to create an interesting focal point.

Whatever tile you choose, remember to seal the grout in your new shower and to maintain it carefully over the years. Water-resistant grout protects the structure of the shower and prolongs its useful life.

Tools & Materials ▸

Tape measure
Circular saw
Hammer
Utility knife
Stapler
2-ft. level
Mortar mixing box
Trowel
Wood float
Felt-tip marker
Ratchet wrench
Expandable stopper
Drill
Tin snips
Torpedo level
Tools & materials for installing tile
2 × 4 and 2 × 10 framing lumber
Thinset mortar (for tiling)

16d galvanized common nails
15# building paper
3-piece shower drain
PVC primer & cement
Galvanized finish nails
Galvanized metal lath
Sand topping mix (concrete)
Latex mortar additive
CPE waterproof membrane & preformed dam corners
CPE membrane solvent glue
CPE membrane sealant
Cementboard & materials
Utility knife
Straightedge

Choosing a custom shower base gives you a myriad of options for the shape and size of your shower.

Cross-Section of a Shower Pan

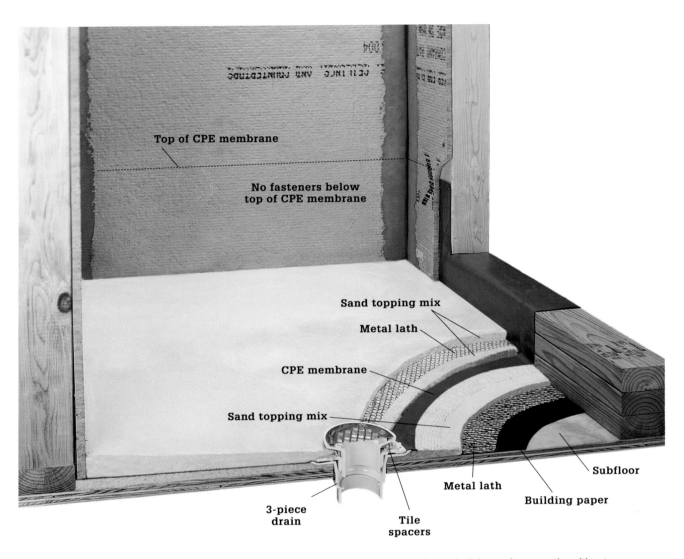

Top of CPE membrane

No fasteners below top of CPE membrane

Sand topping mix

Metal lath

CPE membrane

Sand topping mix

Subfloor

Metal lath

Building paper

3-piece drain

Tile spacers

A custom shower pan is a fairly intricate, multi-layed construction, but choosing to build one gives you the ultimate design flexibility.

Tips for Building a Custom Shower Base ▸

A custom-tiled shower base is built in three layers to ensure proper water drainage: the pre pan, the shower pan, and the shower floor. A mortar pre pan is first built on top of the subfloor, establishing a slope toward the drain of ¼" for every 12" of shower floor. Next, a waterproof chlorinated polyethylene (CPE) membrane forms the shower pan, providing a watertight seal for the shower base. Finally, a second mortar bed reinforced with wire mesh is installed for the shower floor, providing a surface for tile installation. If water penetrates the tiled shower floor, the shower pan and sloped pre pan will direct it to the weep holes of the 3-piece drain.

One of the most important steps in building a custom-tiled shower base is testing the shower pan after installation. This allows you to locate and fix any leaks to prevent costly damage.

How to Build a Custom-tiled Shower Base

Remove building materials to expose subfloor and stud walls. Cut three 2 × 4s for the curb and fasten them to the floor joists and the studs at the shower threshold with 16d galvanized common nails. Also cut 2 × 10 lumber to size and install in the stud bays around the perimeter of the shower base. Install (or have installed) drain and supply plumbing.

Staple 15# building paper to the subfloor of the shower base. Disassemble the 3-piece shower drain and glue the bottom piece to the drain pipe with PVC cement. Partially screw the drain bolts into the drain piece, and stuff a rag into the drain pipe to prevent mortar from falling into the drain.

Mark the height of the bottom drain piece on the wall farthest from the center of the drain. Measure from the center of the drain straight across to that wall, then raise the height mark ¼" for every 12" of shower floor to slope the pre pan toward the drain. Trace a reference line at the height mark around the perimeter of the entire alcove, using a level.

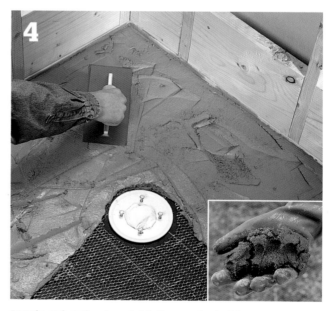

Staple galvanized metal lath over the building paper; cut a hole in the lath ½" from the drain. Mix concrete topping mix or Type N mortar to a fairly dry consistency. The cement mixture should hold its shape when squeezed (inset). Trowel the cement mixture onto the building paper, building the pre-pan from the flange of the drain piece to the height line on the perimeter of the walls.

Continue using the trowel to form the pre pan, checking the slope using a level and filling any low spots with mortar. Finish the surface of the pre pan with a wood float until it is even and smooth. Allow the mortar to cure overnight.

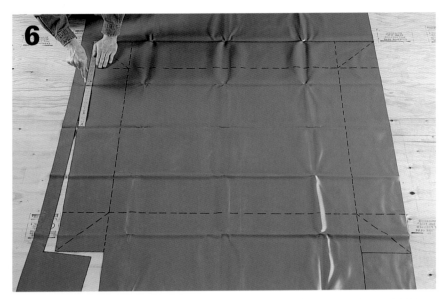

Measure the dimensions of the shower floor, and mark it out on a sheet of CPE waterproof membrane, using a felt-tipped marker. From the floor outline, measure out and mark an additional 8" for each wall and 16" for the curb end. Cut the membrane to size, using a utility knife and straightedge. Be careful to cut on a clean, smooth surface to prevent puncturing the membrane. Lay the membrane onto the shower pan.

Measure to find the exact location of the drain and mark it on the membrane, outlining the outer diameter of the drain flange. Cut a circular piece of CPE membrane roughly 2" larger than the drain flange, then use CPE membrane solvent glue to weld it into place and reinforce the seal at the drain.

Apply CPE sealant around the drain. Fold the membrane along the floor outline. Set the membrane over the pre pan so the reinforced drain seal is centered over the drain bolts. Working from the drain to the walls, carefully tuck the membrane tight into each corner, folding the extra material into triangular flaps.

(continued)

9

Apply CPE solvent glue to one side, press the flap flat, then staple it in place. Staple only the top edge of the membrane to the blocking; do not staple below the top of the curb, or on the curb itself.

10

Dam corner

At the shower curb, cut the membrane along the studs so it can be folded over the curb. Solvent glue a dam corner at each inside corner of the curb. Do not fasten the dam corners with staples.

11

At the reinforced drain seal on the membrane, locate and mark the drain bolts. Press the membrane down around the bolts, then use a utility knife to carefully cut a slit just large enough for the bolts to poke through. Push the membrane down over the bolts.

12

Use a utility knife to carefully cut away only enough of the membrane to expose the drain and allow the middle drain piece to fit in place. Remove the drain bolts, then position the middle drain piece over the bolt holes. Reinstall the bolts, tightening them evenly and firmly to create a watertight seal.

Test the shower pan for leaks overnight. Fill the shower pan with water, to 1" below the top of the curb. Mark the water level and let the water sit overnight. If the water level remains the same, the pan holds water. If the level is lower, locate and fix leaks in the pan using patches of membrane and CPE solvent.

Install cementboard on the alcove walls, using ¼" wood shims to lift the bottom edge off the CPE membrane. To prevent puncturing the membrane, do not use fasteners in the lower 8" of the cementboard. Cut a piece of metal lath to fit around the three sides of the curb. Bend the lath so it tightly conforms to the curb. Pressing the lath against the top of the curb, staple it to the outside face of the curb. Mix enough mortar for the two sides of the curb.

Overhang the front edge of the curb with a straight 1× board so it is flush with the outer wall material. Apply mortar to the mesh with a trowel, building to the edge of the board. Clear away excess mortar, then use a torpedo level to check for plumb, making adjustments as needed. Repeat for the inside face of the curb. *Note: The top of the curb will be finished after tile is installed (step 19). Allow the mortar to cure overnight.*

Attach the drain strainer piece to the drain, adjusting it to a minimum of 1½" above the shower pan. On one wall, mark 1½" up from the shower pan, then use a level to draw a reference line around the perimeter of the shower base. Because the pre pan establishes the ¼" per foot slope, this measurement will maintain that slope.

(continued)

Spread tile spacers over the weep holes of the drain to prevent mortar from plugging the holes. Mix the floor mortar, then build up the shower floor to roughly half the planned thickness of this layer. Cut metal lath to cover the mortar bed, keeping it ½" from the drain (see photo in step 18).

Continue to add mortar, building the floor to the reference line on the walls. Use a level to check the slope, and pack mortar into low spots with a trowel. Leave space around the drain flange for the thickness of the tile. Float the surface using a wood float until it is smooth and slopes evenly to the drain. When finished, allow the mortar to cure overnight before installing the tiles.

Install the tile. At the curb, cut the tiles for the inside to protrude ½" above the unfinished top of the curb, and the tiles for the outside to protrude ⅝" above the top, establishing a ⅛" slope so water drains back into the shower. Use a level to check the tops of the tiles for level as you work.

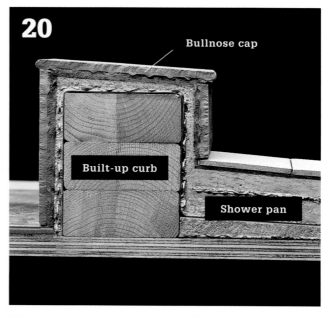

Bullnose cap

Built-up curb

Shower pan

Mix enough mortar to cover the unfinished top of the curb, then pack it in place between the tiles, using a trowel. Screed off the excess mortar flush with the tops of the side tiles. Allow the mortar to cure, then install bullnose cap tile. Install the wall tile, then grout, clean, and seal all the tile. After the grout has cured fully, run a bead of silicone caulk around all inside corners to create control joints.

Textured surfaces improve the safety of tile floors, especially in wet areas such as this open shower. The shower area is designated effectively by a simple shift in color and size.

The raised curb on this open shower keeps most of the water headed toward the drain. But no matter, the entire bathroom is tiled, so stray droplets are no problem.

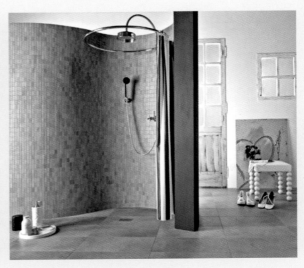

Mosaic tile, with its mesh backing and small shapes, often works well on curved walls such as the one that forms this shower. The rectangular shape of the individual mosaic tiles complements the shape of the post at the corner of the shower.

Alcove Bathtubs

Most of our homes are equipped with an alcove tub that includes a tub surround and shower function. By combining the tub and the shower in one fixture, you conserve precious bathroom floorspace and simplify the initial installation. Plus, you only have one bathing fixture that needs cleaning.

But because tub/showers are so efficient, they do get a lot of use and tend to have fairly limited lifespans. The fact that the most inexpensive tubs on the market are designed for alcove use also reduces the average tub/shower lifespan. Pressed steel tubs have enamel finishes that crack and craze; plastic and fiberglass tubs get grimy and stained; even acrylic and composite tubs show wear eventually (and as with other fixtures, styles, and colors change too).

Plumbing an alcove tub is a relatively difficult job because getting access to the drain lines attached to the tub and into the floor is often very awkward. Although an access panel is required by most codes, the truth is that many tubs were installed without them or with panels that are too small or hard to reach to be of much use. If you are contemplating replacing your tub, the first step in the decision process should be to fid the access panel and determine if it is sufficient. If it is not (or there is no panel at all),

consider how you might enlarge it. Often, this means cutting a hole in the wall on the adjoining room and also in the ceiling below. This creates more work, of course, but compared to the damage caused by a leaky drain from a subpar installation, making an access opening is little inconvenience.

Tools & Materials ▸

Channel-type pliers	Galvanized
Hacksaw	deck screws
Carpenter's level	Drain-waste-
Pencil	overflow kit
Tape measure	1 × 3, 1 × 4,
Saw	2 × 4 lumber
Screwdriver	Galvanized roofing nails
Drill	Galvanized roof
Adjustable wrench	flashing
Trowel	Thinset mortar
Shims	Tub & tile caulk
	Propane torch

By replacing a dingy old alcove tub with a fresh new one, you can make the tub and shower area as pleasant to use as it is efficient.

Tips for Installing Bathtubs ▸

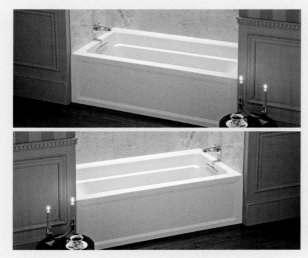

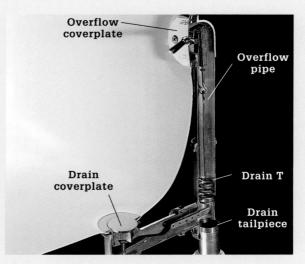

Choose the correct tub for your plumbing setup. Alcove-installed tubs with only one-sided aprons are sold as either "left-hand" or "right-hand" models, depending on the location of the predrilled drain and overflow holes in the tub. To determine which type you need, face into the alcove and check whether the tub drain is on your right or your left.

A Drain-waste-overflow kit with stopper mechanism must be purchased separately and attached after the tub is set. Available in both brass and plastic types, most kits include an overflow coverplate, an overflow pipe that can be adjusted to different heights, a drain T-fitting, an adjustable drain tailpiece, and a drain coverplate that screws into the tailpiece.

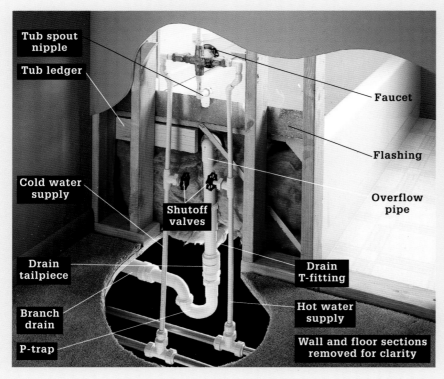

The supply system for a bathtub includes hot and cold supply pipes, shutoff valves, a faucet and handle(s), and a spout. Supply connections can be made before or after the tub is installed.

The drain-waste-overflow system for a bathtub includes the overflow pipe, drain T, P-trap, and branch drain. The overflow pipe assembly is attached to the tub before installation.

How To Remove an Alcove Bathtub

Cut the old supply tubes, if you have access to them, with a reciprocating saw and metal cutting blade or with a hacksaw. Be sure to shut off the water supply at the stop valves first. Cut the shower pipe just above the faucet body and cut the supply tubes just above the stop valves.

Remove the faucet handles, tub spout, shower head and escutcheon, and arm. For the spout, check the underside for a set screw and loosen it if you find one. Then, insert a long screwdriver into the spout and turn the spout counterclockwise.

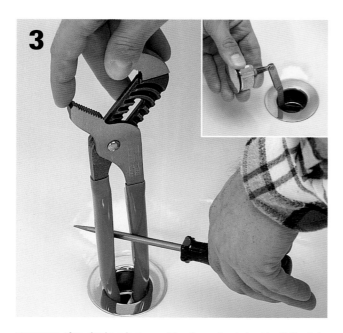

Remove the drain plug, working from the tub side. If the tub has a pop-up drain with linkage, twist the plug to disengage the linkage and remove the plug (inset). Then, insert the handles of a channel-type pliers into the drain opening and past the drain crosspiece. Twist the pliers counterclockwise to remove the plug.

Remove the overflow coverplate (top photo) and then withdraw the pop-up drain linkage through the overflow opening (lower photo).

Disconnect the overflow pipe from the drain assembly and remove both parts (your access may not be as unrestricted as seen here). If you need to cut the pipes, go ahead and do it. In most cases, it is difficult to maneuver the tub out with the DWO assembly still attached.

Cut the wall to a line about 6" above the tub rim. Alcove tubs are fastened to the wall studs with nails driven through or above a flange that protrudes up from the rim. You'll need to remove a bit of the wall covering so you can remove the fasteners.

If you can, pry out fasteners and then pull the tub away from the walls by levering between the back rim of the tub and the back wall of the alcove. If it resists, check for adhesive caulk or even flooring blocking the bottom of the apron. If needed, raise the tub and slide a pair of 1 × 4 runners under the skirt edge (inset photo) to make it easier to slide out.

Option: Cut stubborn tubs in half to wrangle them out of the alcove. This has the added benefit of making the tubs easier to get out the door, down the stairs, and into the dumpster.

How to Install a New Alcove Tub

Prepare for the new tub. Inspect and remove old or deteriorated wall surfaces or framing members in the tub area. With today's mold-resistant wallboard products, it makes extra sense to go ahead and strip off the old alcove wallcoverings and ceiling down to the studs so you can replace them. This also allows you to inspect for hidden damage in the wall and ceiling cavities.

Check the subfloor for level—if it is not level, use pour-on floor leveler compound to correct it (ask at your local flooring store). Make sure the supply and drain pipes and the shutoff valves are in good repair and correct any problems you encounter. If you have no bath fan in the alcove, now is the perfect time to add one.

Check the height of the crossbraces for the faucet body and the showerhead. If your family members needed to stoop to use the old shower, consider raising the brace for the showerhead. Read the instructions for your new faucet/diverter and check to see that the brace for the faucet body will conform to the requirements (this includes distance from the surround wall as well as height). Adjust the brace locations as needed.

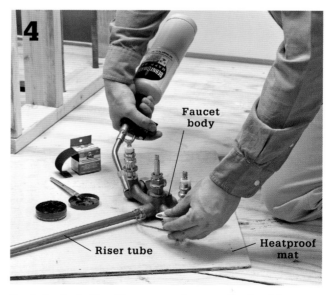

Faucet body

Riser tube

Heatproof mat

Begin by installing the new water supply plumbing. Measure to determine the required height of your shower riser tube and cut it to length. Attach the bottom of the riser to the faucet body and the top to the shower elbow.

Attach the faucet body to the cross brace with pipe hanger straps. Then, attach supply tubing from the stop valves to the faucet body, making sure to attach the hot water to the left port and cold to the right port. Also secure the shower elbow to its cross brace with a pipe strap. Do not attach the shower arm yet.

Slide the bathtub into the alcove. Make sure tub is flat on the floor and pressed flush against the back wall. If your tub did not come with a tub protector, cut a piece of cardboard to line the tub bottom, and tape pieces of cardboard around the rim to protect the finish from shoes and dropped tools.

Mark locations for ledger boards. To do this, trace the height of the top of the tub's nailing flange onto the wall studs in the alcove. Then remove the tub and measure the height of the nailing flange. Measure down this same amount from your flange lines and mark new ledger board location.

Install 1 × 4 ledger boards. Drive two or three 3"-galvanized deck screws through the ledger board at each stud. All three walls should receive a ledger. Leave an open space in the wet wall to allow clearance for the DWO kit.

(continued)

9

Install the drain-waste-overflow (DWO) pipes before you install the tub. Make sure to get a good seal on the slip nuts at the pipe joints. Follow the manufacturer's instructions to make sure the pop-up drain linkage is connected properly. Make sure rubber gaskets are positioned correctly at the openings on the outside of the tub.

10

Drain strainer

Thread the male-threaded drain strainer into the female-threaded drain waste elbow. Wrap a coil of plumber's putty around the drain outlet underneath the plug rim first. Hand tighten only.

11

Attach the overflow coverplate, making sure the pop-up drain controls are in the correct position. Tighten the mounting screws that connect to the mounting plate to sandwich the rubber gasket snugly between the overflow pipe flange and the tub wall. Then, finish tightening the drain strainer against the waste elbow by inserting the handle of a pair of pliers into the strainer body and turning.

12

Place the tub back into the alcove, taking care not to bump the DWO assembly and disturb the connections. You definitely will want a helper for this job. If the drain outlet of the DWO assembly is not directly over the drain pipe when the tub is in position, you'll need to remove it and adjust the drain line location.

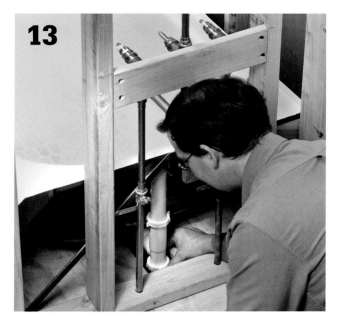

13

Attach the drain outlet from the DWO assembly to the drain P-trap. This is the part of the job where you will appreciate that you spent the time to create a roomy access panel for the tub plumbing. Test the drain and overflow to make sure they don't leak. Also test the water supply plumbing, temporarily attaching the handles, spout, and shower arm so you can operate the faucet and the diverter.

14

Drive a 1½" galvanized roofing nail at each stud location, just over the top of the tub's nailing flange. The nail head should pin the flange to the stud. Be careful here—an errant blow or overdriving can cause the enameled finish to crack or craze. *Option: You may choose to drill guide holes and nail through the flange instead.*

15

Install the wallcoverings and tub surround (see pages for a 3-piece surround installation 81 to 83). You can also make a custom surround from tileboard or cementboard and tile.

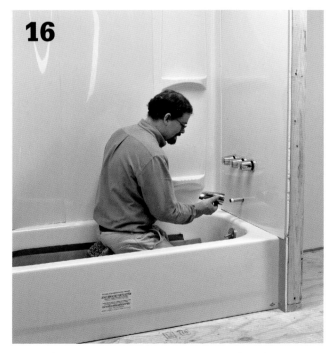

16

Install fittings. First, thread the shower arm into the shower elbow and attach the spout nipple to the valve assembly. Also attach the shower head and escutcheon, the faucet handle/diverter with escutcheon, and the tub spout. Use thread lubricant on all parts.

3-Piece Tub Surrounds

No one wants bathroom fixtures that are aging or yellowed from years of use. A shiny new tub surround can add sparkle and freshness to your dream bath.

Tub surrounds come in many different styles, materials, and price ranges. Choose the features you want and measure your existing bathtub surround for sizing. Surrounds typically come in three or five pieces. A three-panel surround is being installed here, but the process is similar for five-panel systems.

Surface preparation is important for good glue adhesion. Plastic tiles and wallpaper must be removed and textured plaster must be sanded smooth. Surrounds can be installed over ceramic tile that is well attached and in good condition, but it must be sanded and primed. All surfaces must be primed with a water-based primer.

Tools & Materials ▸

Jigsaw	Adhesive
Hole saw	Screwdriver
Drill	Adjustable wrench
Measuring tape	Pry bar
Level	Hammer
Caulking gun	3-piece tub surround
Primer	

Three-piece tub surrounds are inexpensive and come in many colors and styles. The typical unit has two end panels and a back panel that overlap in the corners to form a watertight seal. They are formed from fiberglass, PVC, acrylic, or proprietary resin-based polymers. Five piece versions are also available and typically have more features such as integral soap shelves and even cabinets.

How to Install a 3-Piece Tub Surround

Remove the old plumbing fixtures and wallcoverings in the tub area. In some cases you can attach surround panels to old tileboard or even tile, but it is generally best to remove the wallcoverings down to the studs if you can, so you may inspect for leaks or damage.

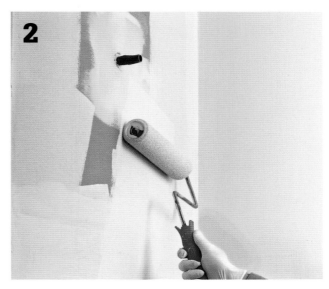

Replace the wallcoverings with appropriate materials, such as water and mold-resistant wallboard or cementboard (for ceramic tile installations). Make sure the new wall surfaces are smooth and flat. Some surround kit manufacturers recommend that you apply a coat of primer to sheet goods such as greenboard to create a better bonding surface for the panel adhesive.

Test-fit the panels before you start; the tub may have settled unevenly or the walls may be out of plumb. Check the manufacturer's directions for distinguishing right and left panels. Place a panel in position on the tub ledge. Use a level across the top of the panel to determine if it is level. Create a vertical reference line to mark the edge of the panel on the plumbing end.

Test-fitting Tip ▶

Ensure a perfect fit by taping the surround panels to the walls in the tub area. Make sure the tops are level when the overlap seams are aligned and that you have a consistent ⅛" gap between the panel bottoms and the tub flange. Mark the panels for cutting if necessary and, once the panels have been removed, make any adjustments to the walls that are needed.

(continued)

Some kits are created to fit a range of bathtub dimensions. After performing the test fit, check the fitting instructions to see if you need to trim any of the pieces. Follow the manufacturer's instructions for cutting. Here, we had to cut the corner panels because the instructions advise not to overlap the back or side panel over the corner panels by more than 3". Cut panels using a jigsaw and a fine-tooth blade that is appropriate for cutting fiberglass or acrylic tileboard. The cut panels should be overlapped by panels with factory edges.

Measure and mark the location of the faucets, spout, and shower outlets. Measure in from the vertical reference line (made in step 3) and up from the top of the tub ledge. Re-measure for accuracy, as any cuts to the surround are final. Place the panel face-up on a sheet of plywood. Mark the location of the holes. Cut the holes ½" larger than the pipe diameter. If your faucet has a recessed trim plate (escutcheon), cut the hole to fit the recess. Using a hole saw or a jigsaw, cut out the plumbing outlets.

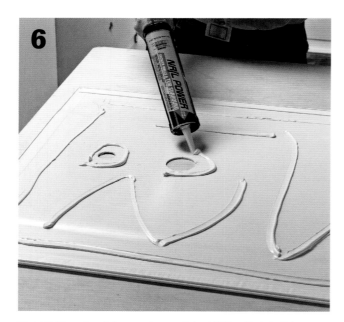

Install the plumbing end panel, test-fitting first. In this surround, the end panels are installed first. Apply adhesive to the back of the plumbing panel. Circle the plumbing outlet holes 1" from the edge. Follow the manufacturer's application pattern. Do not apply adhesive closer than 1" to the double-sided tape or the bottom edge of the panel.

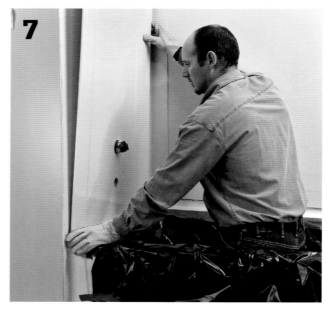

Remove the protective backing from the tape. Carefully lift the panel by the edges and place against the corner and top of the tub ledge. Press firmly from top to bottom in the corner, then throughout the panel.

8

Test-fit the opposite end panel and make any necessary adjustments. Apply the adhesive, remove the protective backing from the tape, and put in place. Apply pressure to the corner first from top to bottom, and then apply pressure throughout.

9

Apply adhesive to the back panel following the manufacturer's instructions. Maintain a 1" space between adhesive tape and the bottom of the panel. Remove protective backing from the tape. Lift the panel by the edges and carefully center between the two end panels. When positioned, firmly press in place from top to bottom.

10

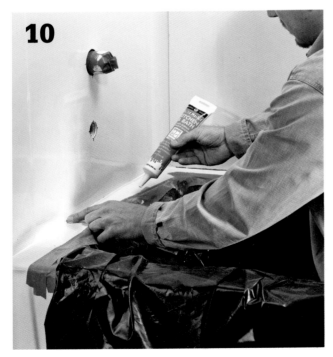

Apply caulk to the bottom and top edges of the panels and at panel joints. Dip your fingertip in water and use it to smooth the caulk to a uniform bead.

11

Apply silicone caulk to escutcheons or trim plates and reinstall them. Allow a minimum of 24 hours for caulk and adhesive to dry thoroughly before using the shower or tub.

Sliding Tub Doors

Curtains on your bathtub shower are a hassle. If you forget to tuck them inside the tub, water flows freely onto your bathroom floor. If you forget to slide them closed, mildew sets up shop in the folds. And every time you brush against them they stick to your skin. Shower curtains certainly don't add much elegance or charm to a dream bath. Neither does a deteriorated door. Clean up the look of your bathroom, and even give it an extra touch of elegance, with a new sliding tub door.

When shopping for a sliding tub door, you have a choice of framed or frameless. A framed door is edged in metal. The metal framing is typically aluminum but is available in many finishes, including those that resemble gold, brass, or chrome. Glass options are also plentiful. You can choose between frosted or pebbled glass, clear, mirrored, tinted, or patterned glass. Doors can be installed on ceramic tile walls or through a fiberglass tub surround.

Tools & Materials ▸

Measuring tape	Masonry bit
Pencil	for tile wall
Hacksaw	Phillips screwdriver
Miter box	Caulk gun
Level	Masking tape
Drill	Silicone sealant
Center punch	& remover
Razor blade	Tub door kit
Marker	Masking tape

A sliding tub door framed in aluminum gives the room a sleek, clean look and is just one of the available options.

How to Install Sliding Tub Doors

Remove the existing door and inspect the walls. Use a razor blade to cut sealant from tile and metal surfaces. Do not use a razor blade on fiberglass surfaces. Remove remaining sealant by scraping or pulling. Use a silicone sealant remover to remove all residue. Remove shower curtain rods, if present. Check the walls and tub ledge for plumb and level.

Measure the distance between the finished walls along the top of the tub ledge. Refer to the manufacturer's instructions for figuring the track dimensions. For the product seen here, ³⁄₁₆" is subtracted from the measurement to calculate the track dimensions.

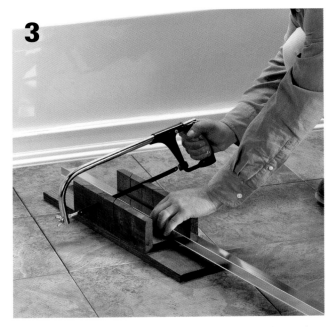

Using a hacksaw and a miter box, carefully cut the track to the proper dimension. Center the track on the bathtub ledge with the taller side out and so the gaps are even at each end. Tape into position with masking tape.

Place a wall channel against the wall with the longer side out and slide into place over the track so they overlap. Use a level to check the channel for plumb, and then mark the locations of the mounting holes on the wall with a marker. Repeat for the other wall channel. Remove the track.

(continued)

5

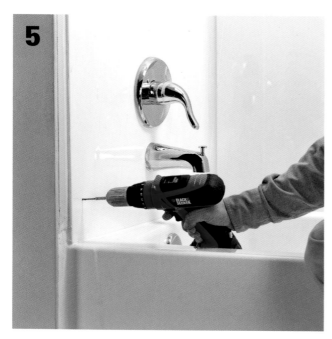

Drill mounting holes for the wall channel at the marked locations. In ceramic tile, nick the surface of the tile with a center punch, use a ¼" masonry bit to drill the hole, and then insert the included wall anchors. For fiberglass surrounds, use a ⅛" drill bit; wall anchors are not necessary.

6

Apply a bead of silicone sealant along the joint between the tub and the wall at the ends of the track. Apply a minimum ¼" bead of sealant along the outside leg of the track underside.

7

Position the track on the tub ledge and against the wall. Attach the wall channels using the provided screws. Do not use caulk on the wall channels at this time.

8

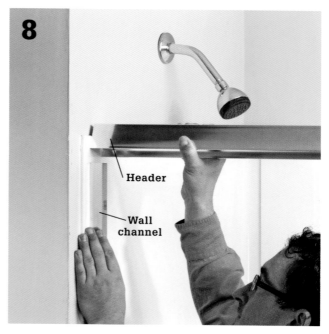

Header

Wall channel

Cut and install the header. At a location above the tops of the wall channels, measure the distance between the walls. Refer to the manufacturer's instructions for calculating the header length. For the door seen here, the length is the distance between the walls minus ¹⁄₁₆". Measure the header and carefully cut it to length using a hacksaw and a miter box. Slide the header down on top of the wall channels until seated.

9

Mount the rollers in the roller mounting holes. To begin, use the second-from-the-top roller mounting holes. Follow the manufacturer's instructions for spacer or washer placement and orientation.

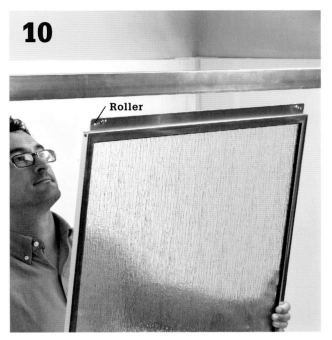

10

Roller

Carefully lift the inner panel by the sides and place the rollers on the inner roller track. Roll the door toward the shower end of the tub. The edge of the panel should touch both rubber bumpers. If it doesn't, remove the door and move the rollers to different holes. Drive the screws by hand to prevent overtightening.

11

Lift the outer panel by the sides with the towel bar facing out from the tub. Place the outer rollers over the outer roller track. Slide the door to the end opposite the shower end of the tub. If the door does not contact both bumpers, remove the door and move the rollers to different mounting holes.

12

Apply a bead of clear silicone sealant to the inside seam of the wall and wall channel at both ends and to the U-shaped joint of the track and wall channels. Smooth the sealant with a fingertip dipped in water.

Jetted Tub

A jetted spa is basically a bathtub that recirculates water, air, or a combination of the two to create an effect known as hydromassage. Hydromassage increases blood flow, relieves pressure on joints and muscles, and relieves tension. Interior hydromassage tubs usually have a water pump that blows a mixture of air and water through jets located in the tub body. Many include an integral water heater.

The product you'll see installed on these pages is a bit different. It is an air-jet tub: a relatively new entry in the jetted spa market that circulates only warm air, not water. This technology makes it safe to use bath oils, bubble bath, and bath salts in the spa. A model with no heater requires only a single 120-volt dedicated circuit. Models with heaters normally require either multiple dedicated 120-volt circuits or a 240-volt circuit.

Like normal bathtubs, jetted tubs can be installed in a variety of ways. Here, we install a drop-in tub (no nailing flange) in a 3-wall alcove. This may require the construction of a new stub wall, like the short wall we plumbed as the wet wall for this installation. Unless you have a lot of wiring and plumbing experience, consider hiring professionals for all or parts of the project.

Tools & Materials ▸

Plumbing tools	Thread lubricant
Utility knife	Shims
4-foot level	1 × 4 lumber
Square-edge trowel	1½" galvanized
Drill or power driver	deck screws
Channel-type pliers	1" galvanized
Hacksaw	roofing nails
Level	Plumber's putty
Circular saw	Dry-set mortar
Drill	Trowel
Screwdriver	Silicone caulk
Adjustable wrench	Jetted tub
Drain-waste-overflow	Faucet
assembly	Plumbing supplies
Rubber gaskets	Joint compound

Air-jet tubs create massaging action, stirring the water with warm air. Air-jets eliminate concerns about stagnant water and bacteria that can remain in the pipes of whirlpool tubs.

Tub Installation Options

Outdoor hot tubs can be inset into a deck or installed in a framed platform that can be built on just about any surface. Many hot tubs come preinstalled in a deck.

Alcove tubs, whether jetted or not, are normally supported by ledgers attached to the side and back walls. The front apron on a jetted tub is removable so you can make hookups and access the tub plumbing.

A framed platform is built to support a drop-in style jetted tub in a corner or island application. The vertical panels installed on the sides of the structure should be easily removable for access to the plumbing and wiring of the tub.

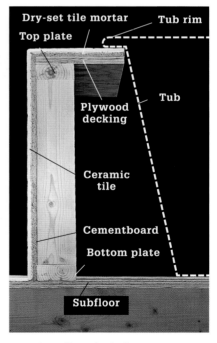

Dry-set tile mortar
Tub rim
Top plate
Plywood decking
Tub
Ceramic tile
Cementboard
Bottom plate
Subfloor

A stub wall can be built to support one or more sides of the tub and is often used in conjunction with ledgers.

How to Install a Jetted Tub

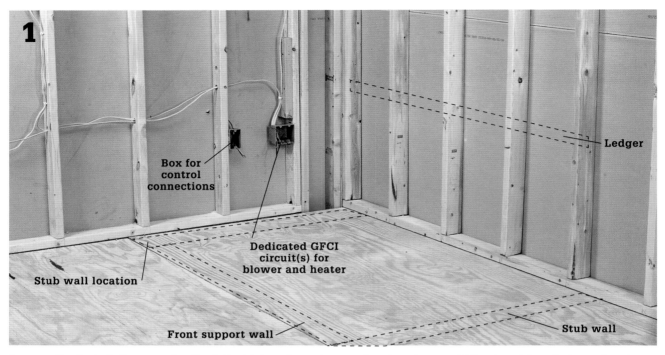

1

Box for control connections

Dedicated GFCI circuit(s) for blower and heater

Stub wall location

Front support wall

Ledger

Stub wall

Prepare the installation area for the jetted tub. Indicate the exact location where you'd like the tub installed as well as the planned wiring, water supply, and drain lines. Also plan for any wall-mounted tub controls, noting that wall-mounted ON/OFF switches or timers generally need to be installed at least 5 ft. away from the tub.

2

Lay out the locations for the drain, supply, and electrical lines, following the dimensions noted in your installation manual. Cut the drain opening in the subfloor making sure the ceneterpoint is exactly aligned with the drain hole in the tub. Cut out drain opening with a jigsaw.

3

Drain line

P-trap

Install a new branch drain line with P-trap for the tub. The P-trap should be centered in the drain cutout area so it will align precisely with the tub's drain tailpiece.

Build support framing as outlined in your installation manual, according to whichever type of installation you are undertaking (see page 89). In this photo, a wet wall is being framed at the head area of the tub. An identically sized stub wall is installed in the corner to support the foot end of the tub. A third stub wall will be constructed to support the front of the tub after the tub is in place.

Install water supply risers with shutoff valves. Make sure to create or allow for an access panel so you can get at the supply and drain plumbing easily. Here, a section of the wallcovering on the room side of the wet wall will be removable. You also need to make sure you have ready access to the motor and pump for the jetted tub. On the model shown here, a removable front apron allows ample access.

Install a 1 × 4 cross brace in the stub wall cavity so you can secure the supply pipes with pipe straps.

Run new wiring circuits and install receptacles as required in your installation manual. You will need a permit for this part of the job. If you do not have significant experience with home wiring, hire a pro for the wiring. In most cases, you'll need a dedicated circuit for the pump and another (often 240-volt) for the motor, and perhaps even a third circuit for accessories and peripherals, such as lights.

(continued)

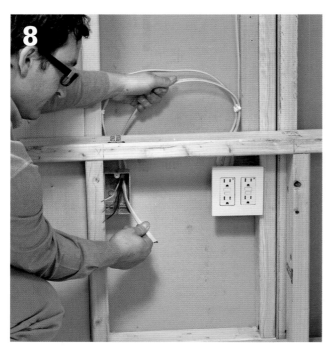

Prepare additional circuits as required for your tub. Here, a circuit is being run from the tub installation area to a remote wall switch that will regulate the air flow. Do as much of the wiring and plumbing installation as you can before the tub is in place.

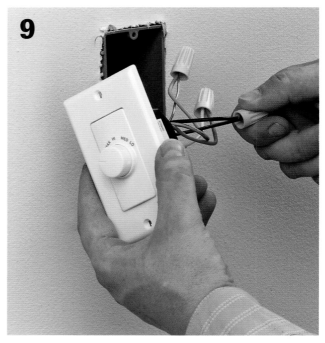

Install wall controls as specified by the manufacturer. Check with your local inspections office. They may want to inspect your wiring and plumbing lines before the tub is installed.

Tip ▸

Check the subfloor to make sure it is level. If you encounter a dip or low area (especially if it is in the area where the tub feet will rest) fill it with floor leveler compound (available at home centers and flooring stores). It is important that the tub be level or have a very slight slope toward the drain.

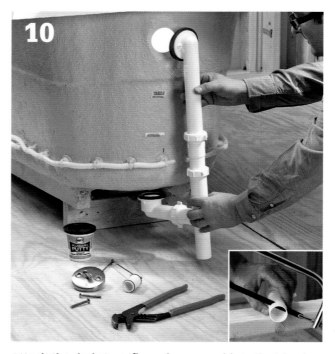

Attach the drain/overflow pipe assembly to the tub prior to installation, using rubber gaskets and pipe joint compound. Measure the distance the drain tailpiece will need to drop to connect with the drain trap and trim the tailpiece to fit (inset photo).

Secure the drain/overflow assembly by tightening the overflow coverplate and the drain strainer onto the assembly, from inside the tub.

Slide or lower the tub into the installation area, taking care not to disturb the drain/overflow assembly. Make sure the drain tailpiece aligns exactly over the P-trap opening.

Check the tub for level. If it is not level, check to make sure it is resting cleanly on the subfloor all around. If needed, shim underneath one of the feet to level the tub. Do not shim under apron if your tub has one that is already installed.

Front stub wall location

Secure the leveled tub in place as directed in your installation manual. Here, 2 × 4 block are screwed to the floor around the perimeter of the bathtub basin to create small curbs that prevent the tub from shifting. Build a 2 × 4 stub wall to support the front tub rim.

(continued)

15

Hook up the drain line by attaching the drain tailpiece to the P-trap in the floor. Use thread lubricant so you can get a good seal on the slip fitting.

16

Test the drain system to make sure it does not leak. Using a hose, first add a small amount of water and visually inspect the slip fittings and the area around the drain body. If it looks good, fill the tub up past the overflow line to make sure the overflow pipe seal does not leak. Drain the tub.

17

Make wiring hookups. Here, the hard work is already done and the blower and pump motors simply need to be plugged into their dedicated receptacles. If this unit had a heater, it would require an additional dedicated circuit. The blower motor also needs to be attached to the lead from the wall regulator installed in step 8.

18

Install wall panels around the tub area. If you will be installing wall tile, use cementboard. If you'll be installing a manufactured surround, mold-resistant drywall will do.

Install the wall surface materials, cutting holes for the spout and valves as needed.

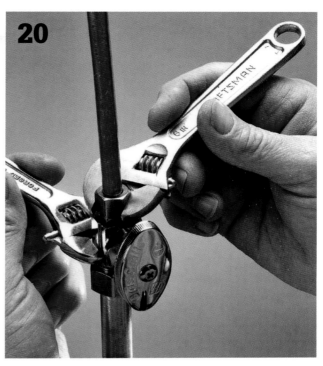

Install the spout supply valves and hook them up to the supply risers. Tubs are not predrilled for faucets as sinks are, so you'll need to decide whether to drill holes for the valves in the tub rim using a step bit, or to mount the faucet in the platform or the rim of the support wall.

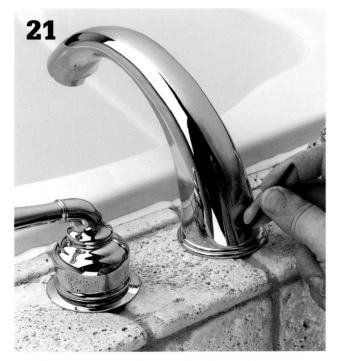

Attach the spout and the valve handles and test the supply system. To clear any debris from the lines, remove the spout aerator and run both hot and cold water for a minute or so.

Attach the removable front apron or replace the access panel covering. Then, fill the tub and have a nice, long soak.

Bidets

Bidets are becoming ever more popular in the United States. Maybe that's because they can give a dream bath that European flare so many of us find alluring. Go to Europe, Asia, or South America and you'll see how much people can come to rely on bidets. Some fans of this bathroom fixture think those who don't use bidets are unhygienic.

With the trend moving toward larger and more luxurious bathrooms, many Americans are becoming intrigued by this personal hygiene appliance. The standard model features hot and cold faucets, and either a movable nozzle located by the faucet handles or a vertical sprayer located near the front of the bowl. Most bidets are outfitted with a pop-up drain. You can also buy a combination toilet and bidet if space is an issue.

Installing a bidet is very much like installing a sink. The only difference is that the bidet can have the waste line plumbed below the floor, like a shower. But like sinks, bidets may have single or multiple deck holes for faucets, so be certain to purchase compatible components.

Tools & Materials ▸

Tape measure	(2) ⅜" supply lines
Drill	P–trap
Adjustable wrench	Tubing cutter
Level	Plumber's putt
Silicone sealant	Thread tape
(2) ⅜" shut off	Bidet
valves	Bidet faucet

A bidet is a useful companion to a toilet, and it is a luxury item you and your family will appreciate. It's also a bit of a novelty you will enjoy sharing. For people with limited mobility, a bidet is an aide to independent personal sanitation.

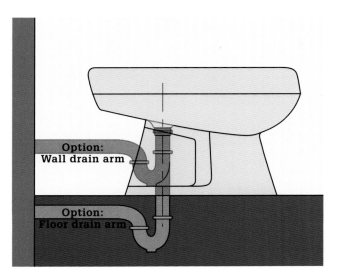

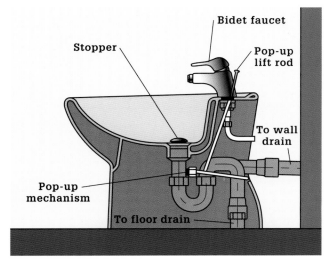

Bidet drains have more in common with sink drains than with toilet drains. Some even attach to a drain arm in the wall, with a P-trap that fits between the fixture drain tailpiece and the arm. Other bidets drain into a floor drain outlet with a trap that's situated between the tailpiece and the branch drain line.

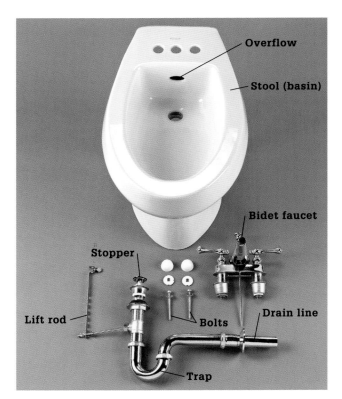

A bidet requires a special faucet that allows you to mix hot and cold water to a temperature you find comfortable. It has a third knob to control the water pressure. The aerator and spout pivot to allow you to adjust the spray to a comfortable height.

You can get all the features of a bidet on your existing toilet with a number of aftermarket bidet seats. These seats feature heaters, sprayers, and dryers in basic or deluxe versions. Installation takes less than an hour and no additional space is needed.

How to Install a Bidet

Rough-in supply and drain lines according to the manufacturer's specifications. If you do not have experience installing home plumbing, hire a plumber for this part of the job. Apply a coil of plumber's putty to the base of the bidet faucet, and then insert the faucet body into the mounting holes. Thread the washers and locknut onto the faucet body shank and hand tighten. Remove any plumber's putty squeeze-out.

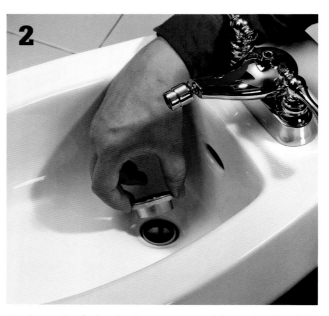

Apply a roll of plumber's putty around the underside of the drain flange. Wrap the bottom ⅔ of the flange threads with three layers of Teflon tape. Make sure to wrap the tape clockwise so that tightening the nut will not bunch up the tape. Insert the flange in the drain hole, place the gasket and washer, and then thread the nut onto the flange. Do not fully tighten.

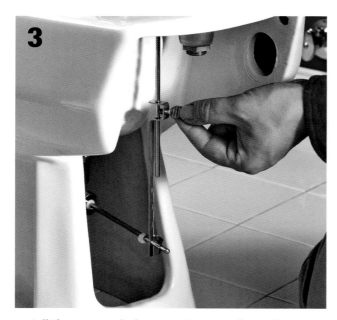

Install the pop-up drain apparatus according to the manufacturer's instructions.

Place the bidet in its final location, checking that supply and drain lines will be in alignment. Mark the locations of the two side-mounting holes through the predrilled holes on the stool and onto the floor.

Remove the bidet and drill ³⁄₁₆" pilot holes at the marks on the floor. Drive the floor bolts (included with the bidet basin) into the holes. Position the bidet so the floor bolts fit into the bolt holes in the base.

Connect the water supply risers to the bidet faucet using compression unions. Make sure to hook the hot and cold risers up to the correct ports on the faucet.

Hook up the drain line by attaching the P-trap to the drain tailpiece. The trap is then attached to a branch drain line coming out of the wall or floor in the same manner as a sink drain.

Remove the aerator so any debris in the supply line will clear and then turn on the water and open both faucets. Check for leaks in lines and fix, if found. Assemble the bolt caps and thread them onto the floor bolts. *Note: Do not dispose of paper in the bidet—return to the toilet to dry off after using the bidet for cleaning.*

Urinals

Most people consider a urinal to be a commercial or industrial bathroom accessory, so why would you want one in your home—and in your dream bathroom no less? The answer is in the many advantages a urinal has to offer and the fact that most major bathroom fixture manufacturers are now producing urinals designed for residential installation. Plumbing for a urinal resembles that of a vanity sink, though it has only a cold water supply.

A urinal doesn't take up much space and it uses much less water per flush than a standard toilet: .5 to 1.0 gallon of water per flush for the urinal, as opposed to the low-flow toilet's 1.6 gallons of water per flush. You also have the option of a waterless urinal, a great option for water conservation. Finally, a urinal is generally easier to keep clean than a toilet because splashing is minimized.

In today's homes, with large multiple bathrooms and his and hers master baths, there are plenty of places you can choose to install a urinal. Of course, the perfect place is where it will get used the most: in the bathroom closest to the TV if the guys congregate at your house to watch sporting events; or in the bathroom closest to boys' bedrooms if you've got a passel of them.

Urinals are great water savers and are becoming increasingly popular in today's dream bathroom.

Tools & Materials ▸

Tape measure	Urinal flushometer
Adjustable wrench	Emery cloth
Pencil	Wire brush
Level	Allen wrench
Sealant tape	Drywall
Utility knife	Drywall tape
Drywall saw	Drywall compound
Tubing cutter	2 × 6 lumber
Hacksaw	PVC 2" drainpipe
Miter box	PVC 2" male threaded
Hex wrenches	drain outlet
Smooth-jawed	½" copper pipe
spud wrench	Urinal
Slotted or phillips	Sealant tape
screwdriver	Pipe sealant

Waterless Urinals ▶

For the ultimate in water-conservation, you can now purchase a home urinal that uses zero water. A waterless urinal is never flushed, so you'll save about a gallon of water per usage. Naturally, waterless urinals are plumbed into your drain line system. But where typical plumbing fixtures rely on fresh water to carry the waste into the system, the waterless system relies simply on gravity for the liquid waste to find its way out of the fixture and into the drain. The secret is a layer of sealing liquid that is heavier than the water and forms a skim coat over the urine. When the urine enters the trap it displaces the sealing liquid, which immediately reforms on the surface to create a layer that seals in odors. The Kohler fixture seen here (see Resources, page 330 is an example of the sealing liquid system. Other waterless urinals use replaceable cartridges.

A layer of sealing liquid forms a skim coat that floats on top of the liquid to trap odors.

Flushing Options for Urinals

A manual flush handle is still the most common and least expensive flushing mechanism for urinals. It is reliable but not as sanitary as touchless types such as the Flushometer on page 105.

Motion sensors automatically flush touchless urinals, which is a great improvement in sanitation. These tend to be more expensive, however, and are more likely to develop problems. Also, because they flush automatically when users step away from the fixture, they don't allow you to conserve water by limiting flushing.

How to Install a Urinal

Remove the drywall or other surface coverings between the urinal location and the closest water supply and waste lines. Remove enough wall surface to reveal half of the stud face on each side of the opening to make patch work simpler.

Following the manufacturer's directions for the urinal and flushometer, determine the mounting height of the urinal and mark the location of the supply and waste lines. For this installation, the 2" waste line is centered 17½" above the finished floor. Cut 5½" × 1½" notches in the wall studs centered at 32" above the finished floor surface, then attach a 2 × 6 mounting board.

Install the copper cold water supply line according to the manufacturer's specifications. Here, it is 4¾" to the side of the fixture centerline and 45" from the finished floor (11½" from the top of the fixture). Cap the stubout 3" from the finished wall surface. Install the 2" drainpipe and vent pipe, making sure that the centerline of the drain outlet is positioned correctly (here, 17½" above the finished floor and 4¾" to the side of the supply line).

Attach the male-threaded waste outlet to the drain pipe. It should extend beyond the finished wall surface. Replace the wall covering and finish as desired.

Attach the mounting brackets 32" above the floor, 3¼" to the sides of the centerline of the waste outlet.

Apply Teflon tape to the waste outlet. Thread the female collar onto the waste outlet until it is firmly seated and the flanges are horizontally level. Place the gasket onto the female collar. The beveled surface of the gasket faces toward the urinal.

Hang the urinal on the brackets, being careful not to bump the porcelain as it chips easily. Thread the screws through the washers, the holes in the urinal, and into the collar. Tighten the screws by hand, then one full turn with an adjustable wrench. Do not overtighten.

Determine the distance from the centerline of the water inlet on the top of the urinal, called the spud, to the finished wall. Subtract 1¼" from this distance and cut the water supply pipe to that length using a tubing cutter. Turn off the water before cutting. After cutting, deburr the inside and outside diameter of the supply pipe. Attach the threaded adapter to the cut pipe.

(continued)

9

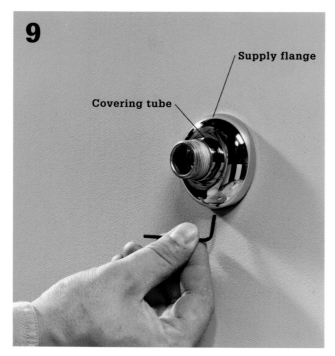

Covering tube

Supply flange

Measure from the wall surface to the first thread of the adapter. Using a hacksaw and a miter box or a tubing cutter, cut the covering tube to this length. Slide the covering tube over the water supply pipe. Slide the supply flange over the covering tube until it rests against the wall. Tighten the setscrew on the flange with an Allen wrench.

10

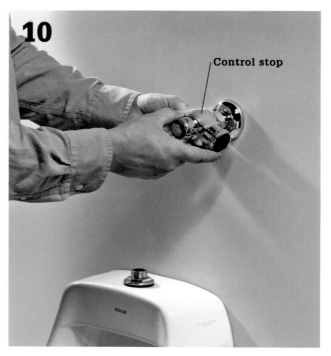

Control stop

Apply a small amount of pipe sealant to the adapter threads, then thread the control stop onto the adapter threads. Position the outlet toward the urinal so that it is horizontally level.

11

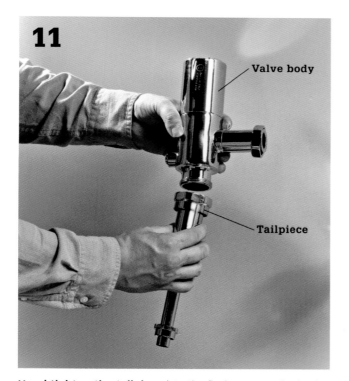

Valve body

Tailpiece

Hand tighten the tailpiece into the flushometer valve body.

12

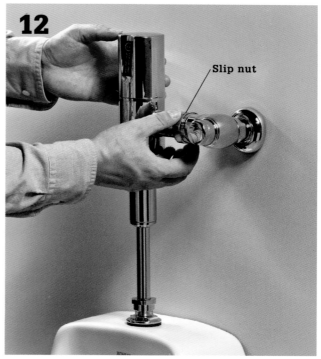

Slip nut

Hand tighten the slip nut that connects the valve body to the control stop.

13

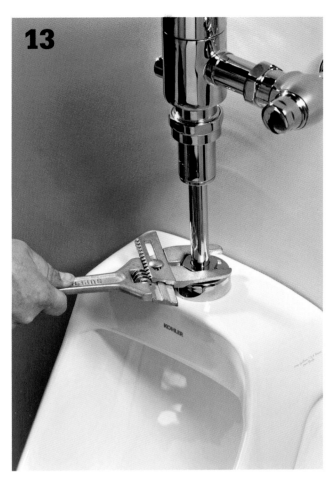

Use a smooth-jawed spud wrench to securely tighten the tailpiece, vacuum breaker, and spud couplings.

Tip ▸

For maximum sanitation, choose a urinal flush mechanism with an electronic sensor, like the Kohler Flushometer being installed here. The electronic eye on this type of flush mechanism senses when a user approaches the fixture and then commands the fixture to flush when the user steps away. This eliminates the need to touch the handle before the user has the opportunity to wash his hands.

While testing the flush, adjust the supply stop screw counterclockwise until adequate flow is achieved.

14

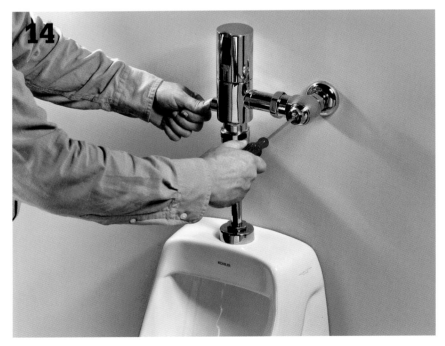

Water Softeners

If your house has hard water coursing through its pipes, then you've got a couple of problems. Not only does your water do a poor job of dissolving soap, but you also have plenty of scale deposits on dishes, plumbing fixtures, and the inside of your water heater.

Softeners fix these problems by chemically removing the calcium and magnesium that are responsible for the hard water (usually described as over 17 grains of minerals per gallon). These units are installed after the water meter but before the water line branches off to appliances or fixtures, with one exception: Piping to outside faucets should branch off the main line before the softener because treating outside water is a waste of money.

Softeners come with an overflow tube and a purge tube to rinse out the minerals that are extracted from the water. These tubes should be attached to the floor drain or to a laundry sink basin, which is the better approach if the sink is close by

Know Your Types of Salt ▸

Salt for water softeners comes in three basic types: rock salt, solar salt (crystals), and evaporated salt (pellets). Rock salt is a mineral that's mined from salt deposits. Solar salt is a crystalline residue left behind when seawater is evaporated naturally. It sometimes is sold as pellets or blocks. Evaporated salt is similar to solar salt, but the liquid in the brine is evaporated using mechanical methods. Rock salt is cheapest but leaves behind the most residue and therefore requires more frequent brine tank cleaning. Evaporated salt pellets are the cleanest and require the least maintenance.

Tools & Materials ▸

Tape measure	Soldering flux
Tubing cutter	Solder
Propane torch	4"-thick
Slip-joint pliers	concrete blocks
Steel wool	

A water softener is a two-part appliance that includes the water softener itself (to the left, above) and an attached salt storage tank (right).

Softened Water ▸

From your plumbing's point-of-view, the best water softening strategy is to position the softener close to the main, cold-only supply line (as seen here). Doing this results in both hot and cold water being softened. But because some homeowners object to the altered taste and increased salinity of softened water, the softener may be installed after the hot and cold lines have split from the main supply line. This way, the water may be softened immediately before it enters the heater, and the cold water remains unsoftened.

Main water supply line to water heater

Cold supply line

How to Install a Water Softener

The first step is to measure the distance between the bypass ports on the tank to the cold water supply line. Cut copper tubing to fit this space and solder appropriate fittings onto both ends.

Install the plastic tubing discharge tube on the head of the water softener following the manufacturer's directions.

(continued)

3

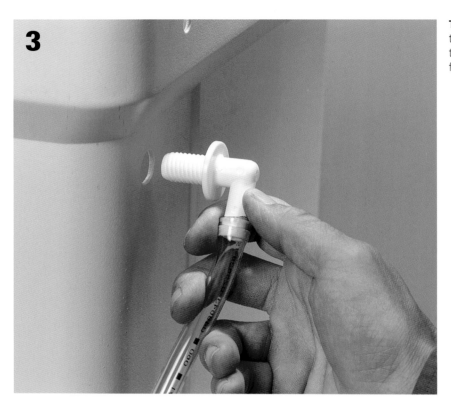

The overflow tube is usually connected to the side of the softener's tank. Run this tube, along with the discharge tube, to a floor drain or a laundry sink.

4

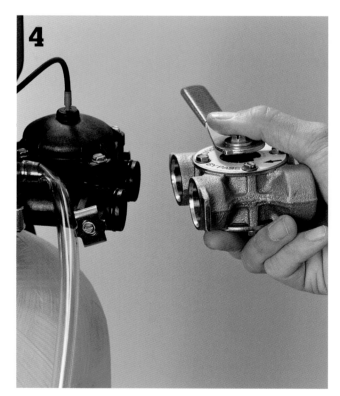

5

Install the bypass valve in the softener's head. One side of the valve goes in the inlet port and the other fits into the outlet port. This valve is held in place with simple plastic clips or threaded couplings. *Note: Check local codes for bypass requirements.*

Attach the copper tubing that supplies the water to the bypass valve. For this unit, the joint is made with a male-threaded union that screws onto the bypass valve ports.

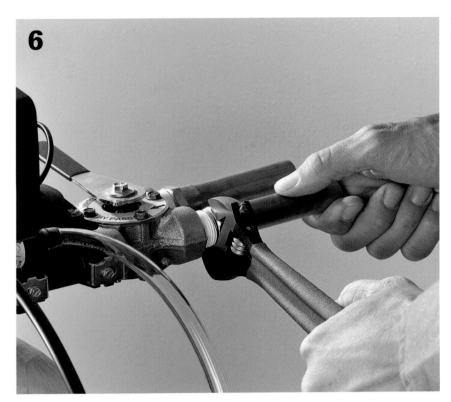

6

Tighten both supply tube nuts with a wrench. Do not over tighten them.

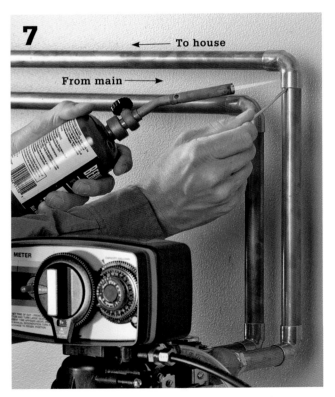

7

← To house

From main →

METER

Connect the copper tubing from the softener to the water supply lines. Clean all fittings and pipes with steel wool. Then, apply soldering flux to the parts and solder them together with a propane torch. For more information on soldering copper, see page 276.

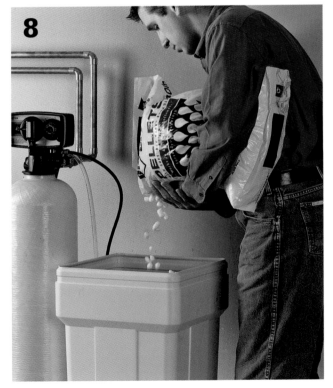

8

Turn on the water supply and make sure the installation works properly. If you see any leaks, fix them. Then add the water softening pellets to the top of the unit in the ratios explained on the package.

Hot Water Dispenser

It's still easy to find a refrigerator without a cold water dispenser in its door, but you have to walk past a lot of product before you see one. This says something about people liking convenience. In many ways, a hot water dispenser is even more convenient than a cold water dispenser. There are boxes and boxes of beverages and food that need only a trickle of hot water to achieve their destiny: coffee, tea, hot chocolate, instant soup, hot cereals, and just plain old hot water and lemon to name a few. And there's no faster way to get this hot water than with a hot water dispenser. These units are designed to fit in the spare hole on many kitchen sink decks. But, if you don't have one, you can replace your spray hose with the dispenser. Or, if you want to keep the hose, just drill an extra hole in your sink or countertop to accommodate the dispenser faucet.

Note: Installing this appliance requires both plumbing and wiring work. If you are unsure of your skills in these areas, hire a professional. (Be sure to check your local codes before starting.)

Tools & Materials ▸

Power drill with ¾"-dia. bit	Wire connectors
Utility knife	Saddle valve
Wire stripper	Brass plug to fill
Screwdrivers	spray hose port on
Adjustable wrench	kitchen faucet
14/2 NM	Teflon tape
electrical cable	Hot water
Flexible cable conduit	dispenser kit
Duplex electrical box	Cable connectors
Conduit box	15-amp circuit
connector	breaker (to
Switched receptacle	match service
Measuring tape	panel breakers)
	Tubing cutter

Switch Receptacle ▸

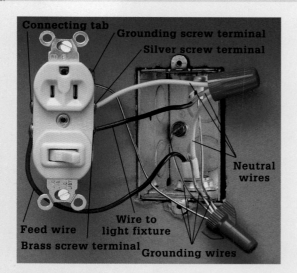

Three wires are connected to the switch/receptacle. One hot wire is the feed wire that brings power into the box. It is connected to the side of the switch that has a connecting tab. The other hot wire carries power out. It is connected to the brass screw terminal on the side that does not have a connecting tab. The white, neutral wire is pigtailed to the silver screw terminal. The grounding wires must be pigtailed to the switch/receptacle green grounding screw and to the grounded metal box.

On-demand hot water is not only a convenience, it can help to conserve both energy and water.

How to Install a Hot Water Dispenser

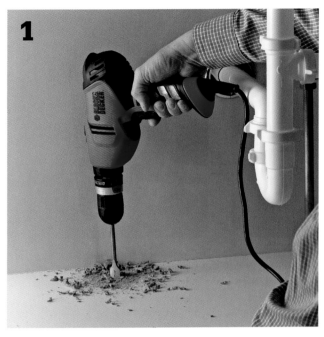

Drill an access hole for a new power cable (in flexible conduit) in the bottom of the sink compartment cabinet. Use a drill and a 3/4"-dia. bit. Go into the basement and drill a hole up through the flooring that will align with the first hole (or make other arrangements to run circuit wire as you see fit).

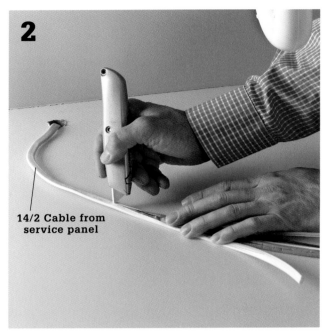

14/2 Cable from service panel

Fish a 14/2 or 12/2 cable from the electric service panel up through the hole in the floor. Strip the sheathing from the cable with a utility knife. Also strip the insulation from the wires with a wire stripper. Do not nick the wire insulation.

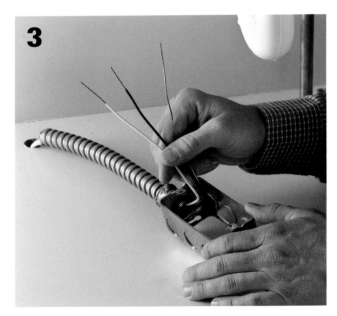

Slide a piece of flexible conduit over the wires, so the wires are protected from the point they leave the cabinet floor to when they enter the electrical box. Attach the conduit to the box with a box connector so at least 8" of wire reaches into the box.

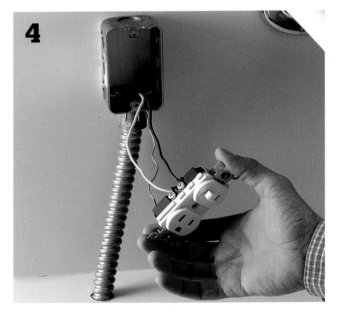

Install a switched receptacle. Mount a duplex metal box on the cabinet wall. Connect the black power wire to the brass screw on the switch. Attach the white neutral wire to the silver screw on the receptacle. Attach the ground wire to the receptacle ground terminal.

(continued)

5

Tie into water supply. Water for the dispenser comes from the cold water supply line under the kitchen sink. Mount a tee on this pipe, below its shutoff valve, by alternately tightening the tee bolts on both sides with a wrench.

6

Determine the best place for the dispenser heater, usually on the back cabinet wall, so its pigtail plug will reach the switched receptacle. Screw its mounting bracket to the wall and hang the heater on this bracket.

7

To replace a spray hose with the dispenser faucet, remove the nut that holds the sprayer to the sink. Then remove the end of the hose from its port on the bottom of the faucet, using an adjustable wrench. This will free the hose so it can be pulled out from above the sink. Plug the spray hose part on the faucet.

8

The dispenser faucet is designed to fit into a standard sink hole. To install it, just squeeze its supply tubes together so they can fit into the hole, and drop it in place. The unit is held securely by a washer and locking screw that is tightened from below the sink.

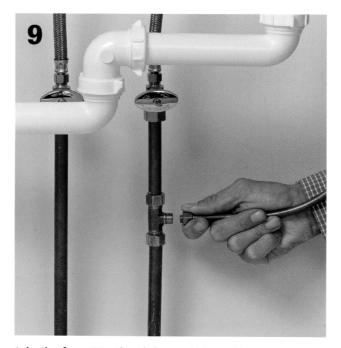

9

Join the faucet to the sink supply tee with a piece of flexible tubing. Measure this piece, make the cut with a tubing cutter, and install compression nuts and ferrules on both ends. Slide one end of the tubing into the valve and tighten the nut with a wrench.

Attach the two copper water tubes to the heater with compression fittings. Tighten them with a wrench. On the model seen here, the heater unit has three tubes. One supplies cold water to the heater, one supplies hot water to the faucet, and a third clear plastic hose acts as a vent and is attached to an expansion tank within the heater.

Slide the end of the plastic vent tube onto the nipple on top of the tank and attach it according to the manufacturer's instructions. On some models a spring clip is used for this job; other models require a hose clamp.

Install the heater power supply cable in the service panel. Begin by turning off the main power breaker. Then, remove the outside door panel and remove one of the knockout plates from the top or side of the box. Install a cable clamp inside this hole, push the cable through the clamp, and tighten the clamp to secure the cable.

Strip the sheathing from the cable inside the panel and remove the insulation from the ends on the black and white cable wires. Loosen a lug screw on the neutral bus bar and push the white wire under the lug. Attach the ground wire to the grounding bus bar. Tighten both these screws securely.

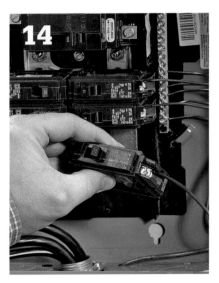

Loosen the lug screw on a standard 15-amp breaker and put the end of the black (hot) cable wire under this lug. Tighten the lug with a screwdriver. Then install the breaker in the hot bus bar by pushing it into place.

Once a new breaker is installed, the service panel cover has to be modified to fit over it. Break out the protective plate that covers the breaker position with pliers. Screw the cover to the panel, and turn on the main breaker. Turn on the water supply to the dispenser and plug it into the receptacle. Turn on the receptacle switch, wait fifteen minutes, and check that the system is working properly.

Icemaker

Most expensive refrigerators come with icemakers as standard equipment, and practically every model features them as an option (a refrigerator with an icemaker usually costs about $100 more). It is also possible to purchase an icemaker as a retrofit feature for your old fridge.

Installing one is a pretty simple job, especially if you buy a kit made by the same manufacturer that built your refrigerator. Most appliance stores can look up the information specific to your fridge, (be sure to have your model number).

Using equipment from the same manufacturer ensures a proper fit. The kit screws fit the fridge holes. The hardest part is running water from a convenient supply line. Because you are working in the kitchen, one sensible source is the cold water line under the kitchen sink. Often by drilling a small hole in the floor, you can access a nearby line in the basement without having to fish your tubing behind (or through) a bank of cabinets.

Most icemakers either come preinstalled or are purchased as an accessory when you buy your new refrigerator. But if you have an older refrigerator with no icemaker and you'd like it to have one, all is not lost. Inspect the back of the unit, behind the freezer compartment. If your refrigerator has the required plumbing to support an icemaker you will see a port or a port that is covered with backing. In that case, all you need to do is take the make and model information to an appliance parts dealer and they can sell you an aftermarket icemaker. Plan to spend $100 to $200.

A built-in icemaker is easy to install as a retrofit appliance in most modern refrigerators. If you want to have an endless supply of ice for home use, you'll wonder how you ever got along without one.

Tools & Materials ▶

Screwdrivers	Duct or masking tape	Channel-type pliers	Saddle valve or
Nut drivers	Electric drill and	Open-end or	T-fitting
Needle-nose pliers	assorted bits	adjustable wrench	(for supply tube)
		Icemaker kit	Putty knife

How Icemakers Work ▸

An icemaker receives its supply of water for making cubes through a ¼" copper supply line that runs from the icemaker to a water pipe. The supply line runs through a valve in the refrigerator and is controlled by a solenoid that monitors the water supply and sends the water into the icemaker itself, where it is turned into ice cubes. The cubes drop down into a bin, and as the ice level rises, they also raise a bail wire that's connected to a shutoff. When the bin is full, the bail wire will be high enough to trigger a mechanism that shuts off the water supply.

Aftermarket automatic icemakers are simple to install as long as your refrigerator is icemaker ready. Make sure to buy the correct model for your appliance and do careful installation work—icemaker water supply lines are very common sources for leaks.

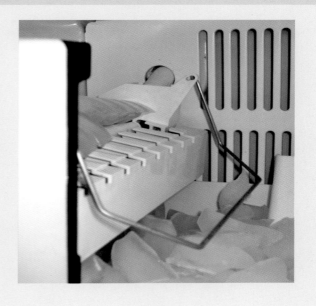

How to Install an Icemaker

Remove all the contents from the refrigerator and freezer compartments and store them in ice chests or in a neighbor's refrigerator. Unplug the unit and pull it out from the wall. Then open the freezer door and remove the icemaker cover plate at the back of the compartment.

On the back side of the refrigerator, remove the backing or unscrew the icemaker access panel that covers the icemaker port.

(continued)

3

Water port

Wiring harness port

Locate and clear the parts. One opening is for the water line. The other is for a wiring harness. Usually, these holes are filled with insulation plugs that keep the cold air inside the freezer from leaking out into the room. Remove these plugs with needle-nose pliers.

4

Install the water tube assembly (part of the icemaker kit) in its access hole on the back of the refrigerator. This assembly features a plastic elbow attached to the plastic tube that reaches into the freezer compartment.

5

Hook up the harness. Icemaker kits usually come with a wiring harness that joins the icemaker motor inside the freezer box to the power supply wires. Push this harness through its access hole and into the freezer compartment. Then seal the hole with the plastic grommet that comes with the harness.

6

Join the end of the icemaker wiring harness to the power connector that was preinstalled on the back of the refrigerator. This connection should lay flat against the back. If it doesn't, just tape it down with some duct tape or masking tape.

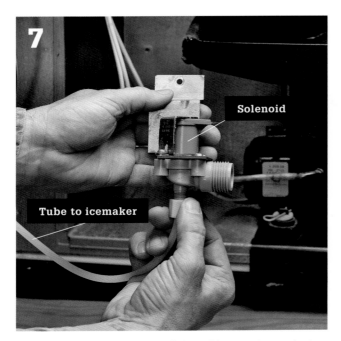

7

Solenoid

Tube to icemaker

The water tube at the top of the refrigerator is attached to the solenoid that is mounted at the bottom with a plastic water line. To install the line, first attach it to the water tube, then run it down the back of the refrigerator and attach it to the solenoid valve with a compression fitting. This job is easier to do before you attach the solenoid assembly to the refrigerator cabinet.

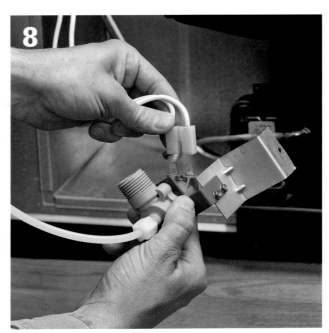

8

The icemaker wiring harness comes with two snap connectors. One goes to the preinstalled wires on the refrigerator and the other is attached to the solenoid. Just push this second connector onto the brass tabs, usually at the top of the solenoid.

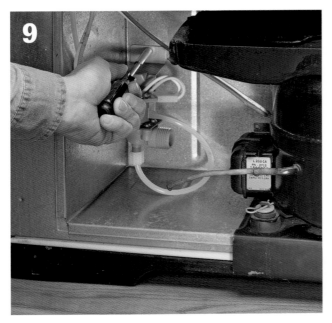

9

Attach the solenoid to a mounting bracket that should be installed on the cabinet wall at the bottom of the refrigerator. Mounting holes may be predrilled in the cabinet for this purpose. But if not, drill holes to match the bracket and the size of the screws. Then attach the bracket and make sure to attach the solenoid ground wire to one of these screws.

10

Install the water-inlet copper tube once the solenoid is mounted. Attach it by tightening the nut on one end with channel-type pliers. The other end of the tube is held to the refrigerator cabinet with a simple clamp. Make sure the end of this tubing is pointing straight up.

(continued)

11

The end of the water-inlet tube is joined to the water supply tubing (from the house plumbing system) with a brass compression coupling. Tighten the compression nuts with an open-end or adjustable wrench.

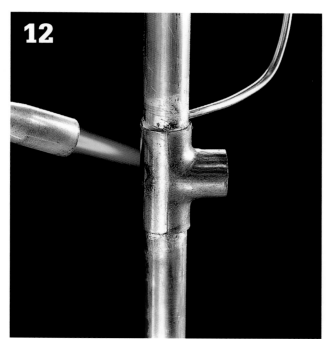

12

Run the water tubing to the kitchen sink cabinet or through the floor to a cold water pipe below. Turn off the water supply at the nearest shutoff valve. Install a T-fitting in the pipe line. Attach the icemaker tubing to the T-fitting with a compression fitting.

13

From inside the freezer compartment, make sure the water tube and the wiring harness (from the back of the refrigerator) are free. If they are caught on the cabinet, loosen them until they are easily accessible.

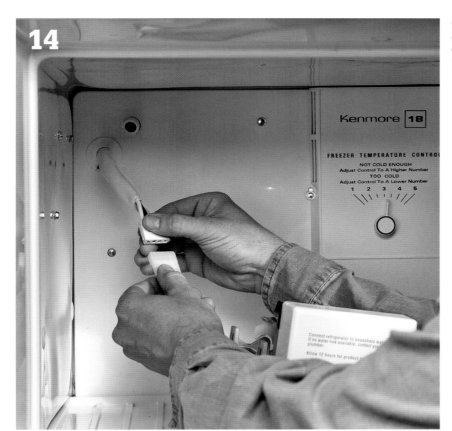

Connect the wire harness to the plug on the icemaker unit. Also connect the water supply tube to the back of the icemaker with a spring clip or hose clamp.

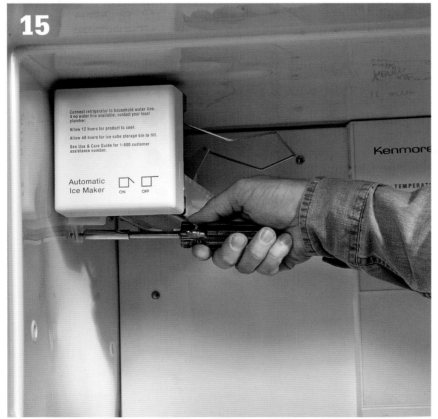

Install the icemaker. Remove any small rubber caps that may be installed in the mounting screw holes with a narrow putty knife. Lift the unit and screw it to the freezer wall. The mounting bracket holes are usually slotted to permit leveling the unit. Plug in the refrigerator and test the icemaker.

Pot Filler

Kitchen design trends are moving ever closer to replicating commercial kitchens in the home. One example of this trend is the pot filler. A long-neck faucet that mounts to the wall behind the cooktop, a pot filler allows you to dispense water directly into large pots on the cooktop. This saves lugging pots of water from the sink to the stove.

Although horizontally mounted models are available, most pot fillers are attached to the wall. Almost all are designed for cold water only. Some have two valves, one at the wall and another at the end of the spout. Other models can be turned on with a foot pedal for safe, hands-free use.

A pot filler will require code-approved supply pipe (½" in most cases) connected with a permanent union at another supply line or the main. The best time to run a new supply is during a remodel. But retrofitting a new supply line and mounting a pot filler is not too difficult as a standalone project. Using PEX supply pipe will make running the new supply line in finished walls easier (see pages 288 to 293 for cutting and fitting PEX).

A pot filler is a cold-water tap that you install above your cooktop so you can add water to large stock pots without having to carry a full pot of water around the kitchen.

Tools & Materials ▶

Hack saw	Pot filler	Reciprocating saw	Wallboard
PEX tools	Protector plates	Wallboard tools	patching materials
PEX pipe	PEX fittings	Pipe joint compound	

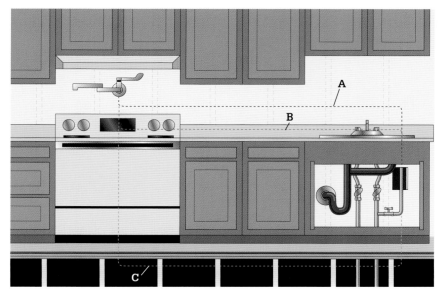

Plan the route for the new supply line. In most cases, you will enter the stud cavity of the wall and run a new line directly upward, past the backsplash height of the countertop (A). If the countertop backsplash is removable, avoid wallboard patching by installing the tubing behind the backsplash (B). You may also be able to run the supply line underneath the kitchen if there is an unfinished basement (C).

How to Install a Pot Filler

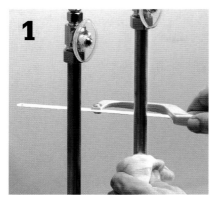

Shut off the water supply and locate the cold water supply riser at the kitchen sink. Cut into the riser and install a T-fitting, or replace the existing shutoff valve on the riser with a multiple-outlet shutoff valve, with an outlet for ½" supply pipe for the pot filler.

Plan the route for the new supply line beginning at the T-fitting and working toward the cooktop area. Determine the height of the new line and then snap chalklines from the sink to the cooktop. With the electrical power shut off, remove wall coverings 2" above and below the chalkline and at the location for the pot filler outlet. Make sure the location is high enough to clear your tallest stockpot.

Drill ¾" holes in the framing for the supply tubes. Install protector plates if the holes are within 1¼" of the stud edge. Run ½" PEX from the supply riser through the holes to the pot filler location (inset).

Attach the new PEX supply line to the T-fitting at the supply riser, installing an accessible shutoff valve on the new line.

At the cooktop, install the faucet union as specified by the manufacturer. Add blocking as needed. The pot filler installed here attaches to a drop-ear L-fitting, mounted to blocking. Apply pipe joint compound to the faucet inlet and thread it on to the L-fitting.

Cut and install the wallboard patch. Fit the flange over the inlet. Apply pipe joint compound to the threads of the faucet body. Assemble and adjust the faucet according to the manufacturer's instructions. Test the faucet before refinishing the wallboard.

Reverse-Osmosis Water Filters

Not all water is created equal. Some water tastes better than other water. Some water looks better than other water. And some has more impurities. Because no one wants to drink bad water, the bottled water business has exploded over the past twenty years. Home filtration systems have also grown by leaps and bounds, in part because there are so many different types of filters available.

For example, sediment filters will remove rust, sand, and suspended minerals, like iron. A carbon filter can remove residual chlorine odors, some pesticides and even radon gas. Distillation filters can remove bacteria and organic compounds, while a traditional water softener can neutralize hard water. But many of the most toxic impurities, heavy metals like mercury, lead, cadmium, and arsenic are best

Reverse-osmosis filters can be highly effective for removing specific contaminants from drinking water. Because the filtration process wastes a lot of fresh water, it's a good idea to have your water professionally tested before investing in an RO system.

removed with a reverse-osmosis (RO) system like the one shown here.

These filters are designed to treat just cooking and drinking water. The system holds the treated water in a storage tank and delivers it to a sink-mounted faucet on demand. RO units feature multiple filter cartridges, in this case a pre-filter unit, followed by the RO membrane, and then a carbon post-filter.

Tools & Materials ▸

Plastic gloves	Teflon tape
Screwdrivers	Saddle valve
Electric drill	Rubber drain saddle
Adjustable wrench	

Point-of-Use Filters ▸

Point-of-use water filtration systems are typically installed in the sink base cabinet, with a separate faucet from the main kitchen faucet. The setup shown here has an extra filter to supply a nearby refrigerator icemaker.

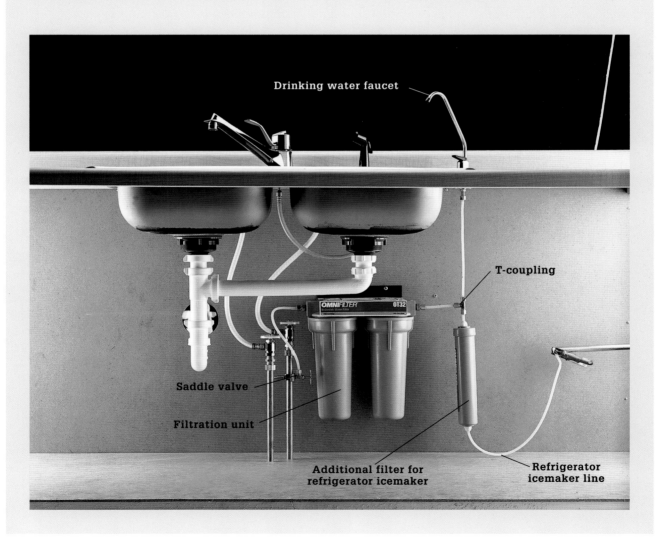

Drinking water faucet

T-coupling

Saddle valve

Filtration unit

Additional filter for refrigerator icemaker

Refrigerator icemaker line

How to Install a Reverse-Osmosis Water Filter

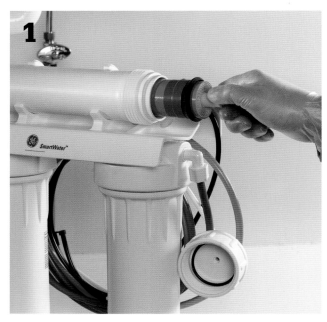

Install the RO membrane filter. It is shipped in a separate bag that is filled with anti-bacterial fluid. Wearing plastic gloves, remove the cartridge from the bag and install it in the filter unit. Make sure to touch only the ends of the cartridge when you handle it or you can damage the membrane.

Follow the manufacturer's instructions to establish the best location for the filter inside your kitchen sink cabinet. Drive mounting screws into the cabinet wall to support the unit.

Assemble the entire filtration system and then hang it on the cabinet wall. The best system layout may be to locate the filter on one wall and the storage tank on the opposite wall.

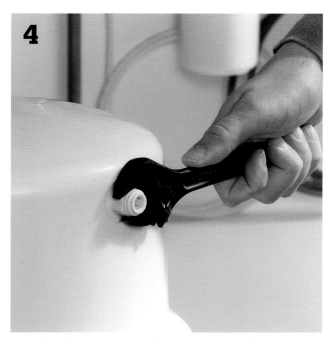

Attach valve to the side of the storage tank. Just wrap its threads a couple of times with Teflon tape and screw the valve into the tank. Finger tighten it, then turn it one more turn with an adjustable wrench.

Connect the filter to the tank with plastic tubing. In most units, the joint between the two is made with a compression fitting. On this filter, the fitting is a push-type collar. Simply insert the hose into the collar until it will not go any farther.

Connect the water storage tank and faucet with plastic tubing. Here, a push-type compression fitting on the end of the tubing was used. To install it, push the end of the fitting over the bottom of the faucet shank until the fitting bottoms out.

Jamb nut

The filter faucet comes with a jamb nut and sometimes a plastic spacer (as with this unit) that goes on the shank of the faucet before the jamb nut. After the nut is finger tight, snug it securely with an adjustable wrench.

Mount the faucet in the sink deck, following the manufacturer's instructions.

(continued)

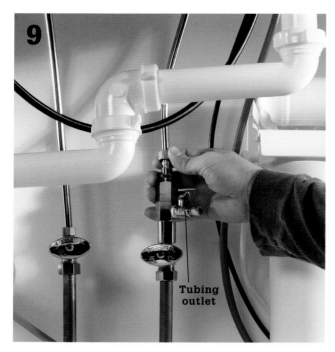

The water supply to the filter comes from the cold-water supply line that services the kitchen sink faucet. The easiest way to tap into the supply line is to replace the shutoff valve at the supply riser with a new valve containing an additional outlet for tubing.

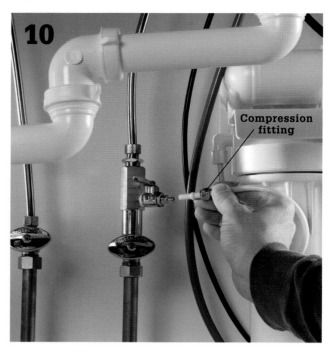

Attach the filter supply tube to the port on the shut off valve with a compression fitting. Push the end of the tubing onto the valve, then push the ferrule against the valve and thread the compression nut into place. Finger tighten it, then turn it one more full turn with a wrench.

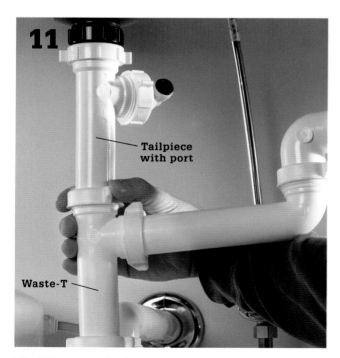

The filter must also be tied into the drain system. The best way to do this is to replace the drain tailpiece with a new drain tailpiece that contains an auxiliary port.

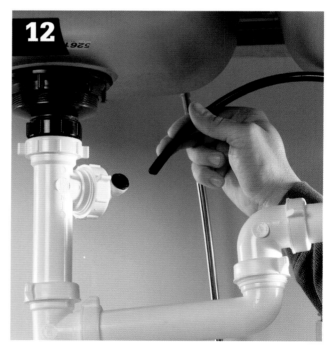

Attach the tubing from the drain to the auxiliary port on the tailpiece. Finish up by turning on the water and checking the system for leaks. Be sure to filter and drain at least two tanks of water, to clean any contaminants from the system, before drinking the water.

Installing a Whole-House Water Filtration System ▶

A whole-house water filtration system is installed along the supply pipe carrying water to the house, located after the water meter, but before any other appliances in the pipe line. A whole-house system reduces the same elements as an undersink system and can also help reduce the iron flowing into the water softener, prolonging its life.

Always follow the manufacturer's directions for your particular unit. If your electrical system is grounded through the water pipes, make sure to install ground clamps on both sides of the filtration unit with a connecting jumper wire. Globe valves should be installed within 6" of the intake and the outtake sides of the filter.

Filters must be replaced every few months, depending on type of manufacturer. The filtration unit cover unscrews for filter access.

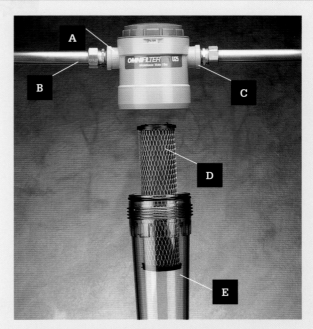

A whole-house water filtration system: (A) intake side, (B) supply pipe from the water meter pipe, (C) outtake side to the house supply pipe, (D) filter, and (E) filtration unit cover.

Shut off main water supply and turn on faucets to drain pipes. Position unit after water meter, but before any other appliances in supply pipe. Measure and mark pipe to accomodate the filtration unit. Cut pipe at marks with a pipe cutter. Join water meter side of pipe with intake side of unit, and house supply side of pipe with outtake side of unit. Tighten with a wrench.

Install a filter and screw filtration unit cover to bottom of the filtration unit. Attach a jumper wire to pipes on other side of unit, using pipe clamps. Open main water supply lines to restore the water supply. Allow faucets to run for a few minutes, as you check to make sure that the system is working properly.

Freezeproof Sillcocks

If you live in a part of the world where sub-freezing temperatures occur for extended periods of time, consider replacing your old sillcock (outdoor faucet) with a frost-proof model. In this project we show you how to attach the new sillcock using compression fittings, so no torch or molten solder is required.

Compression fittings are ok to use in accessible locations, like between open floor joists in a basement. Your building code may prohibit their use in enclosed walls and floors. To see if your sillcock can be replaced according to the steps outlined here, see the facing page.

Tools & Materials ▸

Adjustable wrench	Screwdriver
Frost-proof sillcock	Threaded adapter
Line level	#10 or #8 screws
Silicone caulk	Tubing cutter
Teflon tape	1⅛-inch spade bit
Pipe joint compound	10d nails
Pipe wrench	Board
Tape measure	Electric drill
⅛-in. drill bit	

Did that outside faucet freeze again? Replace it with one that you never have to turn off in the winter.

Anatomy of a Frost-proof Sillcock ▸

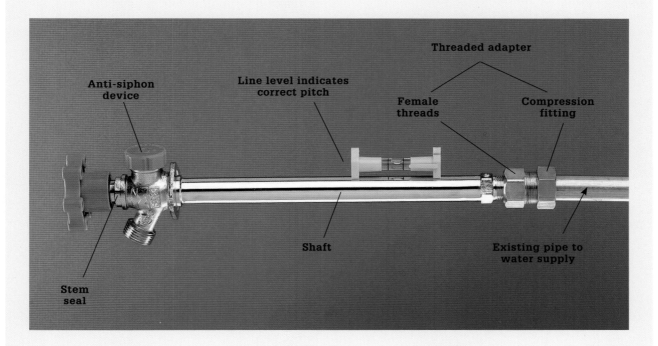

The frost-proof sillcock shown here can stay active all winter because the stem washer turns off the water in the warm interior of the house. The shaft needs to be pitched slightly down toward the outside to allow water to drain from the shaft. This supply pipe is connected to the threaded adapter with a compression fitting, which is secured to the pipe with two wrenches. Do not use the steps that follow if any of the following apply:

- Your pipes are made from steel instead of copper.
- The length of the pipe from the sillcock to where you can comfortably work on it is greater than 12".
- The pipe has a valve or change of direction fitting within ten inches of the existing sillcock.
- The existing supply pipe is ⅝" outside diameter as measured with an adjustable wrench, and you are unable to make the hole in the wall bigger to accommodate the thicker shaft of the frost-proof sillcock. (For example, the hole is in a concrete foundation.)

How to Replace a Hose Bib with a Frost-proof Sillcock

Turn off the water to your outside faucet at a shutoff found inside the house or basement behind the faucet (see page 6 if you have trouble turning off the water). Open the faucet and a bleeder valve on the shutoff to drain any remaining water from the pipe.

When you are sure the water flow has been stopped, use a tubing cutter to sever the supply pipe between the shutoff valve and the faucet. Make this first cut close to the wall. Tighten the tubing cutter onto the pipe. Both wheels of the cutter should rest evenly on the pipe. Turn the cutter around the pipe. The line it cuts should make a perfect ring, not a spiral. If it doesn't track right, take it off and try in a slightly different spot. When the cutter is riding in a ring, tighten the cutter a little with each rotation until the pipe snaps.

Spot where supply tubing was cut

3/4"I.D. / 7/8"O.D.

Remove the screws, holding the flange of the old sillcock to the house, and pull it and the pipe stub out of the hole. Measure the outside diameter of the pipe stub. It should be either ⅝", which means you have ½" nominal pipe, or ⅞", which means you have ¾" nominal pipe. Measure the diameter of the hole in the joist. (If it's less than an inch, you'll probably need to make it bigger.) Measure the length of the pipe stub from the cut end to where it enters the sillcock. This is the minimum length the new sillcock must be to reach the old pipe. Record all this information.

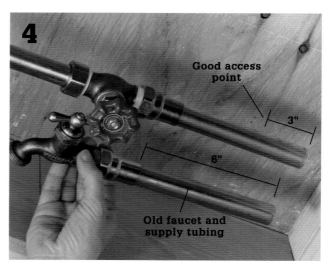

Good access point

3"

6"

Old faucet and supply tubing

Find a spot on the supply pipe where you have good access to work with a fitting and wrenches. The point of this is to help you select a new sillcock that is the best size for your project. In most cases, you'll have only two or three 6" to 12" shaft sizes to pick from. In the example above, we can see that the cut section of pipe is 6" long and the distance from the cut end to a spot with good access on the intact pipe is 3", so a new sillcock that's 9" long will fit perfectly.

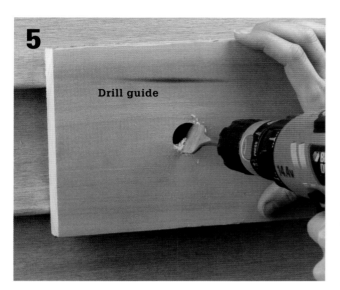

5

Drill guide

If you need to replace old pipe with a larger diameter size, simplify the job of enlarging the sillcock entry hole into your home with a simple drill guide. First, drill a perpendicular 1⅛" diameter hole in a short board. From outside, hold the board over the old hole so the tops are aligned (you can nail or screw it to the siding if you wish). Run the drill through your hole guide to make the new, wider and lower hole in the wall.

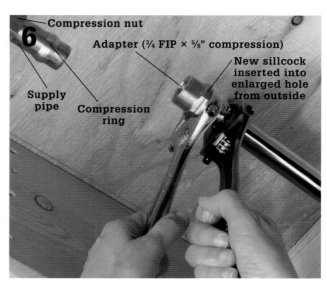

6

Compression nut
Adapter (¾ FIP × ⅝" compression)
New sillcock inserted into enlarged hole from outside
Supply pipe
Compression ring

Insert the sillcock into the hole from the outside. Cut the supply pipe where it will meet the end of the sillcock. From the inside, wrap Teflon tape clockwise onto the threads of the sillcock. Stabilize the sillcock with one wrench and fully tighten the adapter onto the threaded sillcock with the other wrench.

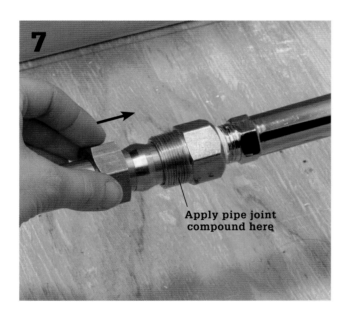

7

Apply pipe joint compound here

Insert the end of the supply pipe into the adapter and pull them together. Spin the sillcock shaft so the faucet outside is oriented correctly (there should be a reference line on the bottom or top of the shaft). Apply pipe joint compound to the male threads on the adapter body. Hand thread the nut onto the adapter body. Stabilize the adapter body with one wrench, then tighten the compression nut with the other about two full turns past hand tight.

8

Turn the water back on. With the sillcock off and then on, check for leaks. Tighten the compression nut a little more if this union drips with the sillcock off. From outside the house, push the sillcock down against the bottom of the entry hole in the wall. Drill small pilot holes into the siding through the slots on the sillcock flange. Now, pull out on the sillcock handle in order to squeeze a thick bead of silicone caulk between the sillcock flange and the house. Attach the sillcock flange to the house with No. 8 or No. 10 corrosion-resistant screws.

Pedestal Sinks

Pedestal sinks move in and out of popularity more frequently than other sink types, but even during times they aren't particularly trendy they retain fairly stable demand. You'll find them most frequently in small half baths, where their little footprint makes them an efficient choice. Designers are also discovering the appeal of tandem pedestal sinks of late, where the smaller profiles allow for his-and-hers sinks that don't dominate visually.

The primary drawback to pedestal sinks is that they don't offer any storage. Their chief practical benefit is that they conceal plumbing some homeowners would prefer not to see.

Pedestal sinks are mounted in two ways. Most of the more inexpensive ones you'll find at home stores are hung in the manner of wall-hung sinks. The pedestal is actually installed after the sink is hung and its purpose is only decorative. But other pedestal sinks (typically on the higher end of the design scale) have structurally important pedestals that do most or all of the bearing for the sink.

Pedestal sinks are available in a variety of styles and are a perfect fit for small half baths. They keep plumbing hidden, lending a neat, contained look to the bathroom.

How to Install a Pedestal Sink

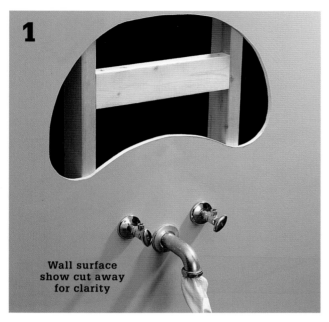

Install 2 × 4 blocking between the wall studs, behind the planned sink location. Cover the wall with water-resistant drywall. Waste and supply lines may need to be moved, depending on the sink.

Set the basin and pedestal in position and brace it with 2 × 4s. Outline the top of the basin on the wall, and mark the base of the pedestal on the floor. Mark reference points on the wall and floor through the mounting holes found on the back of the sink and the bottom of the pedestal.

Set aside the basin and pedestal. Drill pilot holes in the wall and floor at the reference points, then reposition the pedestal. Anchor the pedestal to the floor with lag screws.

Attach the faucet, then set the sink on the pedestal. Align the holes in the back of the sink with the pilot holes drilled in the wall, then drive lag screws and washers into the wall brace using a ratchet wrench. Do not overtighten the screws.

Hook up the drain and supply fittings. Caulk between the back of the sink and the wall when installation is finished.

Wall-Hung Vanities

Think of a wall-mounted sink or vanity cabinet and you're likely to conjure up images of public restrooms where these conveniences are installed to improve access for floor cleaning. However, wall-hung sinks and vanities made for home use are very different from the commercial installations.

Often boasting high design, beautiful modern vanities and sinks come in a variety of styles and materials, including wood, metal, and glass. Some attach with decorative wall brackets that are part of the presentation; others look like standard vanities, just without legs. Install wall-hung sinks and vanities by attaching them securely to studs or wood blocking.

Tools & Materials ▸

Studfinder   Level
Drill   Vanity

Today's wall-hung sinks are stylish and attractive, but they require mounting into studs or added blocking to keep them secure.

How to Install a Wall-Hung Vanity Base

1

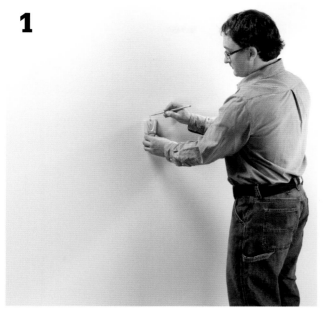

Remove the existing sink or fixture and inspect the wall framing. Also determine if plumbing supply and waste lines will need to be moved to accommodate the dimensions of the new fixture. Locate the studs in the sink location with a stud finder.

2

Hold the sink or cabinet in the installation area and check to see if the studs align with the sink or sink bracket mounting holes. If they do, skip to step 3. If the studs do not align, remove the wallboard behind the mounting area. Install 2 × 6 blocking between studs at the locations of the mounting screws. Replace and repair wallboard.

3

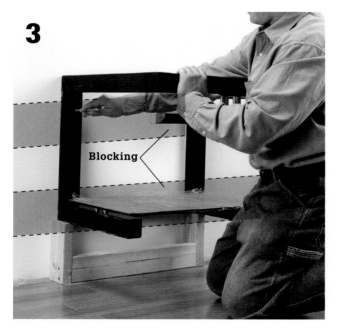

Mark the locations of the mounting holes on the wall using a template or by supporting the sink or vanity against the wall with a temporary brace (made here from scrap 2 × 4s) and marking through the mounting holes.

4

Drill pilot holes at the marks. Have a helper hold the vanity in place while you drive the mounting screws. Hook up the plumbing (see pages 140 to 141).

Vessel Sinks

The vessel sink harkens back to the days of washstands and washbowls. Whether it's round, square, or oval, shallow or deep, the vessel sink offers great opportunity for creativity and proudly displays its style. Vessel sinks are a perfect choice for a powder room, where they will have high visibility.

Most vessel sinks can be installed on any flat surface—from a granite countertop to a wall-mounted vanity to an antique dresser. Some sinks are designed to contact the mounting surface only at the drain flange. Others are made to be partially embedded in the surface. Take care to follow the manufacturer's instructions for cutting holes for sinks and faucets.

A beautiful vessel sink demands an equally attractive faucet. Select a tall spout mounted on the countertop or vanity top or a wall-mounted spout to accommodate the height of the vessel. To minimize splashing, spouts should directly flow to the center of the vessel, not down the side. Make sure your faucet is compatible with your vessel choice. Look for a centerset or single-handle model if you'll be custom drilling the countertop—you only need to drill one faucet hole.

Tools & Materials ▸

Jigsaw	Drill
Trowel	Vanity or countertop
Pliers	Vessel sink
Wrench	Pop-up drain
Caulk gun and caulk	P-trap and drain kit
Sponge	Faucet
	Phillips screwdriver

Vessel sinks are available in countless styles and materials, shapes, and sizes. Their one commonality is that they all need to be installed on a flat surface.

Vessel Sink Options

This glass vessel sink embedded in a "floating" glass countertop is a stunning contrast to the strong and attractive wood frame anchoring it to the wall.

The natural stone vessel sink blends elegantly into the stone countertop and is enhanced by the sleek faucet and round mirror.

The stone vessel sink is complemented by the wall-hung faucet. The rich wood vanity on which it's perched adds warmth to the room.

Vitreous china with a glazed enamel finish is an economical and durable choice for a vessel sink (although it is less durable than stone). Because of the flexibility of both the material and the glaze, the design options are virtually unlimited with vitreous china.

How to Install a Vessel Sink

1

Secure the vanity cabinet or other countertop that you'll be using to mount the vessel sink (see pages 140 to 141).

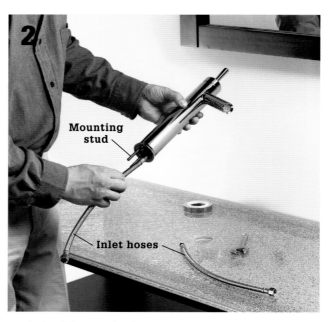

2

Mounting stud

Inlet hoses

Begin hooking up the faucet. Insert the brass mounting stud into the threaded hole in the faucet base with the slotted end facing out. Hand tighten, and then use a screwdriver to tighten another half turn. Insert the inlet hoses into the faucet body and hand tighten. Use an adjustable wrench to tighten another half turn. Do not overtighten.

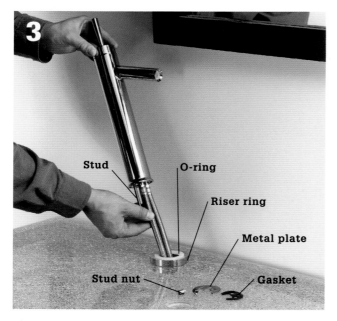

3

Stud   O-ring

Riser ring

Metal plate

Stud nut   Gasket

Place the riser ring on top of the O-ring over the faucet cutout in the countertop. From underneath, slide the rubber gasket and the metal plate over the mounting stud. Thread the mounting stud nut onto the mounting stud and hand tighten. Use an adjustable wrench to tighten another half turn.

4

To install the sink and pop-up drain, first place the small metal ring between two O-rings and place over the drain cutout.

5

Place the vessel bowl on top of the O-rings. In this installation, the vessel is not bonded to the countertop.

6

Put the small rubber gasket over the drain hole in the vessel. From the top, push the pop-up assembly through the drain hole.

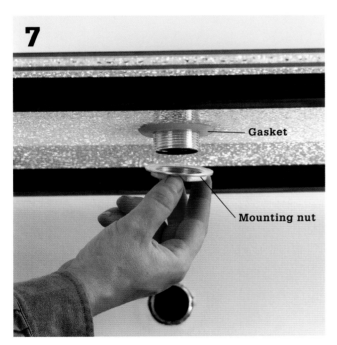

7

Gasket

Mounting nut

From underneath, push the large rubber gasket onto the threaded portion of the pop-up assembly. Thread the nut onto the pop-up assembly and tighten. Use an adjustable wrench or basin wrench to tighten an additional half turn. Thread the tailpiece onto the pop-up assembly.

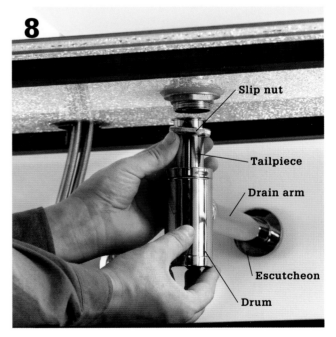

8

Slip nut

Tailpiece

Drain arm

Escutcheon

Drum

Install the drum trap. Loosen the rings on the top and outlet of the drum trap. Slide the drum trap top hole over the tailpiece. Slide the drain arm into the side outlet, with the flat side of the rubber gasket facing away from the trap. Insert the drain arm into the wall outlet. Hand tighten the rings.

Integral Vanity Tops

Most bathroom countertops installed today are integral (one-piece) sink-countertop units made from cultured marble or other solid materials, like solid surfacing. Integral sink-countertops are convenient, and many are inexpensive, but style and color options are limited.

Some remodelers and designers still prefer the distinctive look of a custom-built countertop with a self-rimming sink basin, which gives you a much greater selection of styles and colors. Installing a self-rimming sink is very simple.

For more information regarding countertops and sinks, refer to page 132. For information on installing vanity cabinets see pages 140 to 141.

Pencil · Cardboard
Scissors · Masking tape
Carpenter's level · Plumber's putty
Screwdriver · Lag screws
Channel-type pliers · Tub and tile caulk
Ratchet wrench · Pipe dope
Basin wrench

Integral sink-countertops are made in standard sizes to fit common vanity widths. Because the sink and countertop are cast from the same material, integral sink-countertops do not leak, and do not require extensive caulking and sealing.

How to Install a Vanity Cabinet

Set the sink-countertop unit onto sawhorses. Attach the faucet and slip the drain lever through the faucet body. Place a ring of plumber's putty around the drain flange, then insert the flange in the drain opening.

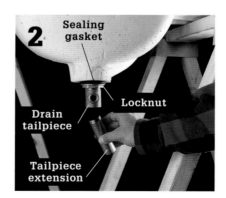

Thread the locknut and sealing gasket onto the drain tailpiece, then insert the tailpiece into the drain opening and screw it onto the drain flange. Tighten the locknut securely. Attach the tailpiece extension. Insert the pop-up stopper linkage.

Place a small amount of pipe dope on all threads. Apply a layer of tub and tile caulk (or adhesive, if specified by the countertop manufacturer) to the top edges of the cabinet vanity, and to any corner braces.

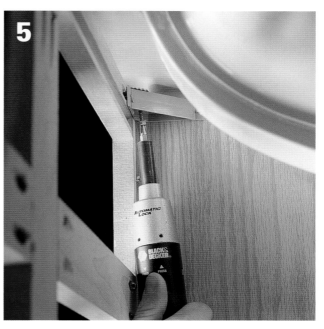

Center the sink-countertop unit over the vanity so the overhang is equal on both sides and the backsplash of the countertop is flush with the wall. Press the countertop evenly into the caulk.

Cabinets with corner braces: Secure the countertop to the cabinet by driving a mounting screw through each corner brace and up into the countertop. *Note: Cultured marble and other hard countertops require predrilling and a plastic screw sleeve.*

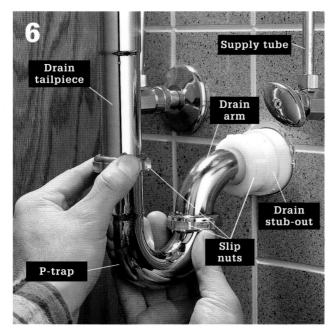

Supply tube

Drain tailpiece

Drain arm

Drain stub-out

Slip nuts

P-trap

Attach the drain arm to the drain stub-out in the wall, using a slip nut. Attach one end of the P-trap to the drain arm, and the other to the tailpiece of the sink drain, using slip nuts. Connect supply tubes to the faucet tailpieces.

Seal the gap between the backsplash and the wall with tub and tile caulk.

Kitchen Sinks

Most drop-in, self-rimming kitchen sinks are easily installed.

Drop-in sinks for do-it-yourself installation are made from cast iron coated with enamel, stainless steel, enameled steel, acrylic, fiberglass, or resin composites. Because cast-iron sinks are heavy, their weight holds them in place and they require no mounting hardware. Except for the heavy lifting, they are easy to install. Stainless steel and enameled-steel sinks weigh less than cast-iron and most require mounting brackets on the underside of the countertop. Some acrylic and resin sinks rely on silicone caulk to hold them in place.

If you are replacing a sink, but not the countertop, make sure the new sink is the same size or larger. All old silicone caulk residue must be removed with acetone or denatured alcohol, or else the new caulk will not stick.

Tools & Materials ▸

Caulk gun	Plumber's putty
Spud wrench	or silicone caulk
Screwdriver	Mounting clips
Sink	Jigsaw
Sink frame	Pen or pencil

Shopping Tips ▸

- When purchasing a sink, you also need to buy strainer bodies and baskets, sink clips, and a drain trap kit.
- Look for basin dividers that are lower than the sink rim—this reduces splashing.
- Drain holes in the back or to the side make for more usable space under the sink.
- When choosing a sink, make sure the predrilled openings will fit your faucet.

Drop-in sinks, also known as self-rimming sinks, have a wide sink flange that extends beyond the edges of the sink cutout. They also have a wide back flange to which the faucet is mounted directly.

How to Install a Self-Rimming Sink

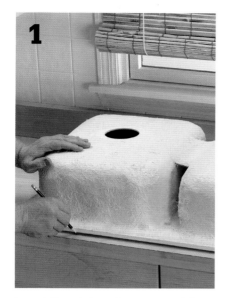

Invert the sink and trace around the edges as a reference for making the sink cutout cutting lines, which should be parallel to the outlines, but about 1" inside of them to create a 1" ledge. If your sink comes with a template for the cutout, use it.

Drill a starter hole and cut out the sink opening with a jigsaw. Cut right up to the line. Because the sink flange fits over the edges of the cutout, the opening doesn't need to be perfect, but as always you should try to do a nice, neat job.

Attach as much of the plumbing as makes sense to install prior to setting the sink into the opening. Having access to the underside of the flange is a great help when it comes to attaching the faucet body, sprayer, and strainer, in particular.

Apply a bead of silicone caulk around the edges of the sink opening. The sink flange most likely is not flat, so try and apply the caulk in the area that will make contact with the flange.

Place the sink in the opening. Try to get the sink centered right away so you don't need to move it around and disturb the caulk, which can break the seal. If you are installing a heavy cast-iron sink, it's best to leave the strainers off so you can grab onto the sink at the drain openings.

For sinks with mounting clips, tighten the clips from below using a screwdriver or wrench (depending on the type of clip your sink has). There should be at least three clips on every side. Don't overtighten the clips—this can cause the sink flange to flatten or become warped.

Undermount Sinks

Undermounted sinks have become quite popular in contemporary kitchens for reasons that are both practical and aesthetic. On the aesthetic side, they look updated and sleek. They are easier to clean than rimmed sinks because you eliminate that area around the rim seal where stuff always collects.

Most sink manufacturers make sinks that are designed for undermounting, and if you don't mind paying the $100 to $200 premium, a true undermount sink is the best choice. But if your decision making is driven more by your frugal side, you can undermount a self-rimming (drop-in) stainless steel sink with little difficulty using readily available undermount clips. (Self-rimmers also come in a much wider range of styles.) *Note: You can undermount any sink you wish, including heavy cast iron models, if you support the sink from below instead of hanging it from clips.*

Not all countertops are suitable for undermounting a sink. The countertop material needs to be contiguous in nature. That is, the edges that are created when you cut through it need to be of the same material as the surface. Solid-surface, granite, butcher block, and concrete are good candidates for undermounting. Post-form and any laminated or tiled countertops are not. (Some new products that claim to seal countertop substrate edges around a sink opening are emerging, but are not yet proven or readily available.)

Tools & Materials ▸

2HP or larger plunge router	Belt sander
½" template following router bit	Solid-surface scraps
	Solid-surface seam adhesive with applicator gun
Roundover bit	
MDF or particleboard for template	Denatured alcohol
	Undermount sink clip hardware
Jigsaw	
Drill and bits	Silicone caulk
Abrasive pads	Pipe clamps
Laminate trimmer	Pad sander

Before

After

Undermounted sinks have a sleek appearance and make clean up easy, but they are only a good idea in countertops that have a solid construction, such as solid surfacing, stone, quartz, or butcher block. Laminate and tile countertops are not compatible with undermounted sinks.

Amateurs and Solid-surface ▶

Solid-surface countertop material is generally installed only by certified installers. But a simple job like mounting a non-solid-surface undermount sink can be done by a skilled amateur if you have access to adhesive and an applicator gun.

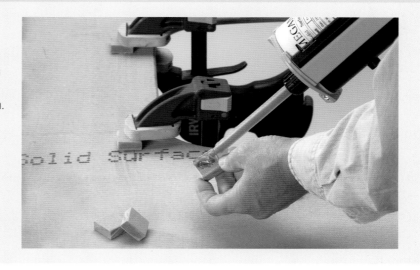

How to Make a Sink Cutout Template

1

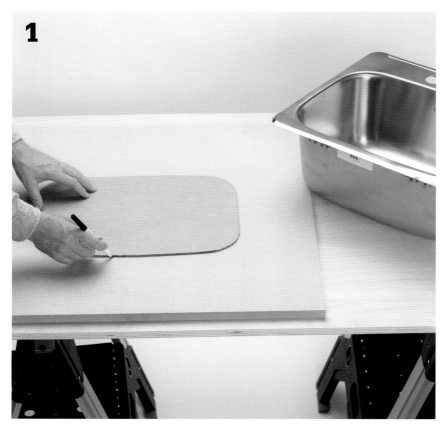

If you are undermounting a self-rimming sink, do not use the sink template provided by the manufacturer. Instead, make your own custom router template to use with a router and pattern-following bit. The template should be sized and shaped so the cutout you make with your pattern-following bit is the same shape and about ⅛" larger than the basin opening in each direction. You can plot the cutout directly onto a piece of MDF, or make a preliminary paper or cardboard template and trace it onto the MDF.

(continued)

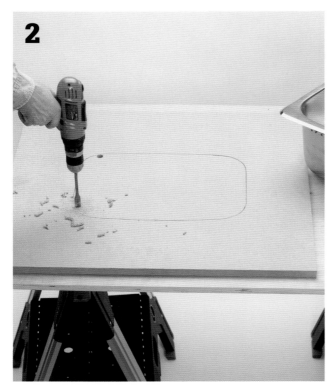

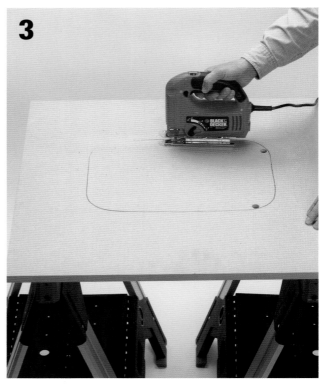

Drill a few starter holes just inside the template outline to create access for your jigsaw blade. If the cutout has sharp radii at the corners, look for a bit or hole cutter of the same radius and carefully drill out the corners.

Connect the starter holes by cutting just inside the cutout line with a jigsaw. You can use a straightedge cutting guide for straight runs if you have little confidence in your ability to cut straight.

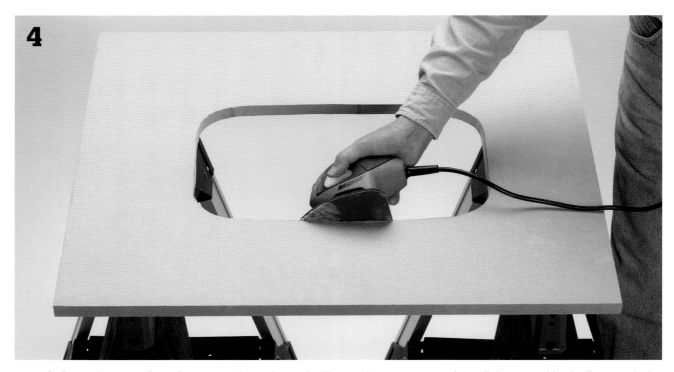

Use a belt sander or pad sander to smooth out the cutting lines and to remove material until the cutout hits the lines precisely. A drum sander attachment mounted in a power drill is useful for smoothing out rounded corners.

How to Undermount a Sink

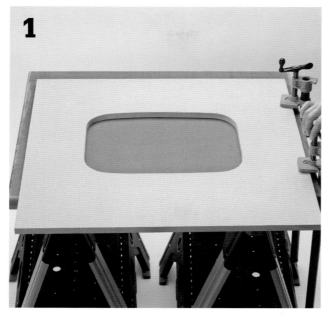

Remove the countertop from the cabinet and transport it to a work area with good light and ventilation. Set the countertop section on sawhorses and then clamp the router template securely so the opening is centered exactly over the planned cutout area. Make sure the router bit won't be cutting into your work area.

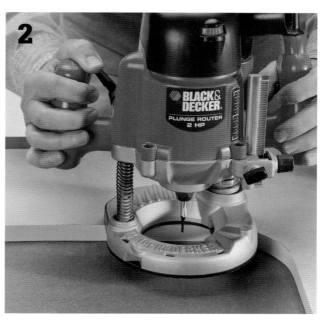

Chuck a two-fluted, ⅛" pattern-following bit (preferably carbide tipped) with a ½" shank into a plunge router with a minimum motor size of 2HP. Retract the bit and position the router so the bit is an inch or so away from the edge of the template. Turn the router on and let it develop to full velocity. Then, plunge the router bit into the countertop material until the bit breaks all the way through.

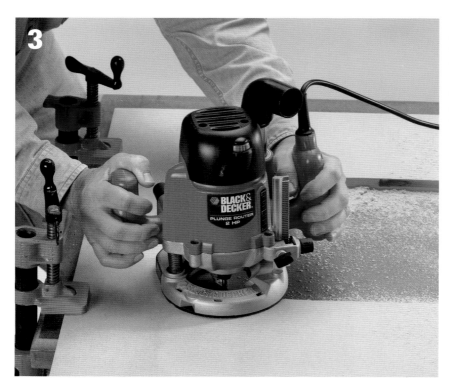

Pull the router bit toward the template edge until the bit sleeve contacts the edge, then slowly cut through the countertop, following the template. Pace is important here: too fast will cause chatter, too slow will cause burning or melting. Cut three continuous sides of the opening, hugging the template edge.

(continued)

4

After routing three side openings, stop routing and screw a support board to the waste piece. The ends of the support board should extend onto the template. Position the support so it is near the center, but not in the way for completing the fourth side of the cut. Then finish the cut. The support board will prevent the waste from breaking off as the cut nears completion.

5

If the sink outline has any chatter or the cutout is not perfectly smooth, make another pass with a straight bit before you remove the template. Remove the template and make a ⅛" roundover cut on both the top and bottom of the sink cutout. If you know exactly where your faucet hole or holes need to be, cut them with a hole saw and round over their tops and bottoms as well.

6

It's easier to mount the sink on the countertop before you reinstall it on the cabinet. Cut several 1 × 1 mounting blocks from the solid-surface waste cutout. You'll also need to purchase some seam adhesive to glue the mounting blocks to the underside of the countertop. After they're cut, break all the block edges with a stationary sander or by clamping a belt sander belt-side up and using it as a stationary sander (breaking the edges reduces the chance that the blocks will crack).

7

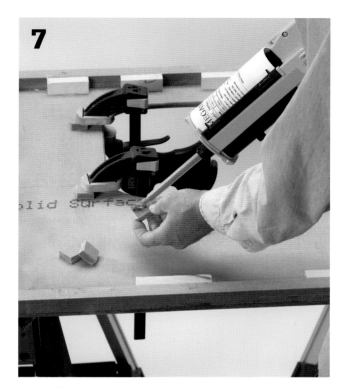

Clean the blocks and the underside of the solid-surface around the cutouts with denatured alcohol. Apply solid-surface seam adhesive to the blocks and bond them to the underside of the countertop, set back ¾" from the cutout. Install three blocks along the long sides of the cutout and two on the front-to-back sides. Clamp the blocks while the adhesive sets up.

8

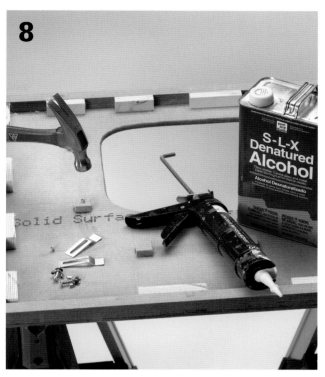

Drill ¼" dia. × ⅜" deep pilot holes for the sink clips into each mounting block. The holes should be in the centers of the mounting blocks. Tap the brass inserts for the mounting clips into the holes in the mounting blocks.

9

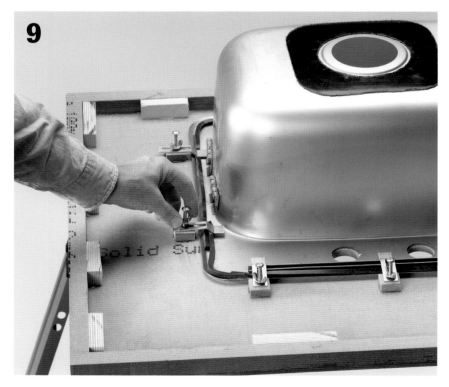

Clean the sink rim and the underside of the countertop with denatured alcohol. When the alcohol has dried, apply a bead of 100 percent silicone adhesive caulk to the sink rim. Carefully center the sink over the opening and press it in place. Hand tighten the wing nuts onto the mounting nuts to secure the clips that hold the sink bowl. Replace the countertop and hook up the faucet and drain. For information on installing a kitchen faucet see pages 142 to 143.

Standpipe Drains

In many houses, the washing machine drain hose is hung loosely over the side of the utility sink, but this configuration is frowned upon by building codes. Instead, you should install a standpipe drain that allows the washing machine to drain directly into the utility sink's drain line. Standpipes with attached P-traps can be purchased at many home centers. A 2"-pipe is required by most building codes. The top of the standpipe should be higher than the highest water level in the washing machine, but not shorter than 34". Hose bibs are installed in the hot and cold supply lines at the utility sink to provide the water supply to the washing machine.

Tools & Materials ▸

Reciprocating saw	Pipe strap
Utility knife	Hose bibs
Waste Y-fitting	Solder
Primer & solvent glue	Threaded T-fittings
90° elbow	Torch
2" standpipe with trap	Sheet metal
2 × 4 backer	Teflon tape
2½" deck screws	Rubber supply hose
½" screws	

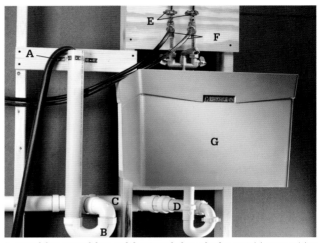

A washing machine with standpipe drain: washing machine drain hose (A), 2" standpipe drain with trap (B), waste line (C), utility sink drain pipe (D), hot and cold supply lines with hose bibs (E), rubber supply hoses to washing machine (F), and utility sink (G).

How to Install a Washing Machine Standpipe Drain

Measure and mark the size and location of a waste Y-fitting in the drain line. Remove the marked section, using a reciprocating saw. Make cuts as straight as possible.

Use a utility knife to remove rough burrs on the cut ends of the pipe. Dry-fit the waste Y-fitting into the drain line to make sure it fits properly, then attach the Y-fitting using primer and solvent glue.

Dry-fit a 90° elbow and a 2" standpipe with trap to the waste Y-fitting. Make sure the standpipe is taller than the highest water level in the washing machine (a minimum of 34"). Solvent-glue all the pipes in place.

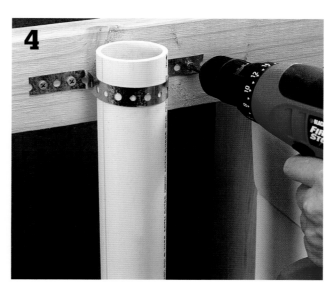

Attach a 2 × 4 backer behind the top of the standpipe for support, using 2½" deck screws. Fasten standpipe to the wood support, using a length of pipe strap and ½" screws. Insert the washing machine's rubber drain hose into the standpipe.

How to Make Water Supply Connections

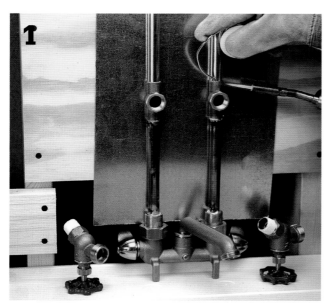

Install hose bibs in the utility sink supply lines. Turn off water main and drain pipes. Cut into each supply pipe 6" to 12" from faucet. Solder threaded T-fittings into each supply line. Protect wood from torch flame with two layers of sheet metal. Wrap Teflon tape around threads of hose bibs, and screw them into T-fittings. Connect a rubber supply hose from each bib to the appropriate intake port on the washing machine.

Recessed washing machine boxes are available for finished utility rooms. The supply pipes and standpipe drain run to one central location. The washing machine's hose bibs, supply hoses, and drain hose must remain easily accessible.

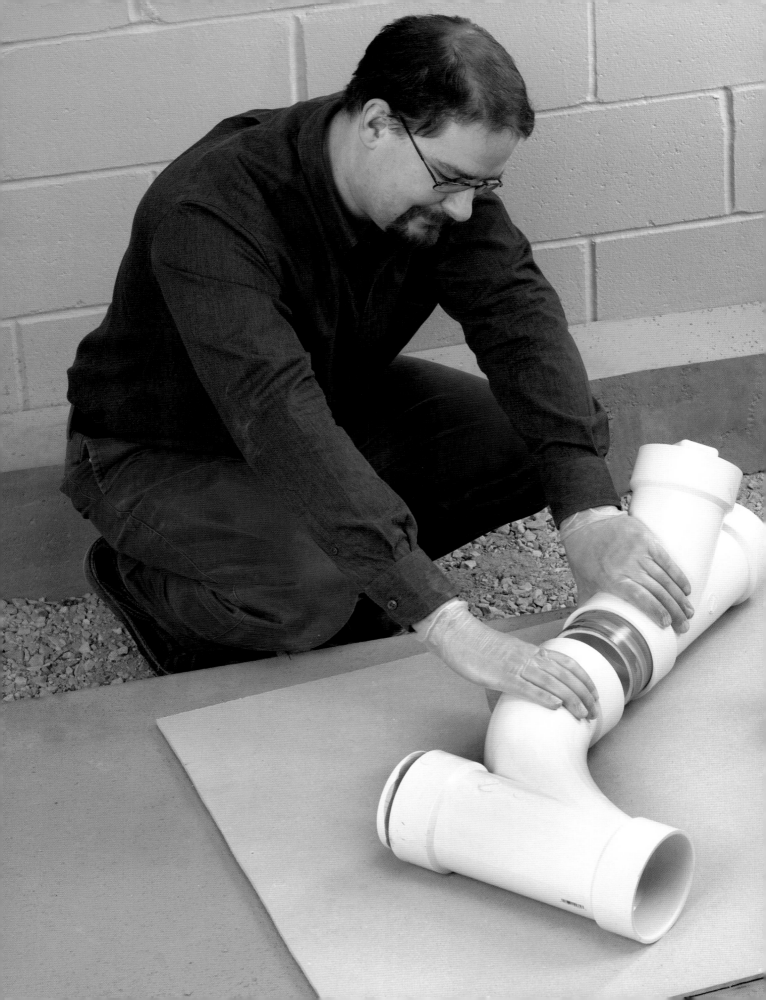

Plumbing Installations

Running new water supply and drain lines is an entirely different pursuit from hooking up fixtures, and in many ways it is more complicated. Because you are installing pipes where none existed before, the need to know all the applicable plumbing codes is critical (as opposed to simply making a one-for-one fixture swap-out). Great care also must be taken to cut new pipes to exactly the right length and make certain all joints are watertight and made with the correct fittings or products.

Choosing the best pipe materials for your job is an important part of the project. In most cases, the best advice is to use the same material that is already present. But you may choose to use a different material as long as you use the correct transition fittings. For example, if you're running a new supply line, you may choose PEX over copper because it is so fast and easy to install. Or, you may choose CPVC over copper for cost reasons.

In this chapter:

- Installation Basics
- Plumbing Routes
- Master Bath
- Basement Bath
- Half Bath
- Kitchen
- New Gas Lines

Installation Basics

A major plumbing project is a complicated affair that often requires demolition and carpentry skills. Bathroom or kitchen plumbing may be unusable for several days while completing the work, so make sure you have a backup bathroom or kitchen space to use during this time.

To ensure that your project goes quickly, always buy plenty of pipe and fittings—at least 25% more than you think you need. Making several extra trips to the building center is a nuisance and can add many hours to your project. Always purchase from a reputable retailer that will allow you to return leftover fittings for credit.

The how-to projects on the following pages demonstrate standard plumbing techniques but should not be used as a literal blueprint for your own work. Pipe and fitting sizes, fixture layout, and pipe routing will always vary according to individual circumstances. When planning your project, carefully read all the information in the planning section. Before you begin work, create a detailed plumbing plan to guide your work and help you obtain the required permits.

Use 2 × 6 studs to frame "wet walls" when constructing a new bathroom or kitchen. Thicker walls provide more room to run drain pipes and main waste-vent stacks, making installation much easier.

Installing New Plumbing

Use masking tape to mark the locations of fixtures and pipes on the walls and floors. Read the layout specifications that come with each sink, tub, or toilet, then mark the drain and supply lines accordingly. Position the fixtures on the floor, and outline them with tape. Measure and adjust until the arrangement is comfortable to you and meets minimum clearance specifications. If you are working in a finished room, prevent damage to wallpaper or paint by using self-adhesive notes to mark the walls.

Consider the location of cabinets when roughing in the water supply and drain stub-outs. You may want to temporarily position the cabinets in their final locations before completing the drain and water supply runs.

Install control valves at the points where the new branch supply lines meet the main distribution pipes. By installing valves, you can continue to supply the rest of the house with water while you are working on the new branches.

(continued)

Framing Member	Maximum Hole Size	Maximum Notch Size
2 × 4 loadbearing stud	1⁷⁄₁₆" diameter	⁷⁄₈" deep
2 × 4 non-loadbearing stud	2½" diameter	1⁷⁄₁₆" deep
2 × 6 loadbearing stud	2¼" diameter	1⅜" deep
2 × 6 non-loadbearing stud	3⁵⁄₁₆" diameter	2³⁄₁₆" deep
2 × 6 joists	1½" diameter	⁷⁄₈" deep
2 × 8 joists	2⅜" diameter	1¼" deep
2 × 10 joists	3¹⁄₁₆" diameter	1½" deep
2 × 12 joists	3¾" diameter	1⅞" deep

The framing member chart shows the maximum sizes for holes and notches that can be cut into studs and joists when running pipes. Where possible, use notches rather than bored holes, because pipe installation is usually easier. When boring holes, there must be at least ⅝" of wood between the edge of a stud and the hole, and at least 2" between the edge of a joist and the hole. Joists can be notched only in the end ⅓ of the overall span; never in the middle ⅓ of the joist. When two pipes are run through a stud, the pipes should be stacked one over the other, never side by side.

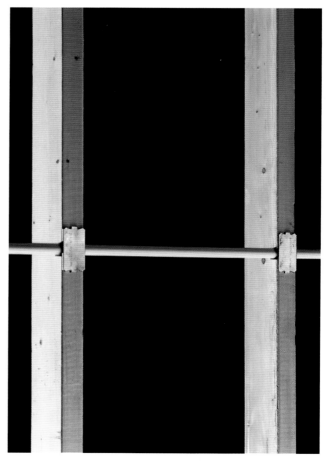

Create access panels so that in the future you will be able to service fixture fittings and shutoff valves located inside the walls. Frame an opening between studs, then trim the opening with wood moldings. Cover the opening with a removable plywood panel the same thickness as the wall surface, then finish it to match the surrounding walls.

Protect pipes from punctures if they are less than 1¼" from the front face of wall studs or joists by attaching metal protector plates to the framing members.

Test-fit materials before solvent-gluing or soldering joints. Test-fitting ensures that you have the correct fittings and enough pipe to do the job, and can help you avoid lengthy delays during installation.

Support pipes adequately. Horizontal and vertical runs of DWV and water supply pipe must be supported at minimum intervals, which are specified by your local plumbing codes. A variety of metal and plastic materials are available for supporting plumbing pipes (pages 272 to 273).

Use plastic bushings to help hold plumbing pipes securely in holes bored through wall plates, studs, and joists. Bushings can help to cushion the pipes, preventing wear and reducing rattling. Always use manufacturer-recommended bushings with metal wall studs (inset).

Install extra T-fittings on new drain and vent lines so that you can pressure-test the system when the building inspector reviews your installation. A new DWV line should have these extra T-fittings near the points where the new branch drains and vent pipes reach the main waste-vent stack.

Planning Plumbing Routes

The first, and perhaps most important, step when replacing old plumbing is to decide how and where to run the new pipes. Since the stud cavities and joist spaces are often covered with finished wall surfaces, finding routes for running new pipes can be challenging.

When planning pipe routes, choose straight, easy pathways whenever possible. Rather than running water supply pipes around wall corners and through studs, for example, it may be easiest to run them straight up wall cavities from the basement. Instead of running a bathtub drain across floor joists, run it straight down into the basement, where the branch drain can be easily extended underneath the joists to the main waste-vent stack.

In some situations, it is most practical to route the new pipes in wall and floor cavities that already hold plumbing pipes, since these spaces are often framed to provide long, unobstructed runs. A detailed map of your plumbing system can be very helpful when planning routes for new plumbing pipes (pages 158 to 161).

To maximize their profits, plumbing contractors generally try to avoid opening walls or changing wall framing when installing new plumbing. But the do-it-yourselfer does not have these limitations. Faced with the difficulty of running pipes through enclosed spaces, you may find it easiest to remove wall surfaces or to create a newly framed space for running new pipes.

On these pages, you will see some common methods used to create pathways for replacing old pipes with new plumbing.

Build a framed chase. A chase is a false wall created to provide space for new plumbing pipes. It is especially effective for installing a new main waste-vent stack. On a two-story house, chases can be stacked one over the other on each floor in order to run plumbing from the basement to the attic. Once plumbing is completed and inspected, the chase is covered with wallboard and finished to match the room.

Planning Pipe Routes

Use existing access panels to disconnect fixtures and remove old pipes. Plan the location of new fixtures and pipe runs to make use of existing access panels, minimizing the amount of demolition and repair work you will need to do.

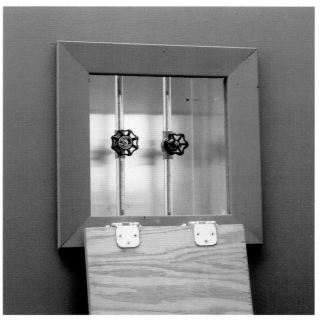

Convert a laundry chute into a channel for running new plumbing pipes. The door of the chute can be used to provide access to control valves, or it can be removed and covered with wall materials, then finished to match the surrounding wall.

Run pipes inside a closet. If they are unobtrusive, pipes can be left exposed at the back of the closet. Or, you can frame a chase to hide the pipes after the installation is completed.

Remove suspended ceiling panels to route new plumbing pipes in joist cavities. Or, you can route pipes across a standard plaster or wallboard ceiling, then construct a false ceiling to cover the installation, provided there is adequate height. Most building codes require a minimum of 7 ft. from floor to finished ceiling.

(continued)

Use a drill bit extension and spade bit or hole saw to drill through wall plates from unfinished attic or basement spaces above or below the wall.

Look for "wet walls." Walls that hold old plumbing pipes can be good choices for running long vertical runs of new pipe. These spaces are usually open, without obstacles such as fireblocks and insulation.

Probe wall and floor cavities with a long piece of plastic pipe to ensure that a clear pathway exists for running new pipe (left photo). Once you have established a route using the narrow pipe, you can use the pipe as a guide when running larger drain pipes up into the wall (right photo).

Remove flooring when necessary. Because replacing toilet and bathtub drains usually requires that you remove sections of floor, a full plumbing replacement job is often done in conjunction with a complete bathroom remodeling project.

Remove wall surfaces when access from above or below the wall is not possible. This demolition work can range from cutting narrow channels in plaster or wallboard to removing the entire wall surface. Remove wall surfaces back to the centers of adjoining studs; the exposed studs provide a nailing surface for attaching repair materials once the plumbing project is completed.

Create a detailed map showing the planned route for your new plumbing pipes. Such a map can help you get your plans approved by the inspector, and it makes work much simpler. If you have already mapped your existing plumbing system (pages 158 to 161), those drawings can be used to plan new pipe routes.

Master Bath

A large bathroom has more plumbing fixtures and consumes more water than any other room in your house. For this reason, a master bath has special plumbing needs.

Frame bathroom "wet walls" with 2 × 6 studs, to provide plenty of room for running 3" pipes and fittings. If your bathroom includes a heavy whirlpool tub, you will likely need to strengthen the floor by installing "sister" joists alongside the existing floor joists underneath the tub. Check with your local codes.

For convenience, our project is divided into the following sequences:

- How to Install DWV Pipes for the Toilet & Sink (pages 163 to 165)
- How to Install DWV Pipes for the Tub & Shower (pages 160 to 167)
- How to Connect Drain Pipes to a Main Waste-Vent Stack (page 168)
- How to Install the Water Supply Pipes (page 169)

Our demonstration bathroom is a second-story master bath. We are installing a 3" vertical drain pipe to service the toilet and the vanity sink, and a 2" vertical pipe to handle the tub and shower drains. The branch drains for the sink and bathtub are 1½" pipes—for the shower, 2" pipe. Each fixture has its own vent pipe extending up into the attic, where they are joined together and connected to the main stack.

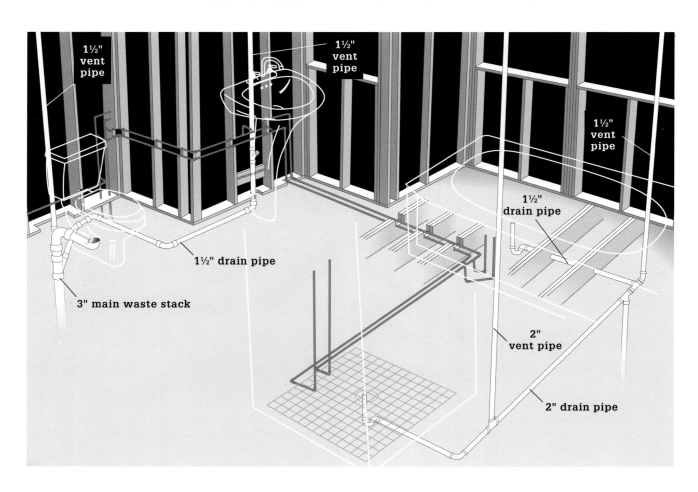

How to Install DWV Pipes for the Toilet & Sink

Use masking tape to outline the locations of the fixtures and pipe runs on the subfloor and walls. Mark the location for a 3" vertical drain pipe on the sole plate in the wall behind the toilet. Mark a 4½"-diameter circle for the toilet drain on the subfloor.

Cut out the drain opening for the toilet, using a hole saw. Mark and remove a section of flooring around the toilet area, large enough to provide access for installing the toilet drain and for running drain pipe from the sink. Use a circular saw with blade set to the thickness of the flooring to cut through the subfloor.

If a floor joist interferes with the toilet drain, cut away a short section of the joist and box-frame the area with double headers. The framed opening should be just large enough to install the toilet and sink drains.

To create a path for the vertical 3" drain pipe, cut a 4½" × 12" notch in the sole plate of the wall behind the toilet. Make a similar cutout in the double wall plate at the bottom of the joist cavity. From the basement, locate the point directly below the cutout by measuring from a reference point, such as the main waste-vent stack.

(continued)

5

Low-heel vent 90° fitting

Y-fitting

Measure and cut a length of 3" drain pipe to reach from the bathroom floor cavity to a point flush with the bottom of the ceiling joists in the basement. Solvent-glue a 3" × 3" × 1½" Y-fitting to the top of the pipe, and a low-heel vent 90° fitting above the Y. The branch inlet on the Y should face toward the sink location; the front inlet on the low-heel should face forward. Carefully lower the pipe into the wall cavity.

Lower the pipe so the bottom end slides through the opening in the basement ceiling. Support the pipe with vinyl pipe strap wrapped around the low-heel vent 90° fitting and screwed to framing members.

7

Use a length of 3" pipe and a 4 × 3 reducing elbow to extend the drain out to the toilet location. Make sure the drain slopes at least ¼" per foot toward the wall, then support it with pipe strap attached to the joists. Insert a short length of pipe into the elbow so it extends at least 2" above the subfloor. After the new drains are pressure tested, this stub-out will be cut flush with the subfloor and fitted with a toilet flange.

Notch out the sole plate and subfloor below the sink location. Cut a length of 1½" plastic drain pipe, then solvent-glue a waste T to the top of the pipe and a sweep 90° elbow to the bottom. *Note: The distance from the subfloor to the center of the waste-T should be 14" to 18". The branch of the T should face out, and the discharge on the elbow should face toward the toilet location. Adjust the pipe so the top edge of the elbow nearly touches the bottom of the sole plate. Anchor it with a ¾"-thick backing board nailed between the studs.*

Dry-fit lengths of 1½" drain pipe and elbows to extend the sink drain to the 3" drain pipe behind the toilet. Use a right-angle drill to bore holes in joists, if needed. Make sure the horizontal drain pipe slopes at least ¼" per foot toward the vertical drain. When satisfied with the layout, solvent-glue the pieces together and support the drain pipe with vinyl pipe straps attached to the joists.

In the top plates of the walls behind the sink and toilet, bore ½"-diameter holes up into the attic. Insert pencils or dowels into the holes, and tape them in place. Enter the attic and locate the pencils, then clear away insulation and cut 2"-diameter holes for the vertical vent pipes. Cut and install 1½" vent pipes running from the toilet and sink drain at least 1 ft. up into the attic.

How to Install DWV Pipes for the Tub & Shower

On the subfloor, use masking tape to mark the locations of the tub and shower, the water supply pipes, and the tub and shower drains, according to your plumbing plan. Use a jigsaw to cut out a 12" square opening for each drain, and drill 1"-diameter holes in the subfloor for each water supply riser.

If installing a large whirlpool tub, cut away the subfloor to expose the full length of the joists under the tub, then screw or bolt a second joist, called a sister, against each existing joist. Make sure both ends of each joist are supported by load-bearing walls.

In a wall adjacent to the tub, establish a route for a 2" vertical waste-vent pipe running from basement to attic. This pipe should be no more than 3½ ft. from the bathtub trap. Then, mark a route for the horizontal drain pipe running from the bathtub drain to the waste-vent pipe location. Cut 3"-diameter holes through the centers of the joists for the bathtub drain.

2" inlet for shower drain

1½" inlet for tub drain

Cut and install a vertical 2" drain pipe running from basement to the joist cavity adjoining the tub location, using the same technique as for the toilet drain (steps 4 to 6, pages 171 to 175). At the top of the drain pipe, use assorted fittings to create three inlets: branch inlets for the bathtub and shower drains and a 1½" top inlet for a vent pipe running to the attic.

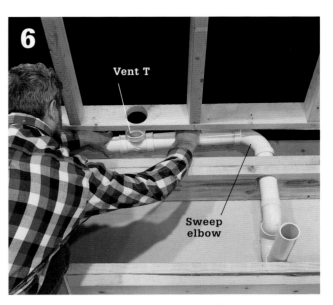

Dry-fit a 1½" drain pipe running from the bathtub drain location to the vertical waste-vent pipe in the wall. Make sure the pipe slopes ¼" per foot toward the wall. When satisfied with the layout, solvent-glue the pieces together and support the pipe with vinyl pipe straps attached to the joists. If local codes require vents for each fixture, add a vent pipe and T-fitting.

Dry-fit a 2" drain pipe from the shower drain to the vertical waste-vent pipe near the tub. Install a solvent-glued trap at the drain location, cut a hole in the sole plate, and insert a 2" × 2" × 1½" vent T within 5 ft. of the trap. Make sure the drain is sloped ¼" per foot downward away from the shower drain. When satisfied with the layout, solvent-glue the pipes together.

Cut and install vertical vent pipes for the bathtub and shower, extending up through the wall plates and at least 1 ft. into the attic. These vent pipes will be connected in the attic to the main waste-vent stack. In our project, the shower vent is a 2" pipe, while the bathtub vent is a 1½" pipe. When you have completed all the DWV piping, cover large cutouts to sill plates with boards and stuff fiberglass insulation or use fire-rated foam insulation to create a fire stop.

How to Connect Drain Pipes to a Main Waste-Vent Stack

In the basement, cut into the main waste-vent stack and install the fittings necessary to connect the 3" toilet-sink drain and the 2" bathtub-shower drain. In our project, we created an assembly made of a waste T-fitting with an extra side inlet and two short lengths of pipe, then inserted it into the existing waste-vent stack using banded couplings. Make sure the T-fittings are positioned so the drain pipes will have the proper downward slope toward the stack.

Dry-fit Y-fittings with 45° elbows onto the vertical 3" and 2" drain pipes. Position the horizontal drain pipes against the fittings, and mark them for cutting. When satisfied with the layout, solvent-glue the pipes together, then support the pipes every 4 ft. with vinyl pipe straps. Make sure to maintain the proper ¼" per foot downward slope in all waste pipes.

How to Connect Vent Pipes to a Main Waste-Vent Stack

In the attic, cut into the main waste-vent stack and install a vent T-fitting, using banded couplings. The side outlet on the vent T should face the new 2" vent pipe running down to the bathroom. Attach a test T-fitting to the vent T. *Note: If your stack is cast iron, make sure to adequately support it before cutting into it (pages 300 to 303).*

Use elbows, vent T-fittings, reducers, and lengths of pipe as needed to link the new vent pipes to the test T-fitting on the main waste-vent stack. Vent pipes can be routed in many ways, but you should make sure the pipes have a slight downward angle to prevent moisture from collecting in the pipes. Support the pipes every 4 ft.

How to Install the Water Supply Pipes

After shutting off the water, cut into existing supply pipes and install T-fittings for new branch lines. Notch out studs and run copper pipes to the toilet and sink locations. Use an elbow and female-threaded fitting to form the toilet stub-out. Once satisfied with the layout, solder the pipes in place.

Cut 1" × 4"-high notches around the wall, and extend the supply pipes to the sink location. Install reducing T-fittings and female-threaded fittings for the sink faucet stub-outs. The stub-outs should be positioned about 18" above the floor, spaced 8" apart. Once satisfied with the layout, solder the joints, then insert ¾" blocking behind the stub-outs and strap them in place.

Extend the water supply pipes to the bathtub and shower. In our project, we removed the subfloor and notched the joists to run ¾" supply pipes from the sink to a whirlpool bathtub, then to the shower. At the bathtub, we used reducing T-fittings and elbows to create ½" risers for the tub faucet. Solder caps onto the risers; after the subfloor is replaced, the caps will be removed and replaced with shutoff valves.

At the shower location, use elbows to create vertical risers where the shower wet wall will be constructed. The risers should extend at least 6" above floor level. Support the risers with a ¾" backer board attached between joists. Solder caps onto the risers. After the shower stall is constructed, the caps will be removed and replaced with shutoff valves.

Basement Bath

Adding a bathroom to an unfinished basement creates a host of new opportunities for finishing the rest of the space. With a convenient bathroom, you can much more easily justify a downstairs recreation room, a wine cellar, a home theater, or additional bedrooms. Many new homes are pre-plumbed with available stub-outs for plumbing at the time the house is built. More likely, you'll need to break up the concrete floor to install new drain and supply plumbing. This is exactly as much work as it sounds like, but with a jackhammer and some help, it is manageable.

Because horizontal plastic pipes cannot be encased in concrete, they must be laid in the granular fill beneath the concrete basement floor. Possible locations for the bathroom, therefore, are limited by how close the main sewer line is to the floor surface when it meets the main drain stack. Check local codes for other specific restrictions in your area.

Plan ahead for this project. Once you cut into the main waste-vent, there can be no drainage in the house until you have fully installed the new branch lines and sealed the joints. Make sure you have extra pipe and fittings on hand.

Sawing and jackhammering concrete (you'll have to do this to run the new pipe line) produces large quantities of dust. Use plastic sheeting to block off other portions of the basement, and wear approved particulate dust masks.

Our demonstration bathroom includes a shower, toilet, and pedestal sink arranged in a line to simplify trenching. A 2" drain pipe services the new shower and sink; a 3" pipe services the new toilet. The drain pipes converge at a Y-fitting joined to the existing main drain. The toilet and sink have individual vent pipes that meet inside the wet wall before extending up into the attic, where they join the main waste-vent stack.

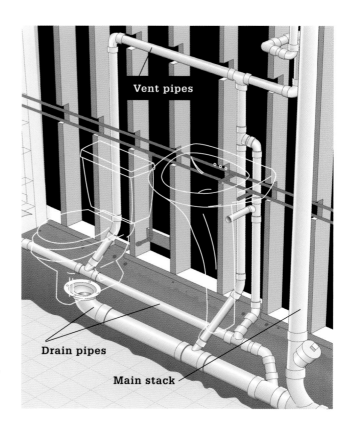

Tools & Materials ▸

Duct tape	2 × 6 lumber
Concrete or circular saw	Duct tape
Cold chisel	Riser clamps
Hand maul	or plastic stack
Plastic sheeting	TY combo
Chalk line	Primer
Jackhammer	Solvent glue
Work & rubber gloves	Banded coupling
Eye & ear protection	Rags
Dust mask	Concrete
Plastic bags	Trowel
4-ft. level	Fiberglass insulation
Reciprocating saw	Power-actuated
2 × 4 lumber	nailer

How to Plumb a Basement Bath

Mark the proposed location of the basement bathroom on the basement floor, using tape. Include the walls, wet wall, and fixture locations. The easiest configuration is to install all the fixtures against the wet wall, which will contain the water supply and vents. The drain lines should run parallel to the wet wall in the most direct route to the main waste-vent stack. Mark the drain line location (typically around 6" out from the wet wall).

Cut out the area around the main stack. Use a concrete saw or a circular saw with a masonry blade to score a 24" × 24" square cutting line around the waste-vent stack. The cut should be at least 1" deep.

Remove concrete and dirt around the main stack. Using a cold chisel and hand maul, strike along the scored cutting lines to chip out the concrete around the main soil stack. If necessary, break up the concrete within the square so it can be removed. Take care not to damage the pipe. Excavate within the square to determine the depth of the sewer line where it meets the main stack. *Tip: Calculate the distance you want the new branch drain to run and multiply by ¼". Add the thickness of concrete floor to this number to find the minimum depth the sewer line must be to accommodate your layout plan. If you excavate an inch or two past this depth, there is no need to dig farther.*

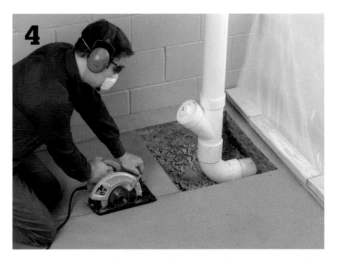

Excavate the drainline trench. Enclose the work area with plastic sheeting to protect the rest of the house from concrete dust. Use a chalk line to lay out a 24"-wide trench centered over the new branch drain location. Score along the lines with a concrete saw or a circular saw with a masonry blade.

(continued)

5

Use a jackhammer to break up the concrete in the trench, taking care not to damage any of the existing plumbing lines. Wear gloves, eye and ear protection, and a dust mask. Remove the concrete for disposal. Remove dirt (technically called granular fill) in the trench, starting at the main waste-vent stack.

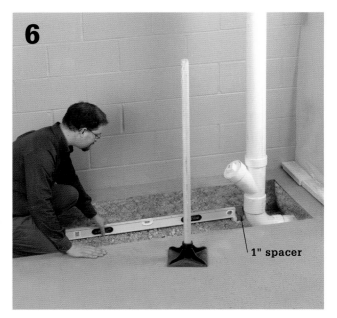

6

1" spacer

Create a flat-bottomed trench that slopes toward the main stack at ¼" per foot. The soil will hold up the drain lines, so it is important to create an even surface. Use a hand tamper to tamp down the soil if it has been disturbed. Tape a 1" spacer to the end of a 4-ft. level to create a handy measuring tool for checking the proper slope. Set the soil aside to use for back fill.

7

Cut the drain line or main stack (depending on how deep the drain line is) using a reciprocating saw (or a snap cutter). Support the main waste-vent stack before cutting. Use a 2 × 4 and duct tape for a plastic stack, or riser clamps for a cast iron stack. If cutting the horizontal drain line, cut as close as possible to the stack.

8

Cleanout

Cut into the stack above the cleanout, and remove the pipe and fittings. Wear rubber gloves, and have a large plastic bag and rags ready, as old pipes and fittings may be coated with sewer sludge. Remember that no waste water can flow in the house while the pipes are cut open. Turn off the water and drain toilets to prevent accidental use.

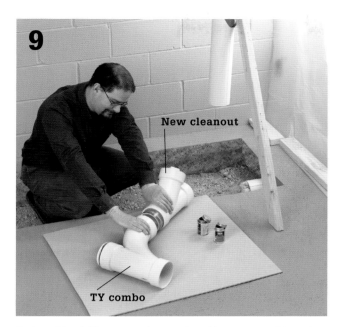

9

New cleanout

TY combo

Cut and test-fit a new cleanout and long sweep TY combo assembly, dry-fitting it to the drain stack and the horizontal drain line to the street. Make any needed adjustments and then solvent-glue the fittings and new pipe into a single assembly.

10

Clean the outside of the old pipes thoroughly and apply primer. Also apply primer and solvent glue to the female surfaces of the union fittings in the assembly. Slide the fitting assembly over the primed ends of the drain stack and the drain line at the same time. This requires a little bit of play in one or both of the lines so you can manipulate the new assembly. If your existing pipes will not move at all, you'll need to use a banded coupling on the drain stack to seal the gap.

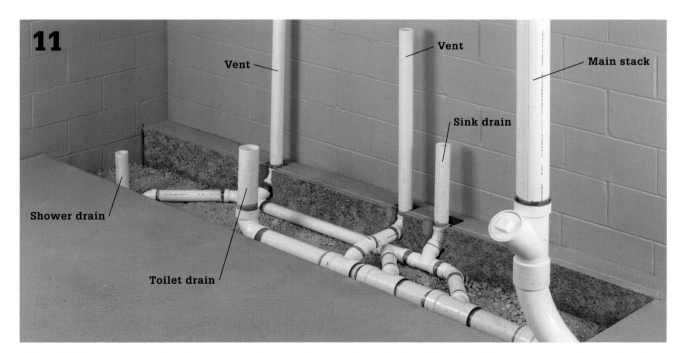

11

Vent

Vent

Main stack

Sink drain

Shower drain

Toilet drain

Cut and fit the components of the new drain line one piece at a time, starting at the stack. Use strings or boards to outline the wet wall, so vent placement is correct. Drain lines underground must be a minimum of 2". Use 3" × 2" reducing Ys to tie the shower drain line and the sink drain line into the toilet drain line. Install vertical drain and vent lines that are long enough to protrude well above the level of the finished floor.

(continued)

Check for leaks by pouring water into each new drain pipe. If the joints appear sound, contact your building department and arrange for your inspection (you must do this prior to covering the pipes). Plug the pipe openings with rags to prevent sewer gas from escaping. *Note: Some local municipalities require an air test as well.*

Backfill around the pipes with the soil dug from the trench. Mix and pour new concrete to cover the trench, and trowel smooth. Allow the concrete to cure for 3 days. Some municipalities may require that isolation membrane be wrapped around vertical pipes where they will be surrounded by concrete—check with your local inspector.

Build the wet wall from 2 × 6 lumber. The sill plate should be pressure treated, but the other members may be SPF. Notch the sill plate so the vent pipes clear it easily. Use masonry anchors or concrete nails and a powder-actuated nailer to attach the plate.

Run 2" vent pipes through notches in the studs. Assemble with vent T and 90° fittings. The 2" pipes are larger than required, but using the same size as the drain lines eliminates the need for reducing fittings, and makes for less waste. The 90° fittings are typically less expensive than the vent elbows.

Route the vent pipe to a point beneath a wall cavity running from the basement to the attic. Or, if there is another vent line closer that you can tie into (not very likely), go ahead and do that.

Pipe hangers

Run vent pipe up through the floors above and either directly out through the roof or tie it to another vent pipe in the attic. Remove sections of wall surface as needed to bore holes for running the vent pipe through wall plates. Feed the vent pipe up into the wall cavity from the basement. Wedge the vent pipe in place while you solvent-glue the fittings. Support the vent pipe at each floor with plastic pipe hangers installed horizontally. Stuff fiberglass insulation into holes around pipes. Do not replace any wallcoverings until you have had your final inspection.

Install the water supply plumbing. Compared to the drain-vent plumbing, this will seem remarkably easy. Follow the instructions on page 169, but adjust the layout to conform to your fixtures.

Nail guard

Half Bath

A first-story half bath is easy to install when located behind a kitchen or existing bathroom, because you can take advantage of accessible supply and DWV lines. It is possible to add a half bath on an upper story or in a location distant from existing plumbing, but the complexity and cost of the project may be increased considerably.

Be sure that the new fixtures are adequately vented. We vented the pedestal sink with a pipe that runs up the wall a few feet before turning to join the main stack. However, if there are higher fixtures draining into the main stack, you would be required to run the vent up to a point at least 6" above the highest fixture before splicing it into the main stack or an existing vent pipe. When the toilet is located within 6 ft. of the stack, as in our design, it requires no additional vent pipe.

The techniques for plumbing a half bath are similar to those used for a master bathroom. Refer to pages 162 to 177 for more detailed information.

In this half bath, the toilet and sink are close to the main stack for ease of installation, but are spaced far enough apart to meet minimum allowed distances between fixtures. Check your local code for any restrictions in your area. Generally, there should be at least 15" from the center of the toilet drain to a side wall or fixture, and a minimum of 21" of space between the front edge of the toilet and the wall.

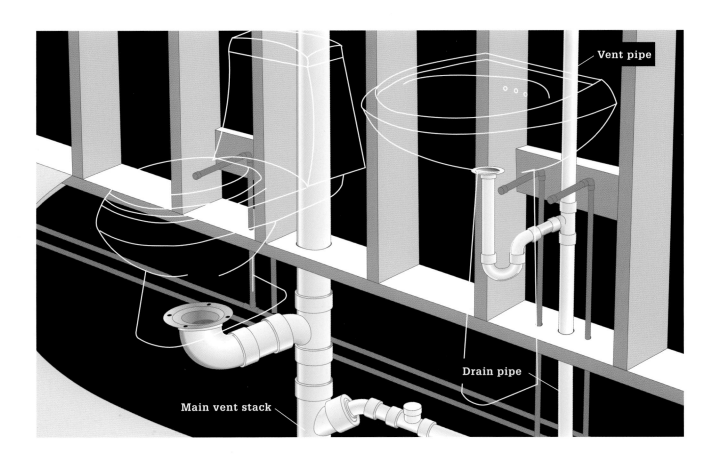

Vent pipe

Drain pipe

Main vent stack

How to Plumb a Half Bath

Locate the main waste-vent stack in the wet wall, and remove the wall surface behind the planned location for the toilet and sink. Cut a 4½"-diameter hole for the toilet flange (centered 12" from the wall for most toilets). Drill two ¾" holes through the sole plate for sink supply lines and one hole for the toilet supply line. Drill a 2" hole for the sink drain.

In the basement, cut away a section of the stack and insert a waste T-fitting with a 3" side inlet for the toilet drain; below that, insert a 3" × 1½" reducing Y and 45, or a 3" × 1½" reducing TY combo for the sink. Install a closet bend and 3" drain pipe for the toilet, and install a 1½" drain pipe with a sweep elbow for the sink. Make sure to maintain the proper ¼" per foot slope of the drain pipes.

Tap into water distribution pipes with ¾" × ½" reducing T-fittings, then run ½" copper supply pipes through the holes in the sole plate to the sink and toilet. Support all pipes at 4-ft. intervals with strapping attached to joists.

Attach drop ear elbows to the ends of the supply pipes, and anchor them to blocking installed between studs. Anchor the drain pipe to the blocking, then run a vertical vent pipe from the waste T-fitting up the wall to a point at least 6" above the highest fixture on the main stack. Then, route the vent pipe horizontally and splice it into the vent stack with a vent T.

Kitchen

Plumbing a remodeled kitchen is a relatively easy job if your kitchen includes only a wall sink. If your project includes an island sink, however, the work becomes more complicated.

An island sink poses problems because there is no wall in which to run a vent pipe. An island sink requires either a complicated configuration known as a loop vent or a device called an air admittance valve (AAV), now approved by most codes. An AAV eliminates the need for a loop vent in most island sink installations. Check with the local plumbing inspector before designing an installation with an AAV or a loop vent.

For our demonstration kitchen, we divided the project into three phases:

- How to Install DWV Pipes for a Wall Sink (pages 180 to 182)
- How to Install DWV Pipes for an Island Sink (pages 183 to 187)
- How to Install New Supply Pipes (pages 190 to 191)

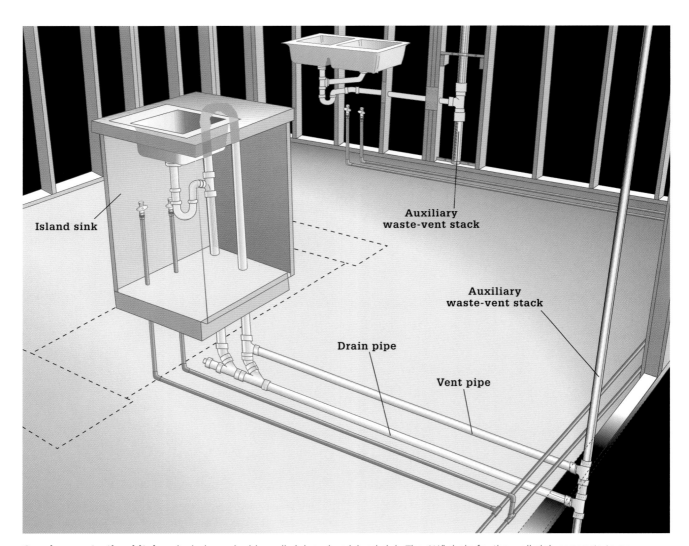

Island sink

Auxiliary
waste-vent stack

Auxiliary
waste-vent stack

Drain pipe

Vent pipe

Our demonstration kitchen includes a double wall sink and an island sink. The 1½" drain for the wall sink connects to an existing 2" galvanized waste-vent stack; since the trap is within 3½ ft. of the stack, no vent pipe is required. The drain for the island sink uses a loop vent configuration connected to an auxiliary waste-vent stack in the basement.

Tips for Plumbing a Kitchen ▸

Insulate exterior walls if you live in a region with freezing winter temperatures. Where possible, run water supply pipes through the floor or interior partition walls, rather than exterior walls.

Use existing waste-vent stacks to connect the new DWV pipes. In addition to a main waste-vent stack, most homes have one or more auxiliary waste-vent stacks in the kitchen that can be used to connect new DWV pipes.

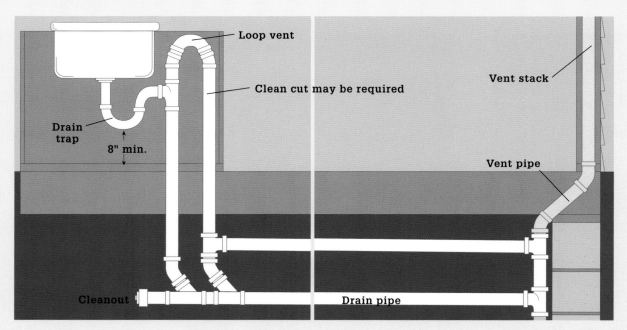

Loop vents makes it possible to vent a sink when there is no adjacent wall to house the vent pipe. The drain is vented with a loop of pipe that arches up against the countertop and away from the drain before dropping through the floor. The vent pipe then runs horizontally to an existing vent pipe. In our project, we have tied the island vent to a vent pipe extending up from a basement utility sink. *Note: Loop vents are subject to local code restrictions. Always consult your building inspector for guidelines on venting an island sink.*

How to Install DWV Pipes for a Wall Sink

Determine the location of the sink drain by marking the position of the sink and base cabinet on the floor. Mark a point on the floor indicating the position of the sink drain opening. This point will serve as a reference for aligning the sink drain stub-out.

Mark a route for the new drain pipe through the studs behind the wall sink cabinet. The drain pipe should angle ¼" per foot down toward the waste-vent stack.

Use a right-angle drill and hole saw to bore holes for the drain pipe. On non-loadbearing studs, such as the cripple studs beneath a window, you can notch the studs with a reciprocating saw to simplify the installation of the drain pipe. If the studs are loadbearing, however, you must thread the run though the bored holes, using couplings to join short lengths of pipe as you create the run.

Measure, cut, and dry-fit a horizontal drain pipe to run from the waste-vent stack to the sink drain stub-out. Create the stub-out with a 45° elbow and 6" length of 1½" pipe. *Note: If the sink trap in your installation will be more than 3½ ft. from the waste-vent pipe, you will have to install a waste-T and run a vent pipe up the wall, connecting it to the vent stack at a point at least 6" above the lip of the sink.*

Remove the neoprene sleeve from a banded coupling, then roll the lip back and measure the thickness of the separator ring.

Attach two lengths of 2" pipe, at least 4" long, to the top and bottom openings on a 2" × 2" × 1½" waste-T. Hold the fitting alongside the waste-vent stack, then mark the stack for cutting, allowing space for the separator rings on the banded couplings.

(continued)

Use riser clamps and 2 × 4 blocking to support the waste-vent stack above and below the new drain pipe, then cut out the waste-vent stack along the marked lines, using a reciprocating saw and metal-cutting blade.

Slide banded couplings onto the cut ends of the waste-vent stack, and roll back the lips of the neoprene sleeves. Position the waste-T assembly, then roll the sleeves into place over the plastic pipes.

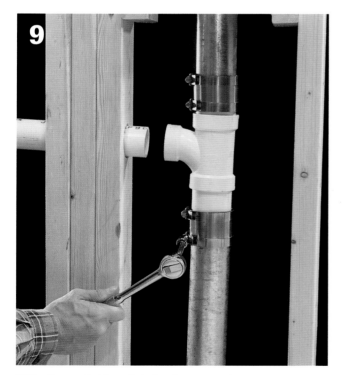

Slide the metal bands into place over the neoprene sleeves, and tighten the clamps with a ratchet wrench or screwdriver.

Solvent-glue the drain pipe, beginning at the waste-vent stack. Use a 90° elbow and a short length of pipe to create a drain stub-out extending about 4" out from the wall.

How to Install DWV Pipes for an Island Sink

Position the base cabinet for the island sink, according to your kitchen plans. Mark the cabinet position on the floor with tape, then move the cabinet out of the way.

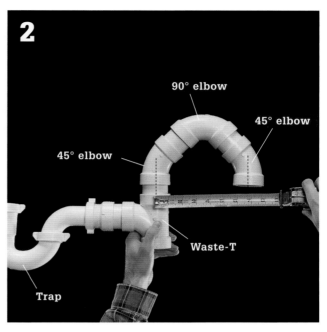

Create the beginning of the drain and loop vent by test-fitting a drain trap, waste-T, two 45° elbows, and a 90° elbow, linking them with 2" lengths of pipe. Measure the width of the loop between the centerpoints of the fittings.

Draw a reference line perpendicular to the wall to use as a guide when positioning the drain pipes. A cardboard template of the sink can help you position the loop vent inside the outline of the cabinet.

Position the loop assembly on the floor, and use it as a guide for marking hole locations. Make sure to position the vent loop so the holes are not over joists.

(continued)

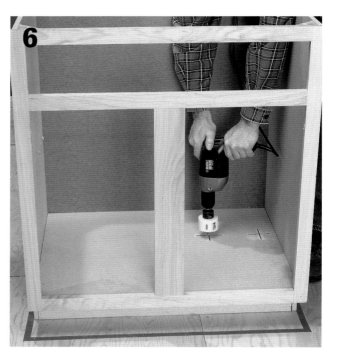

Use a hole saw with a diameter slightly larger than the vent pipes to bore holes in the subfloor at the marked locations. Note the positions of the holes by carefully measuring from the edges of the taped cabinet outline; these measurements will make it easier to position matching holes in the floor of the base cabinet.

Reposition the base cabinet, and mark the floor of the cabinet where the drain and vent pipes will run. (Make sure to allow for the thickness of the cabinet sides when measuring.) Use the hole saw to bore holes in the floor of the cabinet, directly above the holes in the subfloor.

Measure, cut, and assemble the drain and loop vent assembly. Tape the top of the loop in place against a brace laid across the top of the cabinet, then extend the drain and vent pipes through the holes in the floor of the cabinet. The waste-T should be about 18" above the floor, and the drain and vent pipes should extend about 2 ft. through the floor.

In the basement, establish a route from the island vent pipe to an existing vent pipe. (In our project, we used the auxiliary waste-vent stack near a utility sink.) Hold a long length of pipe between the pipes, and mark for T-fittings. Cut off the plastic vent pipe at the mark, then dry-fit a waste T-fitting to the end of the pipe.

Hold a waste-T against the vent stack, and mark the horizontal vent pipe at the correct length. Fit the horizontal pipe into the waste-T, then tape the assembly in place against the vent stack. The vent pipe should angle ¼" per foot down toward the drain.

Fit a 3" length of pipe in the bottom opening on the T-fitting attached to the vent pipe, then mark both the vent pipe and the drain pipe for 45° elbows. Cut off the drain and vent pipes at the marks, then dry-fit the elbows onto the pipes.

Extend both the vent pipe and drain pipe by dry-fitting 3" lengths of pipe and Y-fittings to the elbows. Using a level, make sure the horizontal drain pipe will slope toward the waste-vent at a pitch of ¼" per foot. Measure and cut a short length of pipe to fit between the Y-fittings.

(continued)

Cut a horizontal drain pipe to reach from the vent Y-fitting to the auxiliary waste-vent stack. Attach a waste-T to the end of the drain pipe, then position it against the drain stack, maintaining a downward slope of ¼" per foot. Mark the auxiliary stack for cutting above and below the fittings.

Cut out the auxiliary stack at the marks. Use the T-fittings and short lengths of pipe to assemble an insert piece to fit between the cutoff ends of the auxiliary stack. The insert assembly should be about ½" shorter than the removed section of stack.

Slide banded couplings onto the cut ends of the auxiliary stack, then insert the plastic pipe assembly and loosely tighten the clamps.

At the open inlet on the drain pipe Y-fitting, insert a cleanout fitting.

16

Solvent-glue all pipes and fittings found in the basement, beginning with the assembly inserted into the existing waste-vent stack, but do not glue the vertical drain and vent pipes running up into the cabinet. Tighten the banded couplings at the auxiliary stack. Support the horizontal pipes every 4 ft. with strapping nailed to the joists, then detach the vertical pipes extending up into the island cabinet. The final connection for the drain and vent loop will be completed as other phases of the kitchen remodeling project are finished.

17

After installing flooring and attaching cleats for the island base cabinet, cut away the flooring covering the holes for the drain and vent pipes.

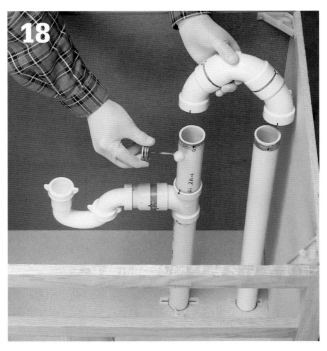

18

Install the base cabinet, then insert the drain and vent pipes through the holes in the cabinet floor, and solvent-glue the pieces together.

Air Admittance Valves ▸

The loop vent (page 135) is approved by code in any jurisdiction and is a reliable way to vent your island sink. But in many parts of the country, you'll find another option that is far simpler, if not as time-tested: the air admittance valve (AAV). Invented in the 1970s, AAVs let the necessary amount of air enter a DWV system when water is draining, but they close when the line has emptied to keep sewer gases from escaping.

The advantage of AAVs is that you can install them to vent individual fixtures, reducing the amount of vent piping needed, as well as the number of roof penetrations. You can also install them on branch vent lines to service more than one fixture.

Be sure to check with your local building department before installing them anywhere. Any vent system containing AAVs also must have at least one standard vent outlet to the exterior of the building.

The first AAVs on the market were spring-activated, and you can still purchase these today through wholesale plumbing suppliers or the Internet. Later versions are gravity activated. In these AAVs, the valve is opened by negative line pressure in the drain line created by flushing or draining. When the valve opens, the pressure in the line equalizes.

AAVs can be installed into PVC systems like any other solvent-glued fitting. Always install AAVs according to the manufacturer's specification.

Air admittance valves are designed to allow air into the vent system when needed, but to keep it from exiting when the system should remain closed.

Shown cutaway

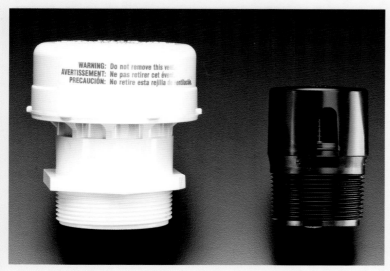

The original air admittance valves were spring loaded (right) but advancing technology is replacing these versions with gravity-activated AAVs (left).

Common AAV Applications

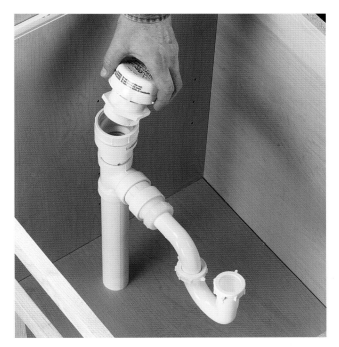

By installing an AAV in a plumbed kitchen island, you can do away with almost all of the complicated loop-vent plumbing. But be sure to check with your local plumbing inspector first. AAVs are allowed in all 50 states but not in some municipalities in selected states.

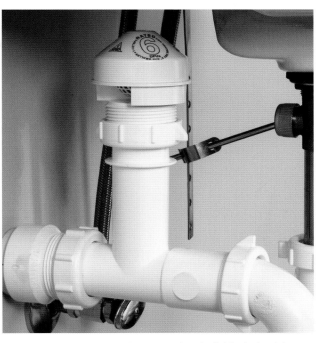

An AAV connected to the trap of an individual plumbing fixture can eliminate great amounts of vent-plumbing work. In many large public stadiums, for example, each bathroom fixture is vented with an AAV to cut down on the number of long vent runs.

An AAV can be installed on a branch drain servicing as many as six fixtures (check local code), as long as the DWV system has at least one outlet through the roof and outside of the building.

How to Install New Supply Pipes

Drill two 1"-diameter holes, spaced about 6" apart, through the floor of the island base cabinet and the underlying subfloor. Position the holes so they are not over floor joists. Drill similar holes in the floor of the base cabinet for the wall sink.

Turn off the water at the main shutoff and drain the pipes. Cut out any old water supply pipes that obstruct new pipe runs, using a tubing cutter or hacksaw. In our project, we removed the old pipe back to a point where it was convenient to begin the new branch lines.

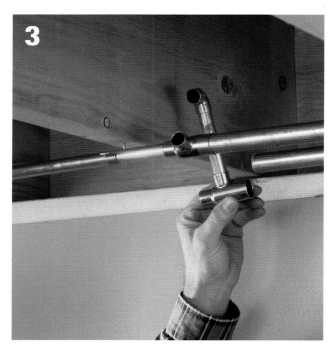

Dry-fit T-fittings on each supply pipe (we used ¾" × ½" × ½" reducing T-fittings). Use elbows and lengths of copper pipe to begin the new branch lines running to the island sink and the wall sink. The parallel pipes should be routed so they are between 3" and 6" apart.

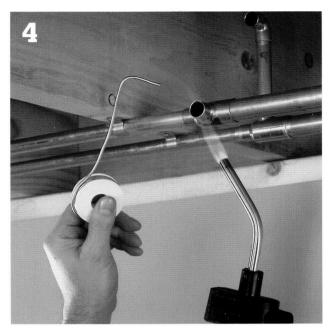

Solder the pipes and fittings together, beginning at the T-fittings. Support the horizontal pipe runs with copper pipe straps attached to the joists at least every 6 ft. (Check your local codes for specific strap spacing requirements.)

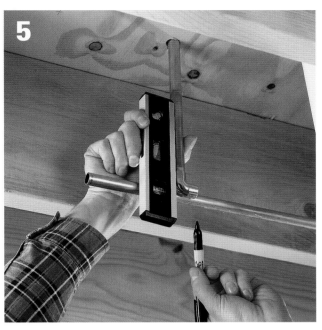

Extend the branch lines to points directly below the holes leading up into the base cabinets. Use elbows and lengths of pipe to form vertical risers extending at least 12" into the base cabinets. Use a small level to position the risers so they are plumb, then mark the pipe for cutting.

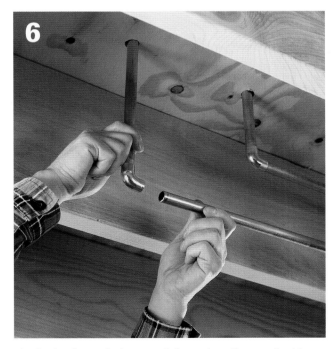

Fit the horizontal pipes and risers together, and solder them in place. Install blocking between joists, and anchor the risers to the blocking with pipe straps.

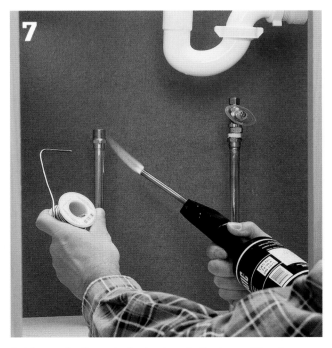

Solder male-threaded adapters to the tops of the risers, then screw threaded shutoff valves onto the fittings.

New Gas Lines

Do you want to enjoy the efficiency and control of cooking on a gas range, but your kitchen only supports an electric model? Or perhaps you've been meaning to move the range to improve the workflow. Would you like to add a supplementary gas water heater closer to your master bath? Are you planning to add a permanent heat source in your garage? Or do you simply want to save money by converting from electricity to gas fuel for a few of your major appliances? Any of these projects is within your grasp as long as your home already has natural gas service. You simply need to install a new branch gas line.

Installing a gas line isn't difficult, but it is dangerous and in many areas you simply aren't allowed to do it yourself. Please read the discussion of whether or not to tackle a gas-related project on pages 314 to 316 before you make your decision. Also refer to the basic materials and handling information in the same location.

If you choose to proceed with the new line installation, begin by mapping out where the new line will run and calculating what lengths of pipe and which fittings you will need. Begin at the supply pipe you'll be tying into and work forward. Also check with your local building department to find out which types of pipe are allowed and which types they recommend for your job.

The number of gas appliances a branch line can support is limited by the diameter of the branch and length of runs, so you'll need to know exactly which other appliances are serviced by the branch you're tying into and how much fuel they consume (see chart, next page). You will need to obtain a permit and have your work inspected, so it's good to involve the inspections department up front.

Running new pipe lines allows you to enjoy the practical and cost-savings benefits of natural gas in all areas of your home.

Notes for Installing Gas Lines ▸

- In most areas, a shut-off valve (usually a ball valve) must be accessible within 3 ft. of the appliance and in the same room.
- If you are relocating a line and cannot remove the existing branch supply line because of limited access, you will need to cap the gas stub out.
- If you live in an area that allows flexible copper or flexible stainless steel connectors you will have more room for error in your measurements. If you must connect only using rigid black pipe, you may need to have some pipe lengths cut and threaded to fit.
- Most areas allow Type K and Type L copper tubing for installation in an LP gas or natural gas line. But always check with your local building department.
- Never use standard plumbing fittings with gas pipe. Use only gas-rated, cast brass stopcocks for smaller pipe (less than 3" dia.) and use gas-rated globe or gate valves for larger pipe.

Gas Consumption of Household Appliances ▸

Appliance	Avg. Btu's per hour	Gas consumption per hour*
50-gallon water heater	50,000	50 cu. ft.
Furnace	200,000	200 cu. ft.
Clothes dryer	35,000	35 cu. ft.
Range/oven	65,000	65 cu. ft.

*Based on output rate of 1,000 Btu per cubic foot of fuel per hour. Your actual rate will likely differ. Check with your energy company.

Determine the flow rate for a branch line by adding the gas consumption per hour (use above data only if specific information is not printed on your appliance label) of each appliance. Although appliances may not run concurrently, it is advisable to select pipe size based on 100% flow rate. Note that distance traveled also plays an important role in selecting pipe size diameter (½", ¾", 1", 1¼", or 1½").

Horizontal pipe runs must be pitched downward slightly, either by using progressively thicker shims between pipe and the attachment surface, or by making progressively deeper cutouts in a support member, or drilling access holes that become progressively lower in joists.

Tips for Running Gas Pipe ▶

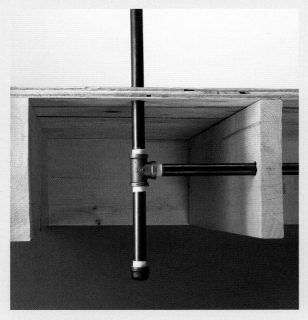

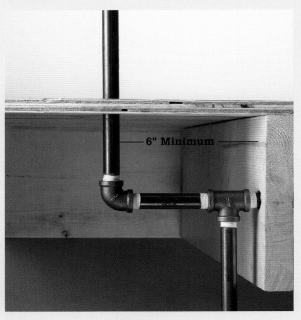

Horizontal pipe runs should terminate in a drip nipple that drops from the end to capture moisture and impurities.

Make branch connections at the side or top of the pipe you are tying into. If you need to drop down or up, run a branch line at least 6" long straight out from the side of the pipe and then drop down or go up with a 90° union.

Protect pipes running in enclosed wall cavities with steel protector plates to stop nails or screws before they reach the pipe. Pipes in enclosed walls must be at least ½" in diameter.

How to Install a Branch Gas Line

Begin layout at the end of the run. Pull the appliance away from the wall slightly in the new location and mark the most convenient spot for the new gas line to enter the room. The easiest installation is up through the floor. Drill a hole through the floor and thread a wire through the hole to mark the location of the proposed gas line.

From the basement, locate the wire and determine whether the placement is feasible. Adjust the placement to work around joists or other supply lines if necessary. Drill a 1" hole up through the floor.

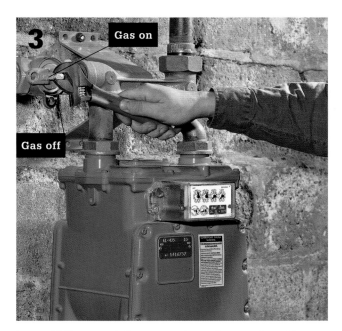

Turn off the gas at the gas meter, using an adjustable wrench. The valve does not have a stop, so it can rotate indefinitely. The gas is off when the bar is perpendicular to the pipe.

Disconnect the existing appliance. If a flexible stainless steel connector was used, discard it, as they can only be installed once. Remove the gas stub-out or flexible copper line back to the supply line.

(continued)

Begin fitting the new pipe. Apply pipe compound or gas-rate, yellow PTFE tape to all male threads. Hand tighten each joint, then tighten each pipe and fitting at least one turn before moving on to the next section. You may need to tighten more than one turn to get the proper alignment. Wipe any excess joint compound from the exposed threads.

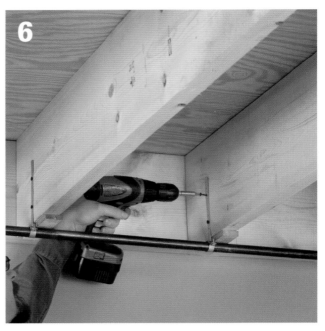

Support pipe runs with pipe hangers rated for use with your pipe material. Make sure that the line has a slight downward slope from the source toward the appliance.

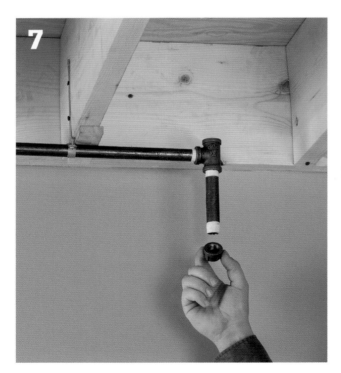

Install a T at the point where the pipe turns up to go through the floor. Connect a short nipple and a cap on the crossbar of the T pointing down. This creates a drip nipple to trap any moisture or impurities in the gas line.

Push the riser stub-out pipe up through the hole in the floor. To prevent contamination, cover the end of the riser nipple with tape or plastic.

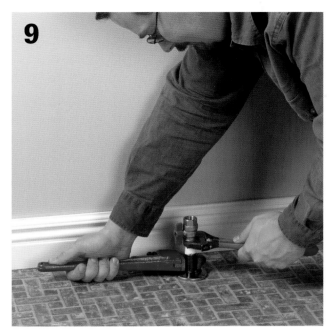

9

Attach an approved ¼"-turn gas valve to the riser stub-out. Apply pipe compound to the male threads. Use an adjustable wrench, not a pipe wrench, to tighten the valve onto the stubout. If desired, slip an escutcheon plate over the riser pipe before you attach the valve (you can also install a split plate later). With the valve off, restore gas to the line at the meter and test all joints with leak detector solution (see page 315).

10

Attach a male-threaded-to-flare adapter to the valve. Use two adjustable wrenches—one holding the valve in place and one tightening the fitting.

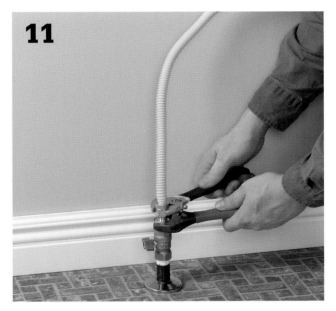

11

Attach the appliance connector tube to the valve. Make sure to buy a connector with ends that match the valve and the appliance port. In most cases, you may now use flexible stainless steel connectors instead of soft copper tubing that requires flaring. But soft copper is allowed if you have the equipment to make a flare fitting joint (see page 317) and want to save a few dollars.

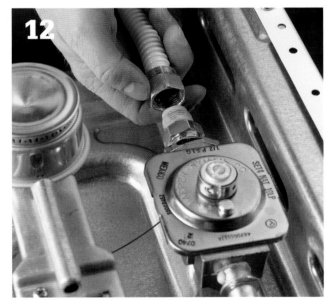

12

Hook up the appliance by attaching the other flare nut to the threaded gas inlet port on the appliance. Plug in the appliance's power cord. Turn on gas at the main meter and at the stop valve and test the flare fittings for leaks. Once you're certain all the joints are good, carefully slide the appliance into place.

Plumbing Repairs

Making plumbing repairs is a good deal easier today than it was a generation ago. Back then, a leaky faucet was repaired by disassembling the valve and repacking it with messy string. Today, you simply remove the old cartridge and pop in a new one. In older times, if your toilet was running you replaced a rubber gasket or washer. Today, you're more likely to simply remove and replace the entire flush mechanism, which is actually a good deal easier to do than fixing one discreet piece of the mechanism. But convenience always comes at a price. Locating the correct replacement parts can get tricky, and instead of a cheap washer or bit of graphite string, you usually have to pay for the whole replacement parts package.

Faucets and drains are the parts of your plumbing system that are most likely to need repairs. Faucets leak or drip and drains clog. If you add these repairs to fixing toilet problems, you've covered almost everything you're likely to face. This chapter includes thorough information on these common repairs, as well as several that you're less likely to encounter—but in the event that you do, you'll be prepared.

In this chapter:

- Common Toilet Problems
- Toilet Flanges
- Toilet Drain Lines
- Sinks
- Sprayers & Aerators
- Leaky Plumbing
- Tubs & Showers
- Sink Drains
- Branch & Main Drains
- Branch Drains & Vents
- Main Stacks
- Supply Pipes
- Burst Pipes
- Noisy Pipes

Common Toilet Problems

A clogged toilet is one of the most common plumbing problems. If a toilet overflows or flushes sluggishly, clear the clog with a plunger or closet auger. If the problem persists, the clog may be in the main waste-vent stack (pages 254 to 258).

Most other toilet problems are fixed easily with minor adjustments that require no disassembly or replacement parts. You can make these adjustments in a few minutes, using simple tools (pages 268 to 271).

If minor adjustments do not fix the problem, further repairs will be needed. The parts of a standard toilet are not difficult to take apart, and most repair projects can be completed in less than an hour.

A recurring puddle of water on the floor around a toilet may be caused by a crack in the toilet base or in the tank. A damaged toilet should be replaced. Installing a new toilet is an easy project that can be finished in three or four hours.

A standard two-piece toilet has an upper tank that is bolted to a base. This type of toilet uses a simple gravity-operated flush system and can easily be repaired using the directions on the following pages. Some one-piece toilets use a complicated, high-pressure flush valve.

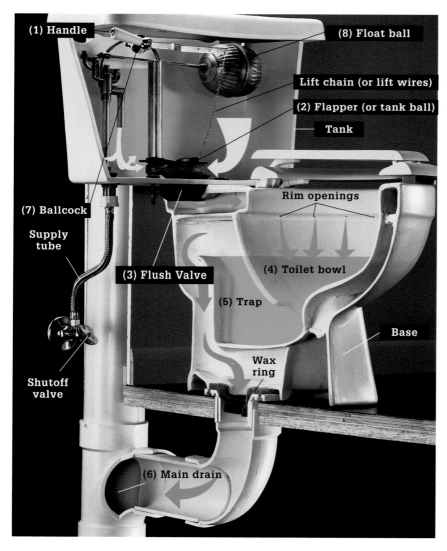

(1) Handle
(8) Float ball
Lift chain (or lift wires)
(2) Flapper (or tank ball)
Tank
(7) Ballcock
Supply tube
Rim openings
(3) Flush Valve
(4) Toilet bowl
(5) Trap
Base
Shutoff valve
Wax ring
(6) Main drain

How a toilet works: When the handle (1) is pushed, the lift chain raises a rubber seal, called a flapper or tank ball (2). Water in the tank rushes down through the flush valve opening (3) in the bottom of the tank and into the toilet bowl (4). Waste water in the bowl is forced through the trap (5) into the main drain (6). When the toilet tank is empty, the flapper seals the tank, and a water supply valve, called a ballcock (7), refills the toilet tank. The ballcock is controlled by a float ball (8) that rides on the surface of the water. When the tank is full, the float ball automatically shuts off the ballcock.

Problems	Repairs
Toilet handle sticks or is hard to push.	1. Adjust lift wires (page 202). 2. Clean and adjust handle (page 202).
Handle must be held down for entire flush.	1. Adjust handle (page 202). 2. Shorten lift chain or wires (page 202). 3. Replace waterlogged flapper.
Handle is loose.	1. Adjust handle (page 202). 2. Reattach lift chain or lift wires to lever (page 202).
Toilet will not flush at all.	1. Make sure water is turned on. 2. Adjust lift chain or lift wires (page 202).
Toilet does not flush completely.	1. Adjust lift chain (page 202). 2. Adjust water level in tank (page 204). 3. Increase pressure on pressure-assisted toilet.
Toilet overflows or flushes sluggishly.	1. Clear clogged toilet (page 212). 2. Clear clogged main waste-vent stack (page 211).
Toilet runs continuously.	1. Adjust lift wires or lift chain (page 202). 2. Replace leaky float ball (page 204). 3. Adjust water level in tank (page 204). 4. Adjust and clean flush valve (page 208). 5. Replace flush valve (page 208). 6. Repair or replace ballcock. 7. Service pressure-assist valve (page 204).
Water on floor around toilet.	1. Tighten tank bolts and water connections (page 214). 2. Insulate tank to prevent condensation. 3. Replace wax ring (page 214). 4. Replace cracked tank or bowl (pages 12 to 17).
Toilet noisy when filling.	1. Open shutoff valve completely. 2. Replace ballcock and float valve. 3. Refill tube is disconnected.
Weak flush.	1. Clean clogged rim openings (page 205). 2. Replace old low-flow toilet.
Toilet rocks.	1. Replace wax ring and bolts (page 214). 2. Replace toilet flange (page 215).

Making Minor Adjustments

Many common toilet problems can be fixed by making minor adjustments to the handle and the attached lift chain (or lift wires).

If the handle sticks or is hard to push, remove the tank cover and clean the handle-mounting nut. Make sure the lift wires are straight.

If the toilet will not flush completely unless the handle is held down, you may have to remove excess slack in the lift chain.

If the toilet will not flush at all, the lift chain may be broken or may have to be reattached to the handle lever.

A continuously running toilet (page opposite) can be caused by bent lift wires, kinks in a lift chain, or lime buildup on the handle mounting nut. Clean and adjust the handle and the lift wires or chain to fix the problem.

Tools & Materials ▶

Adjustable wrench
Needlenose pliers
Screwdriver
Scissors

Hacksaw
Spray Lubricant
Small wire brush
Vinegar

How to Adjust a Toilet Handle & Lift Chain (or Lift Wires)

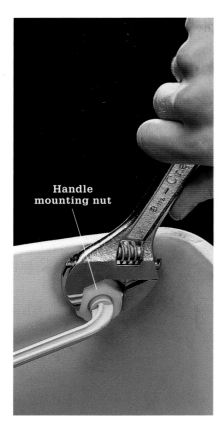

Clean and adjust handle-mounting nut so handle operates smoothly. Mounting nut has reversed threads. Loosen nut by turning clockwise; tighten by turning counterclockwise. Remove lime buildup with a brush dipped in vinegar.

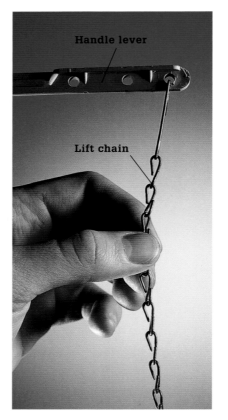

Adjust lift chain so it hangs straight from handle lever, with about ½" of slack. Remove excess slack in chain by hooking the chain in a different hole in the handle lever or by removing links with needlenose pliers. A broken lift chain must be replaced.

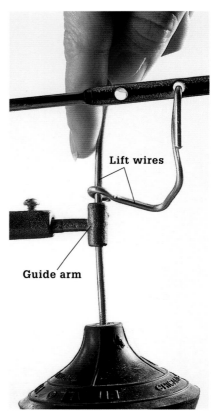

Adjust lift wires (found on toilets without lift chains) so that wires are straight and operate smoothly when handle is pushed. A sticky handle often can be fixed by straightening bent lift wires.

Seat loose? Loose seats are almost always the result of loose nut on the seat bolts. Tighten the nuts with pliers. If the nut is corroded or stripped, replace the bolts and nuts or replace the whole seat.

Seat uncomfortably low? Instead of going to the trouble of raising the toilet or replacing it with a taller model, you can simply replace the seat with a thicker, extended seat.

Tank fills too slowly? The first place to check is the shutoff valve where the supply tube for the toilet is connected. Make sure it is fully open. If it is, you may need to replace the shutoff—these fittings are fairly cheap and frequently fail to open fully.

Toilet running? Running toilets are usually caused by faulty or misadjusted fill valves, but sometimes the toilet runs because the tank is leaking water into the bowl. To determine if this is happening with your toilet, add a few drops of food coloring to the tank water. If, after a while, the water in the bowl becomes colored, then you have a leak and probably need to replace the rubber gasket at the base of your flush valve.

Reset Tank Water Level

Tank water flowing into the overflow pipe is the sound we hear when a toilet is running. Usually, this is caused by a minor misadjustment that fails to tell the water to shut off when the toilet tank is full. The culprit is a float ball or cup that is adjusted to set a water level in the tank that's higher than the top of the overflow pipe, which serves as a drain for excess tank water. The other photos on this page show how to fix the problem.

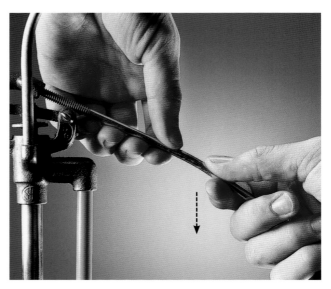

A ball float is connected to a float arm that's attached to a plunger on the other end. As the tank fills, the float rises and lifts one end of the float arm. At a certain point, the float arm depresses the plunger and stops the flow of water. By simply bending the float arm downward a bit, you can cause it to depress the plunger at a lower tank water level, solving the problem.

A diaphragm fill valve usually is made of plastic and has a wide bonnet that contains a rubber diaphragm. Turn the adjustment screw clockwise to lower the water level and counterclockwise to raise it.

Spring clip

A float cup fill valve is made of plastic and is easy to adjust. Lower the water level by pinching the spring clip with fingers or pliers and moving the clip and cup down the pull rod and shank. Raise the water level by moving the clip and cup upward.

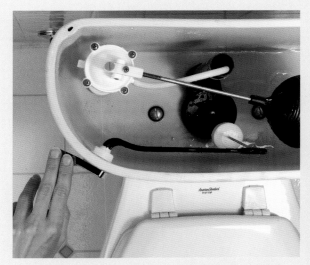

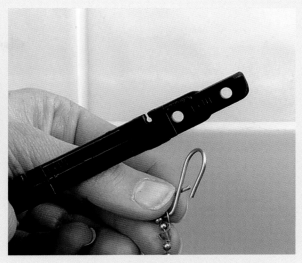

Sometimes there is plenty of water in the tank, but not enough of it makes it to the bowl before the flush valve shuts off the water from the tank. Modern toilets are designed to leave some water in the tank, since the first water that leaves the tank does so with the most force. (It's pressed out by the weight of the water on top.) To increase the duration of the flush, shorten the length of the chain between the flapper and the float (yellow in the model shown).

The handle lever should pull straight up on the flapper. If it doesn't, reposition the chain hook on the handle lever. When the flapper is covering the opening, there should be just a little slack in the chain. If there is too much slack, shorten the chain and cut off excess with the cutters on your pliers.

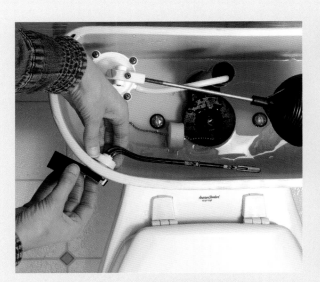

If the toilet is not completing flushes and the lever and chain for the flapper or tank ball are correctly adjusted, the problem could be that the handle mechanism needs cleaning or replacement. Remove the chain/linkage from the handle lever. Remove the nut on the backside of the handle with an adjustable wrench. It unthreads clockwise (the reverse of standard nuts). Remove the old handle from the tank.

Unless the handle parts are visibly broken, try cleaning them with an old toothbrush dipped in white vinegar. Replace the handle and test the action. If it sticks or is hard to operate, replace it. Most replacement handles come with detailed instructions that tell you how to install and adjust them.

How to Replace a Fill Valve

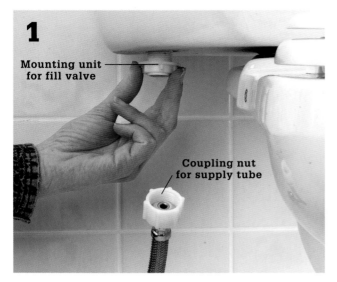

Mounting unit for fill valve

Coupling nut for supply tube

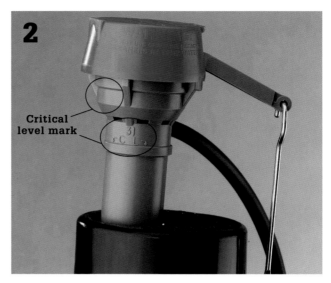

Critical level mark

Toilet fill valves degrade eventually and need to be replaced. Before removing the old fill valve, shut off the water supply at the fixture stop valve located on the tube that supplies water to the tank. Flush the toilet and sponge out the remaining water. Then, remove the old fill valve assembly by loosening and removing the mounting nut on the outside of the tank wall that secures the fill valve.

Fill valves need to be coordinated with the flush valve so the tank water level is not higher than the overflow pipe and so the fill valve is not low enough in the tank that it creates a siphoning hazard. New fill valves have a "critical level" mark ("CL") near the top of the valve.

The new fill valve must be installed so the critical level ("CL") mark is at least 1" above the overflow pipe. Slip the shank washer on the threaded shank of the new fill valve and place the valve in the hole so the washer is flat on the tank bottom. Compare the locations of the "CL" mark and the overflow pipe.

Adjust the height of the fill valve shank so the "CL" line and overflow pipe will be correctly related. Different products are adjusted in different ways—the fill valve shown here telescopes when it's twisted.

5

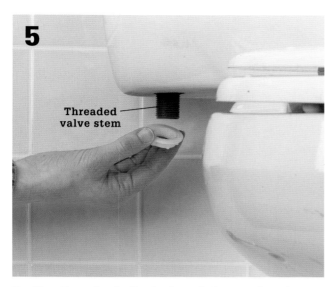

Threaded valve stem

Position the valve in the tank. Push down on the valve shank (not the top) while hand tightening the locknut onto the threaded valve stem (thread the mounting nut on the exterior side of tank). Hand tighten only.

6

Hook up the water by attaching the coupling nut from the supply riser to the threaded shank at the bottom end of the new fill valve. Hand tighten only.

7

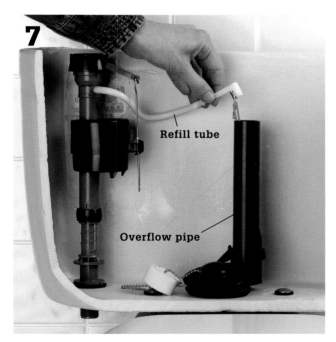

Refill tube

Overflow pipe

If the overflow pipe has a cap, remove it. Attach one end of the refill tube from the new valve to the plastic angle adapter and the other end to the refill nipple near the top of the valve. Attach the angle adapter to the overflow pipe. Cut off excess tubing with scissors to prevent kinking. *Warning: Don't insert the refill tube into the overflow pipe. The outlet of the refill tube needs to be above the top of pipe for it to work properly.*

8

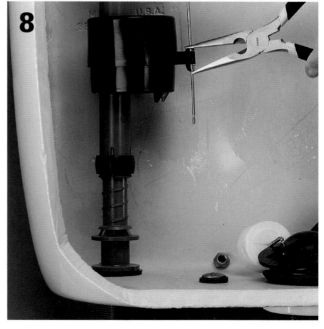

Turn the water on fully. Slightly tighten any fitting that drips water. Adjust the water level in the tank by squeezing the spring clip on the float cup with needlenose pliers and moving the cup up or down on the link bar. Test the flush.

How to Replace a Flush Valve

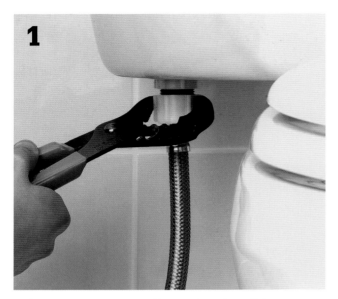

Before removing the old flush valve, shut off the water supply at the fixture stop valve located on the tube that supplies water to the tank. Flush the toilet and sponge out the remaining water. To make this repair you'll need to remove the tank from the bowl. Start by unscrewing the water supply coupling nut from the bottom of the tank.

Unscrew the bolts holding the toilet tank to the bowl by loosening the nuts from below. If you are having difficulty unscrewing the tank bolts and nuts because they are fused together by rust or corrosion, apply penetrating oil or spray lubricant to the threads, give it a few minutes to penetrate, and then try again. If that fails, slip an open-ended hacksaw (or plain hacksaw blade) between the tank and bowl and saw through the bolt (inset photo).

Unhook the chain from the handle lever arm. Remove the tank and carefully place it upside-down on an old towel. Remove the spud washer and spud nut from the base of the flush valve using a spud wrench or large channel-type pliers. Remove the old flush valve.

Place the new flush valve in the valve hole and check to see if the top of the overflow pipe is at least 1" below the critical level line (see page 206) and the tank opening where the handle is installed. If the pipe is too tall, cut it to length with a hacksaw.

5

Spud nut

Spud washer

Position the flush valve flapper below the handle lever arm and secure it to the tank from beneath with the spud nut. Tighten the nut one-half turn past hand tight with a spud wrench or large channel-type pliers. Overtightening may cause the tank to break. Put the new spud washer over the spud nut, small side down.

6

Intermediate nut goes between tank and bowl

With the tank lying on its back, thread a rubber washer onto each tank bolt and insert it into the bolt holes from inside the tank. Then, thread a brass washer and hex nut onto the tank bolts from below and tighten them to a quarter turn past hand tight. Do not overtighten.

7

Intermediate nut

With the hex nuts tightened against the tank bottom, carefully lower the tank over the bowl and set it down so the spud washer seats neatly over the water inlet in the bowl and the tank bolts fit through the holes in the bowl flange. Secure the tank to the bowl with a rubber washer, brass washer, and nut or wing nut at each bolt end. Press the tank to level as you hand-tighten the nuts. Hook up the water supply at the fill valve inlet.

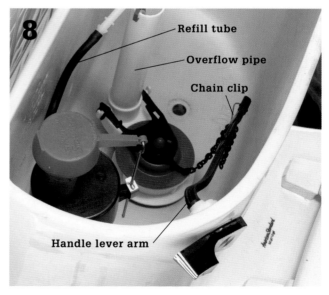

8

Refill tube

Overflow pipe

Chain clip

Handle lever arm

Connect the chain clip to the handle lever arm and adjust the number of links to allow for a little slack in the chain when the flapper is closed. Leave a little tail on the chain for adjusting, cutting off remaining excess. Attach the refill tube to the top of the overflow pipe the same way it had been attached to the previous refill pipe. Turn on the water supply at the stop valve and test the flush. (Some flush valve flappers are adjustable.)

Clogged Toilets

The toilet is clogged and has overflowed. Have patience. Now is the time for considered action. A second flush is a tempting but unnecessary gamble. First, do damage control. Mop up the water if there's been a spill. Next, consider the nature of the clog. Is it entirely "natural" or might a foreign object be contributing to the congestion? Push a natural blockage down the drain with a plunger. A foreign object should be removed, if possible, with a closet auger. Pushing anything more durable than toilet paper into the sewer may create a more serious blockage in your drain and waste system.

If the tub, sink, and toilet all back up at once, the branch drainline that serves all the bathroom fixtures is probably blocked and your best recourse is to call a drain clearing service.

Tools & Materials ▶

Towels
Closet auger

Plunger with foldout
skirt (force cup)

A blockage in the toilet bowl leaves flush water from the tank nowhere to go but on the floor.

The trap is the most common catching spot for toilet clogs, Once the clog forms, flushing the toilet cannot generate enough water power to clear the trap, so flush water backs up. Traps on modern 1.6-gallon toilets have been redesigned to larger diameters and are less prone to clogs than the first generation of 1.6-gallon toilets.

Plunger | Force cup

Not all plungers were created equal. The standard plunger (left) is simply an inverted rubber cup and is used to plunge sinks, tubs, and showers. The flanged plunger, also called a force cup, is designed to get down into the trap of a toilet drain. You can fold the flange up into the flanged plunger cup and use it as a standard plunger.

Drain Clearers ▸

The home repair marketplace is filled with gadgets and gimmicks, as well as well-established products, that are intended to clear drains of all types. Some are caustic chemicals, some are natural enzymes, others are more mechanical in nature. Some help, some are worthless, some can even make the problem worse. Nevertheless, if you are the type of homeowner who is enamored with new products and the latest solutions, you may enjoy testing out new drain cleaners as they become available. In this photo, for example, you'll see a relatively new product that injects blasts of compressed CO_2 directly into your toilet, sink, or tub drain to dislodge clogs. It does not cause any chemicals to enter the waste stream, and the manufacturers claim the CO_2 blast is very gentle and won't damage pipes. As with any new product, use it with caution. But if a plunger or a snake isn't working, it could save you the cost of a house call.

How to Plunge a Clogged Toilet

Plunging is the easiest way to remove "natural" blockages. Take time to lay towels around the base of the toilet and remove other objects to a safe, dry location, since plunging may result in splashing. Often, allowing a very full toilet to sit for twenty or thirty minutes will permit some of the water to drain to a less precarious level.

Tip ▸

A flanged plunger (force cup) fits into the mouth of the toilet trap and creates a tight seal so you can build up enough pressure in front of the plunger to dislodge the blockage and send it on its way.

There should be enough water in the bowl to completely cover the plunger. Fold out the skirt from inside the plunger to form a better seal with the opening at the base of the bowl. Pump the plunger vigorously half-a-dozen times, take a rest, and then repeat. Try this for 10 to 15 cycles.

If you force enough water out of the bowl that you are unable to create suction with the plunger, put a controlled amount of water in the bowl by lifting up on the flush valve in the tank. Resume plunging. When you think the drain is clear, you can try a controlled flush, with your hand ready to close the flush valve should the water threaten to spill out of the bowl. Once the blockage has cleared, dump a five-gallon pail of water into the toilet to blast away any residual debris.

How to Clear Clogs with a Closet Auger

Place the business end of the auger firmly in the bottom of the toilet bowl with the auger tip fully withdrawn. A rubber sleeve will protect the porcelain at the bottom bend of the auger. The tip will be facing back and up, which is the direction the toilet trap takes.

Tip ▶

A closet auger is a semirigid cable housed in a tube. The tube has a bend at the end so it can be snaked through a toilet trap (without scratching it) to snag blockages.

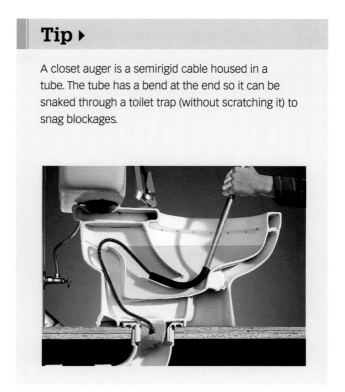

Rotate the handle on the auger housing clockwise as you push down on the rod, advancing the rotating auger tip up into the back part of the trap. You may work the cable backward and forward as needed, but keep the rubber boot of the auger firmly in place in the bowl. When you feel resistance, indicating you've snagged the object, continue rotating the auger counterclockwise as you withdraw the cable and the object.

Fully retract the auger until you have recovered the object. This can be frustrating at times, but it is still a much easier task than the alternative—to remove the toilet and go fishing.

Toilet Flanges

If your toilet rocks it will eventually leak. The rocking means that the bolts are no longer holding the toilet securely to the floor. If you have tightened the bolts and it still rocks, it is possible that a bolt has broken a piece of the flange off and is no longer able to hold. Rocking might also be because an ongoing leak has weakened the floor and it is now uneven. Whatever the reason, a rocking toilet needs to be fixed.

If your flange is connected to cast iron piping, use a repair flange. This has a rubber compression ring that will seal the new flange to the cast iron pipe.

Use a flange repair kit for a quick fix to a broken flange. The new flange piece from the kit is simply screwed to the floor after it has been oriented correctly over the broken flange.

Tools & Materials ▸

Drill
Wrench
Internal pipe cutter
Solvent-glue

#10 stainless steel
flathead wood
screws
Marker

Toilets that rock often only need to have the nuts on the closet bolts tightened. But if you need to tighten the bolts on an ongoing basis, you very likely have a problem with the closet flange.

How to Replace a PVC Closet Flange

Begin by removing the toilet and wax ring. Cut the pipe just below the bottom of the flange using an internal pipe cutter (inset, available at plumbing supply stores). Remove the flange.

If your flange is attached to a closet bend you will need to open up the floor around the toilet to get at the horizontal pipe connecting the bend to the stack to make the repair. If it is connected to a length of vertical plastic pipe, use a repair coupling and a short length of pipe to bring the pipe back up to floor level. Glue the new pipe into the repair coupling first and allow it to set. Clean the old pipe thoroughly before gluing.

Cut the replacement pipe flush with the floor. Dry-fit the new flange into the pipe. Turn the flange until the side cut-out screw slots are parallel to the wall. (Do not use the curved keyhole slots, as they are not as strong.) Draw lines to mark the location of the slots on the floor.

Prime and solvent-glue the pipe and flange, inserting the flange slightly off the marks and twisting it to proper alignment. Secure the flange to the floor with #10 stainless steel flathead wood screws.

Toilet Drain Lines

If your existing toilet drain line is heavily deteriorated, replace it. You will also need to replace the drain line if you are relocating and replacing the main drain stalk or if you are moving the toilet to a different spot in the bathroom.

Replacing a toilet drain is sometimes a troublesome task, mostly because the cramped space makes it difficult to route the large, 3" or 4" pipe. You likely will need to remove flooring around the toilet and wall surface behind the toilet.

Replacing a toilet drain may require framing work, as well, if you find it necessary to cut into joists in order to route the new pipes. When possible, plan your project to avoid changes to the framing members.

Tools & Materials ▶

Drill
Circular saw
Reciprocating saw
Pipe
Exterior-grade
  plywood
Screws

Replacing a toilet drain usually requires that you remove flooring and wall surface to gain access to the pipes.

How to Replace a Toilet Drain Line

Remove the toilet, then unscrew the toilet flange from the floor and remove it from the drain pipe. You can also use an internal pipe cutter to cut plastic drain pipe (see previous page, top left).

Joist location

Cut away the flooring around the toilet drain along the center of the floor joists, using a circular saw with the blade set to a depth ⅛" more than the thickness of the subfloor. The exposed joist will serve as a nailing surface when the subfloor is replaced.

Cut away the old closet bend as close as possible to the old waste-vent stack, using a reciprocating saw with metal-cutting blade, or a cast iron cutter.

If a joist obstructs the route to a new waste-vent stack, cut away a section of the floor joist. Install double headers and metal joist hangers to support the ends of the cut joist.

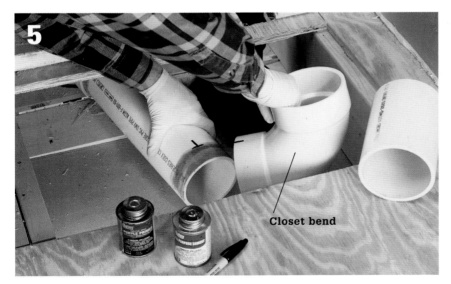

Closet bend

Create a new toilet drain running to the waste-vent stack, using a closet bend and a straight length of pipe. Position the drain so there will be at least 15" of space between the center of the bowl and side wall surfaces when the toilet is installed. Make sure the drain slopes at least ¼" per ft. toward the stack, then support the pipe with plastic pipe strap attached to framing members. Insert a 6" length of pipe in the top inlet of the closet bend; once the new drain pipes have been tested, this pipe will be cut off with a handsaw and fitted with a toilet flange.

Cut a piece of exterior-grade plywood to fit the cutout floor area, and use a jigsaw to cut an opening for the toilet drain stub-out. Position the plywood, and attach it to joists and blocking with 2" screws.

Sinks

It's not surprising that sink faucets leak and drip. Any fitting that contains moving mechanical parts is susceptible to failure. But add to the equation the persistent force of water pressure working against the parts, and the real surprise is that faucets don't fail more quickly or often. It would be a bit unfair to say that the inner workings of a faucet are regarded as disposable by manufacturers, but it is safe to say that these parts have become more easy to remove and replace.

The most important aspect of sink faucet repair is identifying which type of faucet you own. In this chapter we show all of the common types and provide instructions on repairing them. In every case, the easiest and most reliable repair method is to purchase a replacement kit with brand new internal working parts for the model and brand of faucet you own.

Tools & Materials ▸

Pliers
Needlenose pliers
Heatproof grease
Channel-type pliers
Utility knife
White Vinagar
Old toothbrush
Tape measure
Repair kit
  (exact type varies)
Teflon tape
Screwdrivers
Pipe joint compound
Plumber's putty
Rag

Eventually, just about every faucet develops leaks and drips. Repairs can usually be accomplished simply by replacing the mechanical parts inside the faucet body (the main trick is figuring our which kind of parts your faucet has).

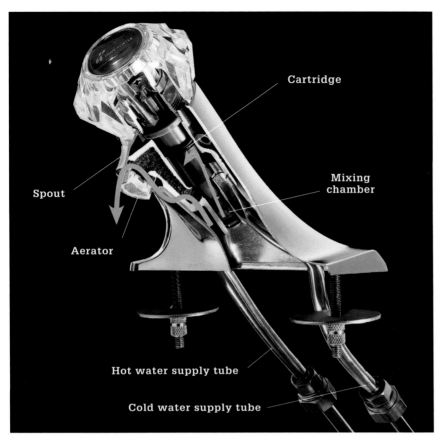

Cartridge

Spout

Mixing chamber

Aerator

Hot water supply tube

Cold water supply tube

Almost all leaks are caused by malfunctioning faucet valve mechanisms. Whether your sink faucet is a one-handle cartridge type (left) or a two-handle compression type or anything in between, the solution to fixing the leak is to clean or replace the parts that seal off the hot and cold water inlets from the spout.

Common Problems and Repairs ▶

Problems	Repairs
Faucet drips from the end of the spout or leaks around the base.	1. Identify the faucet design (page 220), then install replacement parts, using directions on the following pages.
Old worn-out faucet continues to leak after repairs are made.	1. Replace the old faucet (pages 48 to 53).
Water pressure at spout seems low, or water flow is partially blocked.	1. Clean faucet aerator (page 227). 2. Replace corroded galvanized pipes with copper.
Water pressure from sprayer seems low, or sprayer leaks from handle.	1. Clean sprayer head (page 227). 2. Fix diverter valve (page 233).
Water leaks onto floor underneath faucet.	1. Replace cracked sprayer hose (page 229). 2. Tighten water connections, or replace supply tubes and shutoff valves. 3. Fix leaky sink strainer (page 274).
Hose bib or valve drips from spout or leaks around handle.	1. Take valve apart and replace washers and O-rings (pages 238 to 239).

Common Faucet Types

A leaky faucet is the most common home plumbing problem. Leaks occur when washers, O-rings, or seals inside the faucet are dirty or worn. Fixing leaks is easy, but the techniques for making repairs will vary, depending on the design of the faucet. Before beginning work, you must first identify your faucet design and determine what replacement parts are needed.

There are four basic faucet designs: ball-type, cartridge, disc, and compression. Many faucets can be identified easily by outer appearance, but others must be taken apart before the design can be recognized.

The compression design is used in many double-handle faucets. Compression faucets all have washers or seals that must be replaced from time to time. These repairs are easy to make, and replacement parts are inexpensive.

Ball-type, cartridge, and disc faucets are all known as washerless faucets. Many washerless faucets are controlled with a single handle, although some cartridge models use two handles. Washerless faucets are more trouble-free than compression faucets and are designed for quick repair.

When installing new faucet parts, make sure the replacements match the original parts. Replacement parts for popular washerless faucets are identified by brand name and model number. To ensure a correct selection, you may want to bring the worn parts to the store for comparison.

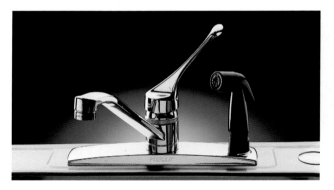

Ball-type faucet has a single handle over a dome-shaped cap. If your single-handle faucet is made by Delta® or Peerless®, it is probably a ball-type faucet. See page 224 to fix a ball-type faucet.

Cartridge faucets are available in single-handle or double-handle models. Popular cartridge faucet brands include Price Pfister™, Moen, Valley, and Aqualine. See page 223 to fix a cartridge faucet.

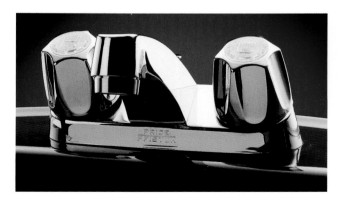

Compression faucet has two handles. When shutting the faucet off, you usually can feel a rubber washer being squeezed inside the faucet. Compression faucets are sold under many brand names. See page 222 to fix a compression faucet.

Disc faucet has a single handle and a solid, chromed-brass body. If your faucet is made by American Standard or Reliant, it may be a disc faucet. See page 225 to fix a disc faucet.

Faucet Repair Kits

Repair kit for a ball-type faucet includes rubber valve seats, springs, cam, cam washer, and spout O-rings. Kit may also include small Allen wrench tool used to remove faucet handle. Make sure kit is made for your faucet model. Replacement ball can be purchased separately but is not needed unless old ball is obviously worn.

Replacement cartridges come in dozens of styles. Cartridges are available for popular faucet brands, including (from left) PricePfister™, Moen, and Kohler. O-ring kits may be sold separately.

Universal washer kit contains parts needed to fix most types of compression faucets. Choose a kit that has an assortment of neoprene washers, O-rings, packing washers, and brass stem screws.

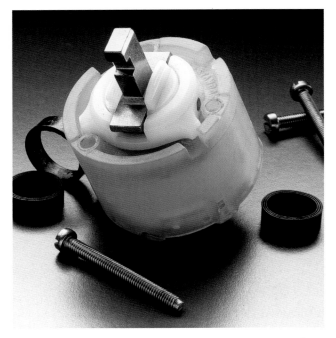

Replacement cylinder for disc faucet is necessary only if faucet continues to leak after cleaning. Continuous leaking is caused by cracked or scratched ceramic discs. Replacement cylinders come with neoprene seals and mounting screws.

Compression Faucets

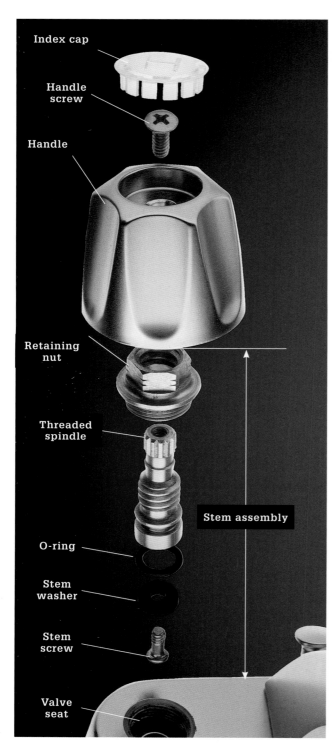

Index cap

Handle screw

Handle

Retaining nut

Threaded spindle

O-ring

Stem washer

Stem screw

Valve seat

Stem assembly

A compression faucet has a stem assembly that includes a retaining nut, threaded spindle, O-ring, stem washer, and stem screw. Dripping at the spout occurs when the washer becomes worn. Leaks around the handle are caused by a worn O-ring.

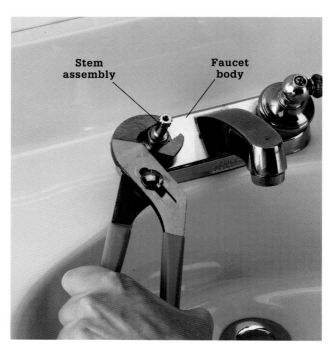

Stem assembly

Faucet body

Remove the faucet handles so you can grasp the retaining nut for the stem assembly with pliers. Loosen the nut and remove the entire stem assembly.

Stem washer

O-ring

Remove the old O-ring and replace it with a new one. Also replace the stem washer. Clean all parts with white vinegar, scrubbing with an old toothbrush if necessary. Coat the new O-ring and stem washer with heatproof grease and reassemble the valve.

Cartridge Faucets

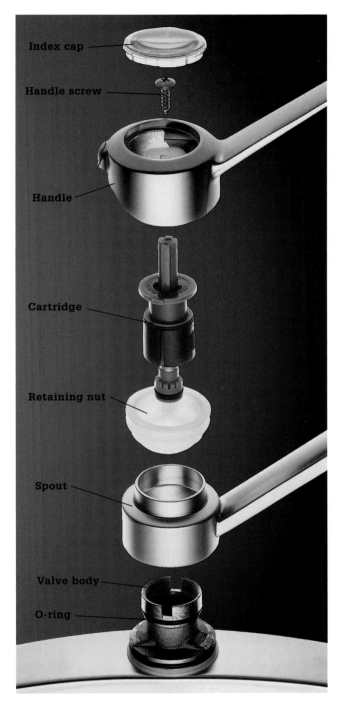

Index cap

Handle screw

Handle

Cartridge

Retaining nut

Spout

Valve body

O-ring

Retaining nut

Remove the faucet handle and withdraw the old cartridge. Make a note of how the cartridge is oriented before you remove it. Purchase a replacement cartridge.

Install the replacement cartridge. Clean the valve seat first and coat the valve seat and O-rings with heatproof grease. Be sure the new cartridge is in the correct position, with its tabs seated in the slotted body of the faucet. Re-assemble the valve and handles.

Both one- and two-handle faucets are available with replaceable plastic cartridges inside the faucet body. These cartridges (used by PricePfister™, Sterling, Kohler, Moen, and others) regulate the flow of water through the spout, and in single-handle faucets they also mix the hot and cold water to alter the temperature out of the spout. To locate the correct replacement cartridge for your faucet, knowing the manufacturer and model number is a great help.

Ball Faucets

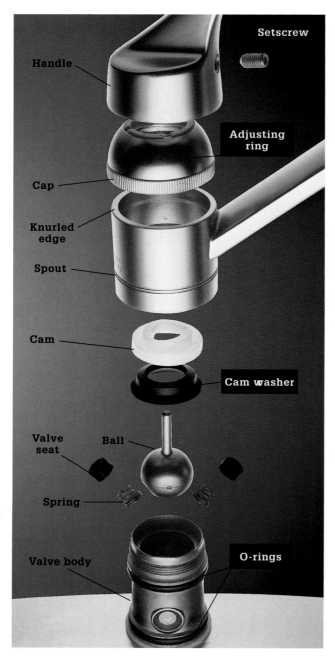

Remove the old ball and cam after removing the faucet handle and ball cap. Some faucets may require a ball faucet tool to remove the handle. Otherwise, simply use a pair of channel-type pliers to twist off the ball cap.

The ball-type faucet is used by Delta, Peerless, and a few others. The ball fits into the faucet body and is constructed with three holes (not visible here)—a hot inlet, a cold inlet, and the outlet, which fills the valve body with water that then flows to the spout or sprayer. Depending on the position of the ball, each inlet hole is open, closed, or somewhere in-between. The inlet holes are sealed to the ball with valve seats, which are pressed tight against the ball with springs. If water drips from the spout, replace the seats and springs. Or go ahead and purchase an entire replacement kit and replace all or most of the working parts.

Pry out the neoprene valve seals and springs and replace them with new parts. Also replace the O-rings on the valve body. You may want to replace the ball and cam, too, especially if you're purchasing a repair kit. Coat all rubber parts in heatproof grease, and reassemble the faucet.

Disc Faucets

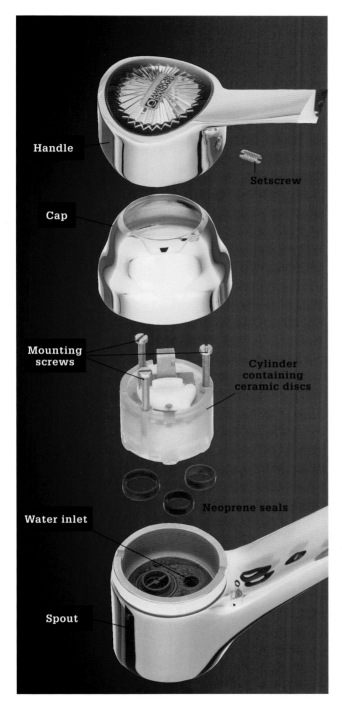

Handle

Setscrew

Cap

Mounting screws

Cylinder containing ceramic discs

Neoprene seals

Water inlet

Spout

The disc-type faucet used by American Standard, among others, has a wide disc cartridge hidden beneath the handle and the cap. Mounting screws hold the cartridge in the valve body. Two tight-fitting ceramic discs with holes in them are concealed inside the cartridge. The handle slides the top disc back and forth and from side to side over the stationary bottom disc. This brings the holes in the disks into and out of alignment, adjusting the flow and mix of hot and cold water.

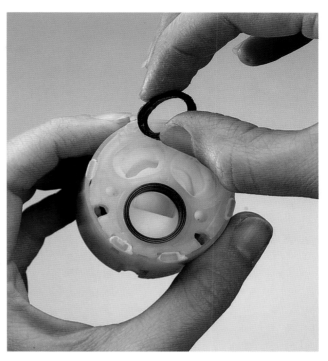

Disassemble the faucet handle and remove the old disc. You'll need to unscrew the three long mounting screws all the way to get the cylinder containing the ceramic discs out of the faucet.

Replace the cylinder with a new one, coating the rubber parts with heatproof grease before installing the new cylinder. Make sure the rubber seals fit correctly in the cylinder openings before you install the cylinder. Assemble the faucet handle.

Sprayers & Aerators

If water pressure from a sink sprayer seems low, or if water leaks from the handle, it is usually because lime buildup and sediment have blocked small openings inside the sprayer head. To fix the problem, first take the sprayer head apart and clean the parts. If cleaning the sprayer head does not help, the problem may be caused by a faulty diverter valve. The diverter valve inside the faucet body shifts water flow from the faucet spout to the sprayer when the sprayer handle is pressed. Cleaning or replacing the diverter valve may fix water pressure problems.

Whenever making repairs to a sink sprayer, check the sprayer hose for kinks or cracks. A damaged hose should be replaced.

If water pressure from a faucet spout seems low, or if the flow is partially blocked, take the spout aerator apart and clean the parts. The aerator is a screw-on attachment with a small wire screen that mixes tiny air bubbles into the water flow. Make sure the wire screen is not clogged with sediment and lime buildup. If water pressure is low throughout the house, it may be because galvanized iron water pipes are corroded. Corroded pipes should be replaced with copper (pages 274 to 277).

Tools & Materials ▸

Screwdriver
Channel-type pliers
Needlenose pliers
Small brush
Vinegar

Universal washer kit
Heatproof grease
Replacement
    sprayer hose

Kitchen sprayers are very convenient and, in theory, quite simple. Yet, they break down with surprising regularity. Fixing or replacing one is an easy job, however.

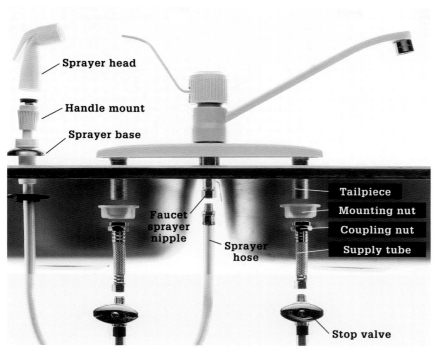

Sprayer head

Handle mount

Sprayer base

Faucet sprayer nipple

Sprayer hose

Tailpiece

Mounting nut

Coupling nut

Supply tube

Stop valve

The standard sprayer hose attachment is connected to a nipple at the bottom of the faucet valve. When the lever of the sprayer is depressed, water flows from a diverter valve in the faucet body out to the sprayer. If your sprayer stream is weak or doesn't work at all, the chances are good that the problem lies in the diverter valve.

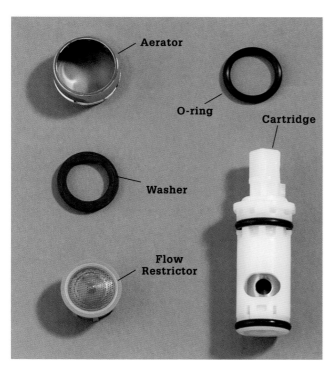

Aerator

O-ring

Cartridge

Washer

Flow Restrictor

Diverter valves and aerators differ from faucet to faucet, so you'll need to know the make and model if your faucet to purchase replacement. However, if you bring the old parts in to the plumbing supply store, they can probably find the right replacements for you.

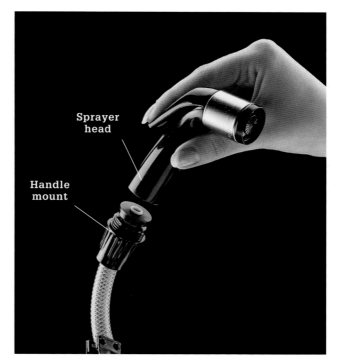

Sprayer head

Handle mount

Sprayer heads can be removed from the sprayer hose, usually by loosening a retaining nut. By removing the head, disassembling it as much as you can and cleaning it you may be able to solve a weak spray problem.

How to Repair a Sprayer

Shut off the water at the stop valves and remove the faucet handle to gain access to the faucet parts. Disassemble the faucet handle and body to expose the diverter valve. Ball-type faucets like the one shown here require that you also remove the spout to get at the diverter.

Locate the diverter valve, seen here at the base of the valve body. Because different types and brands of faucets have differently configured diverters, do a little investigating beforehand to try and locate information about your faucet. The above faucet is a ball type.

Pull the diverter valve from the faucet body with needlenose pliers. Use a toothbrush dipped in white vinegar to clean any lime buildup from the valve. If the valve is in poor condition, bring it to the hardware store and purchase a replacement.

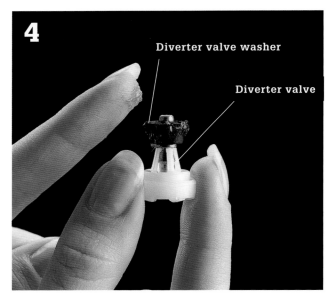

Coat the washer or O-ring on the new or cleaned diverter valve with heatproof grease. Insert the diverter valve back into the faucet body. Reassemble the faucet. Turn on the water and test the sprayer. If it still isn't functioning to your satisfaction, remove the sprayer tip and run the sprayer without the filter and aerator in case any debris has made its way into the sprayer line during repairs.

How to Repair a Kitchen Sprayer

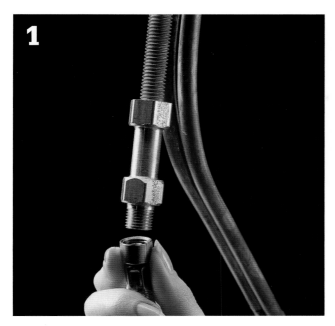

To replace a sprayer hose, start by shutting off the water at the shutoff valves. Clear out the cabinet under your sink and put on eye protection. Unthread the coupling nut that attaches the old hose to a nipple or tube below the faucet spout. Use a basin wrench if you can't get your channel-type pliers on the nut.

Unscrew the mounting nut of the old sprayer from below and remove the old sprayer body. Clean the sink deck and then apply plumber's putty to the base of the new sprayer. Insert the new sprayer tailpiece into the opening in the sink deck.

From below, slip the friction washer up over the sprayer tailpiece. Screw the mounting nut onto the tailpiece and tighten with a basin wrench or channel-type pliers. Do not overtighten. Wipe away any excess plumber's putty.

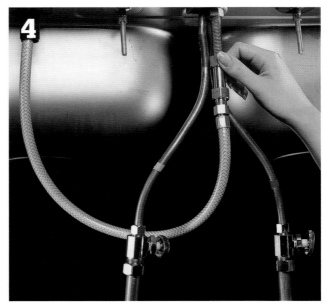

Screw the coupling for the sprayer hose onto the hose nipple underneath the faucet body. For a good seal, apply pipe joint compound to the nipple threads first. Tighten the coupling with a basin wrench, turn on the water supply at the shutoff valves, and test the new sprayer.

Leaky Plumbing

Tub and shower faucets have the same basic designs as sink faucets, and the techniques for repairing leaks are the same as described in the faucet repair section of this book (pages 218 to 229). To identify your faucet design, you may have to take off the handle and disassemble the faucet.

When a tub and shower are combined, the showerhead and the tub spout share the same hot and cold water supply lines and handles. Combination faucets are available as three-handle, two-handle, or single-handle types (next page). The number of handles gives clues as to the design of the faucets and the kinds of repairs that may be necessary.

With combination faucets, a diverter valve or gate diverter is used to direct water flow to the tub spout or the showerhead. On three-handle faucet types, the middle handle controls a diverter valve. If water does not shift easily from tub to showerhead, or if water continues to run out the spout when the shower is on, the diverter valve probably needs to be cleaned and repaired (pages 230 to 231).

Two-handle and single-handle types use a gate diverter that is operated by a pull lever or knob on the tub spout. Although gate diverters rarely need repair, the lever occasionally may break, come loose, or refuse to stay in the up position. To repair a gate diverter set in a tub spout, replace the entire spout.

Tub and shower faucets and diverter valves may be set inside wall cavities. Removing them may require a deep-set ratchet wrench.

If spray from the showerhead is uneven, clean the spray holes. If the showerhead does not stay in an upright position, remove the head and replace the O-ring.

To add a shower to an existing tub, install a flexible shower adapter. Several manufacturers make complete conversion kits that allow a shower to be installed in less than one hour.

Tub/shower plumbing is notorious for developing drips from the tub spout and the showerhead. In most cases, the leak can be traced to the valves controlled by the faucet handles.

Tub & Shower Combination Faucets

Three-handle faucet (page 232) has valves that are either compression or cartridge design.

Two-handle faucet (page 234) has valves that are either compression or cartridge design.

Single-handle faucet (pages 236 to 237) has valves that are cartridge, ball-type, or disc design.

Fixing Three-handle Tub & Shower Faucets

A three-handle faucet type has two handles to control hot and cold water, and a third handle to control the diverter valve and direct water to either a tub spout or a shower head. The separate hot and cold handles indicate cartridge or compression faucet designs. To repair them, refer to page 220.

If a diverter valve sticks, if water flow is weak, or if water runs out of the tub spout when the flow is directed to the showerhead, the diverter needs to be repaired or replaced. Most diverter valves are similar to either compression or cartridge faucet valves. Compression-type diverters can be repaired, but cartridge types should be replaced.

Remember to turn off the water before beginning work.

Tools & Materials ▸

Screwdriver
Adjustable wrench
  or channel-type
  pliers
Deep-set
  ratchet wrench
Small wire brush

Replacement
  diverter cartridge
  or universal
  washer kit
Heatproof grease
Vinegar

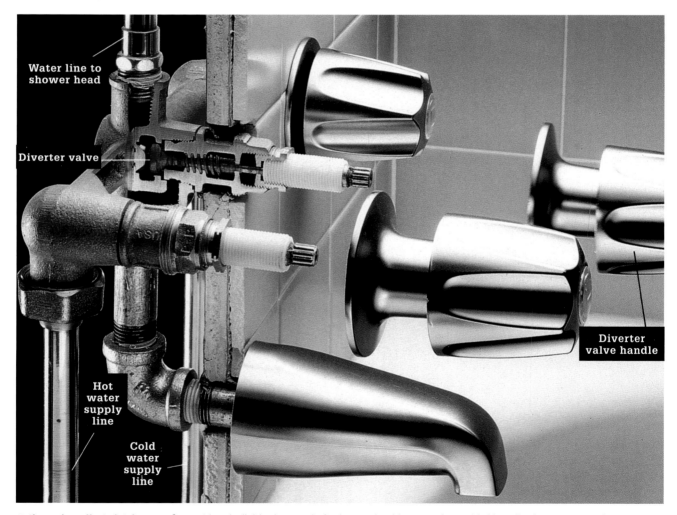

Water line to shower head

Diverter valve

Hot water supply line

Cold water supply line

Diverter valve handle

A three-handle tub/shower faucet has individual controls for hot and cold water plus a third handle that operates the diverter valve.

How to Repair a Compression Diverter Valve

Remove the diverter valve handle with a screwdriver. Unscrew or pry off the escutcheon.

Remove bonnet nut with an adjustable wrench or channel-type pliers.

Unscrew the stem assembly, using a deep-set ratchet wrench. If necessary, chip away any mortar surrounding the bonnet nut.

Remove brass stem screw. Replace stem washer with an exact duplicate. If stem screw is worn, replace it.

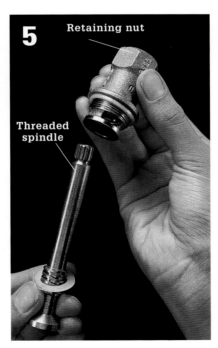

Unscrew the threaded spindle from the retaining nut.

Clean sediment and lime buildup from nut, using a small wire brush dipped in vinegar. Coat all parts with heatproof grease, and reassemble diverter valve.

Fixing Two-handle Tub & Shower Faucets

Two-handle tub and shower faucets are either cartridge or compression design. They may be repaired following the directions on pages 222 to 223. Because the valves of two-handle tub and shower faucets may be set inside the wall cavity, a deep-set socket wrench may be required to remove the valve stem.

Two-handle tub and shower designs have a gate diverter. A gate diverter is a simple mechanism located in the tub spout. A gate diverter closes the supply of water to the tub spout and redirects the flow to the shower head. Gate diverters seldom need repair. Occasionally, the lever may break, come loose, or refuse to stay in the up position.

If the diverter fails to work properly, replace the tub spout. Tub spouts are inexpensive and easy to replace.

Remember to turn off the water before beginning any work.

Tools & Materials ▸

Screwdriver
Allen wrench
Pipe wrench
Channel-type pliers
Small cold chisel
Ball-peen hammer

Deep-set
  ratchet wrench
Masking tape or cloth
Pipe joint compound
Replacement faucet
  parts, as needed

Water line to shower head

Bonnet nut

Valve stem

Diverter lever

Cold water supply line

Hot water supply line

Gate diverter

A two-handle tub/shower faucet can operate with compression valves, but more often these days they contain cartridges that can be replaced. Unlike a three-handled model, the diverter is a simple gate valve that operated by a lever.

Tips on Replacing a Tub Spout ▸

Check underneath tub spout for a small access slot. The slot indicates the spout is held in place with an Allen screw. Remove the screw, using an Allen wrench. Spout will slide off.

Unscrew faucet spout. Use a pipe wrench, or insert a large screwdriver or hammer handle into the spout opening and turn spout counterclockwise.

Spread pipe joint compound on threads of spout nipple before replacing spout.

How to Remove a Deep-set Faucet Valve

Remove handle and unscrew the escutcheon with channel-type pliers. Pad the jaws of the pliers with masking tape to prevent scratching the escutcheon.

Chip away any mortar surrounding the bonnet nut, using a ball-peen hammer and a small cold chisel.

Unscrew the bonnet nut with a deep-set ratchet wrench. Remove the bonnet nut and stem from the faucet body.

Fixing Single-handle Tub & Shower Faucets

A single-handle tub and shower faucet has one valve that controls both water flow and temperature. Single-handle faucets may be ball-type, cartridge, or disc designs.

If a single-handle control valve leaks or does not function properly, disassemble the faucet, clean the valve, and replace any worn parts. Use the repair techniques described on page 224 for ball-type, or page 225 for ceramic disc. Repairing a single-handle cartridge faucet is shown on the opposite page.

Direction of the water flow to either the tub spout or the showerhead is controlled by a gate diverter. Gate diverters seldom need repair. Occasionally, the lever may break, come loose, or refuse to stay in the up position. If the diverter fails to work properly, replace the tub spout (page 235).

Tools & Materials ▸

Screwdriver
Adjustable wrench
Channel-type pliers

Replacement faucet
parts, as needed

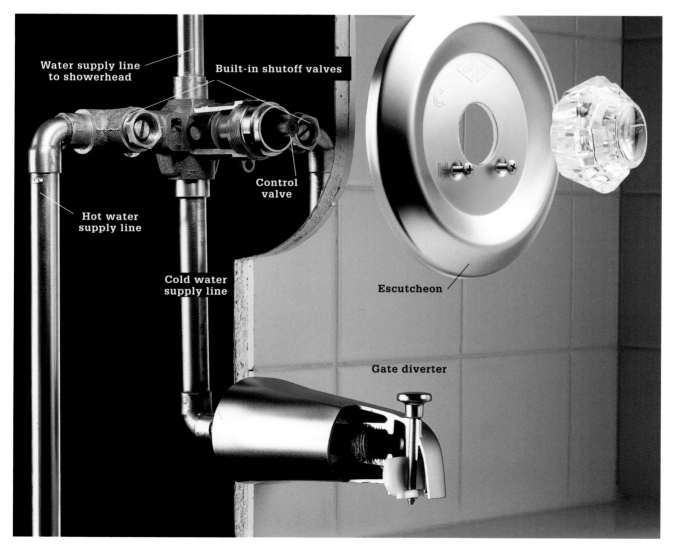

Water supply line to showerhead

Built-in shutoff valves

Control valve

Hot water supply line

Cold water supply line

Escutcheon

Gate diverter

A single-handle tub/shower faucet is the simplest type to operate and to maintain. The handle controls the mixing ratio of both hot and cold water, and the diverter is a simple gate valve.

How to Repair a Single-handle Cartridge Tub & Shower Faucet

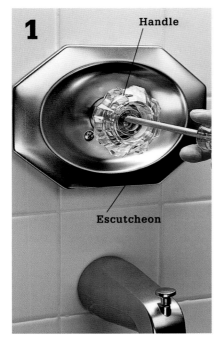

Use a screwdriver to remove the handle and escutcheon.

Turn off water supply at the built-in shutoff valves or the main shutoff valve.

Unscrew and remove the retaining ring or bonnet nut, using adjustable wrench.

Remove the cartridge assembly by grasping the end of the valve with channel-type pliers and pulling gently.

Flush the valve body with clean water to remove sediment. Replace any worn O-rings. Reinstall the cartridge and test the valve. If the faucet fails to work properly, replace the cartridge.

Fixing & Replacing Showerheads

If spray from the showerhead is uneven, clean the spray holes. The outlet or inlet holes of the showerhead may get clogged with mineral deposits. Showerheads pivot into different positions. If a showerhead does not stay in position, or if it leaks, replace the O-ring that seals against the swivel ball.

A tub can be equipped with a shower by installing a flexible shower adapter kit. Complete kits are available at hardware stores and home centers.

Tools & Materials ▸

Adjustable wrench
or channel-type
pliers
Pipe wrench
Drill
Glass and tile bit
Mallet
Screwdriver

Masking tape
Thin wire (paper clip)
Heatproof grease
Rag
Replacement O-rings
Masonry anchors
Flexible shower adapter
kit (optional)

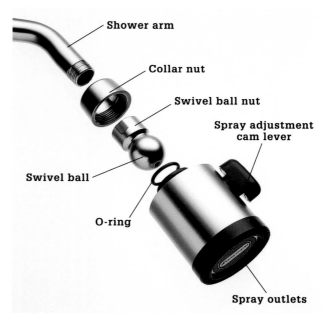

A typical showerhead can be disassembled easily for cleaning and repair. Some showerheads include a spray adjustment cam lever that is used to change the force of the spray.

How to Clean & Repair a Showerhead

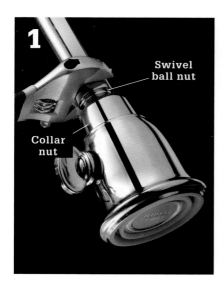

Unscrew the swivel ball nut, using an adjustable wrench or channel-type pliers. Wrap jaws of the tool with masking tape to prevent marring the finish. Unscrew collar nut from the showerhead.

Clean outlet and inlet holes of showerhead with a thin wire. Flush the head with clean water.

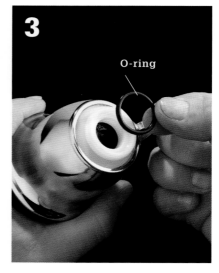

Replace the O-ring, if necessary. Lubricate the O-ring with heatproof grease before installing.

How to Install a Flexible Shower Adapter

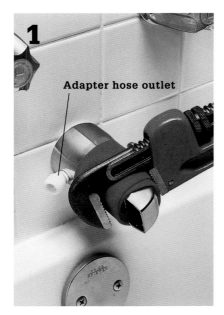

Remove old tub spout (page 235). Install new tub spout from kit, using a pipe wrench. New spout will have an adapter hose outlet. Wrap the tub spout with a rag to prevent damage to the chrome finish.

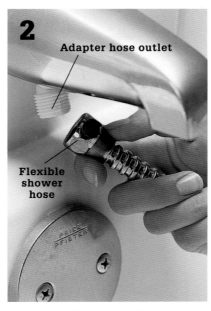

Attach flexible shower hose to the adaptor hose outlet. Tighten with an adjustable wrench or channel-type pliers.

Determine location of showerhead hanger. Use hose length as a guide, and make sure shower-head can be easily lifted off hanger.

Mark hole locations. Use a glass and tile bit to drill holes in ceramic tile for masonry anchors.

Insert anchors into holes, and tap into place with a wooden or rubber mallet.

Fasten showerhead holder to the wall, and hang showerhead.

Tubs & Showers

Tub or shower not draining? First, make sure it's only the tub or shower. If your sink is plugged, too, it may be a coincidence or it may be that a common branch line is plugged. A sure sign of this is when water drains from the sink into the tub. This could require the help of a drain cleaning service, or a drum trap that services both the sink and tub needs cleaning.

If the toilet also can't flush (or worse, water comes into the tub when you flush the toilet), then the common drain to all your bathroom fixtures is plugged. Call a drain cleaning service. If you suspect the problem is only with your tub or shower, then read on. We'll show you how to clear drainlines and clean and adjust two types of tub stopper mechanisms. Adjusting the mechanism can also help with the opposite problem: a tub that drains when you're trying to take a bath.

As with bathroom sinks, tub and shower drain pipes may become clogged with soap and hair. The drain stopping mechanisms can also require cleaning and adjustment.

Tools & Materials ▸

Phillips Screwdriver   Toothbrush
Plunger   Needlenose pliers
Scrub brush   Dishwashing brush
White Vinager   Heatproof grease

Maintenance Tip ▸

Like bathroom sinks, tubs and showers face an ongoing onslaught from soap and hair. When paired, this pesky combination is a sure-fire source of clogs. The soap scum coagulates as it is washed down the drain and binds the hair together in a mass that grows larger with every shower or bath. To nip these clogs in the bud, simply pour boiling hot clean water down the drain from time to time to melt the soapy mass and wash the binder away.

Using Hand Augers ▸

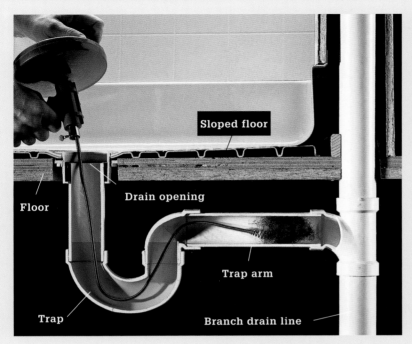

Floor

Drain opening

Sloped floor

Trap arm

Trap

Branch drain line

On shower drains, feed the head of the auger in through the drain opening after removing the strainer. Crank the handle of the auger to extend the cable and the auger head down into the trap and, if the clog is farther downline, toward the branch drain. When clearing any drain, it is always better to retrieve the clog than to push it farther downline.

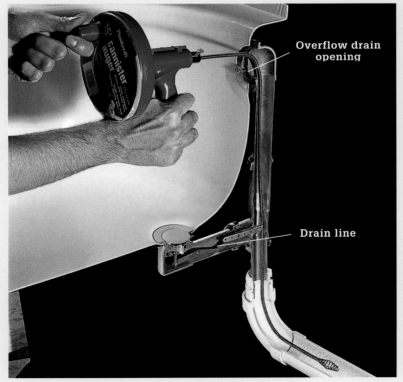

Overflow drain opening

Drain line

On combination tub/showers, it's generally easiest to insert the auger through the overflow opening after removing the coverplate and lifting out the drain linkage. Crank the handle of the auger to extend the cable and the auger head down into the trap and, if the clog is farther downline, toward the branch drain. When clearing any drain, it is always better to retrieve the clog than to push it farther downline.

How to Fix a Plunger-Type Drain

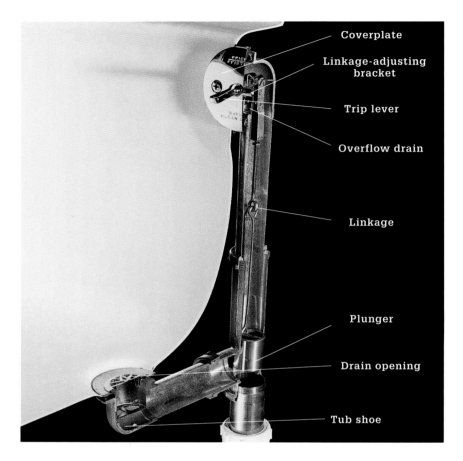

Coverplate

Linkage-adjusting bracket

Trip lever

Overflow drain

Linkage

Plunger

Drain opening

Tub shoe

1

A plunger-type tub drain has a simple grate over the drain opening and a behind-the-scenes plunger stopper. Remove the screws on the overflow coverplate with a slotted or Phillips screwdriver. Pull the coverplate, linkage, and plunger from the overflow opening.

2

Clean hair and soap off the plunger with a scrub brush. Mineral buildup is best tackled with white vinegar and a toothbrush or a small wire brush.

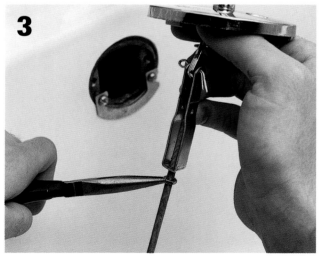

3

Adjust the plunger. If your tub isn't holding water with the plunger down, it's possible the plunger is hanging too high to fully block water from the tub shoe. Loosen the locknut with needlenose pliers, then screw the rod down about ⅛". Tighten the locknut down. If your tub drains poorly, the plunger may be set too low. Loosen the locknut and screw the rod in an ⅛" before retightening the locknut.

How to Fix a Pop-up Drain

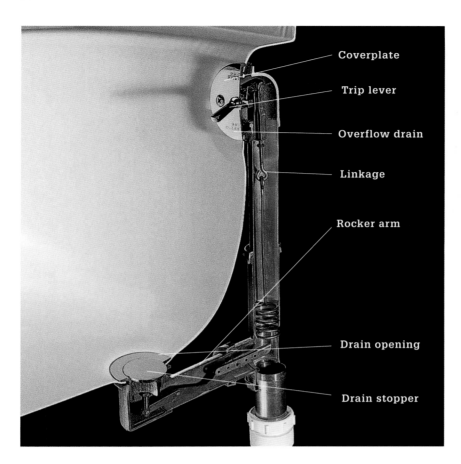

- Coverplate
- Trip lever
- Overflow drain
- Linkage
- Rocker arm
- Drain opening
- Drain stopper

Raise the trip lever to the open position. Pull the stopper and rocker arm assembly from the drain. Clean off soap and hair with a dishwashing brush in a basin of hot water. Clean off mineral deposits with a toothbrush or small wire brush and white vinegar.

Remove the screws from the cover plate. Pull the trip lever and the linkage from the overflow opening. Clean off soap and hair with a brush in a basin of hot water. Remove mineral buildup with white vinegar and a wire brush. Lubricate moving parts of the linkage and rocker arm mechanism with heatproof grease.

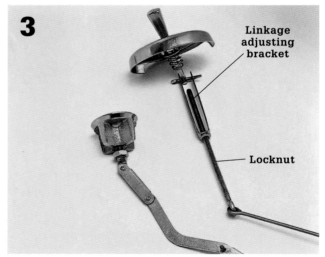

Linkage adjusting bracket

Locknut

Adjust the pop-up stopper mechanism by first loosening the locknut on the lift rod. If the stopper doesn't close all the way, shorten the linkage by screwing the rod ⅛" farther into the linkage-adjusting bracket. If the stopper doesn't open wide enough, extend the linkage by unscrewing the rod ⅛". Tighten the locknut before replacing the mechanism and testing your adjustment.

Sink Drains

Every sink has a drain trap and a fixture drain line. Sink clogs usually are caused by a buildup of soap and hair in the trap or fixture drain line. Remove clogs by using a plunger, disconnecting and cleaning the trap (page 245), or using a hand auger (page 213).

Many sinks hold water with a mechanical plug called a pop-up stopper. If the sink will not hold standing water, or if water in the sink drains too slowly, the pop-up stopper must be cleaned and adjusted (page 243).

Tools & Materials ▸

Plunger
Channel-type pliers
Small wire brush
Screwdriver
Flashlight

Rag
Bucket
Replacement gaskets
Teflon tape

Clogged lavatory sinks can be cleared with a plunger (not to be confused with a flanged force-cup). Remove the pop-up drain plug and strainer first, and plug the overflow hole by stuffing a wet rag into it, allowing you to create air pressure with the plunger.

How to Clear a Sink Trap

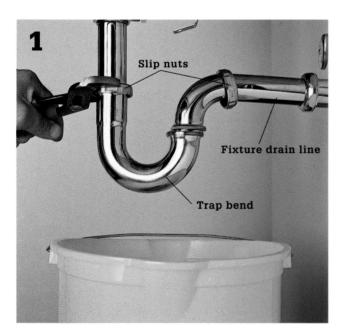

1

Slip nuts

Fixture drain line

Trap bend

Place bucket under trap to catch water and debris. Loosen slip nuts on trap bend with channel-type pliers. Unscrew nuts by hand and slide away from connections. Pull off trap bend.

2

Dump out debris. Clean trap bend with a small wire brush. Inspect slip nut washers for wear, and replace if necessary. Reinstall trap bend and tighten slip nuts.

How to Clear a Kitchen Sink

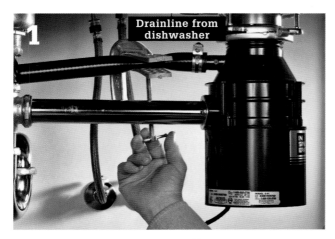

Plunging a kitchen sink is not difficult, but you need to create an uninterrupted pressure lock between the plunger and the clog. If you have a dishwasher, the drain tube needs to be clamped shut and sealed off at the disposer or drainline. The pads on the clamp should be large enough to flatten the tube across its full diameter (or you can clamp the tube ends between small boards).

If there is a second basin, have a helper hold a basket strainer plug in its drain or put a large pot or bucket full of water on top of it. Unfold the skirt within the plunger and place this in the drain of the sink you are plunging. There should be enough water in the sink to cover the plunger head. Plunge rhythmically for six repetitions with increasing vigor, pulling up hard on the last repitition. Repeat this sequence until the clog is removed. Flush out a cleared clog with plenty of hot water.

How to Use a Hand Auger at the Trap Arm

If plunging doesn't work, remove the trap and clean it out (see previous page). With the trap off, see if water flows freely from both sinks (if you have two). Sometimes clogs will lodge in the T-fitting or one of the waste pipes feeding it. These may be pulled out manually or cleared with a bottlebrush or wire. When reassembling the trap, apply Teflon tape clockwise to the male threads of metal waste pieces. Tighten with your channel-type pliers. Plastic pieces need no tape and should be hand tightened only.

If you suspect the clog is downstream of the trap, remove the trap arm from the fitting at the wall. Look in the fixture drain with a flashlight. If you see water, that means the fixture drain is plugged. Clear it with a hand auger (see page 213).

Branch & Main Drains

If using a plunger or a hand auger does not clear a clog in a fixture drain line, it means that the blockage may be in a branch line, the main waste-vent stack, or the sewer service line.

First, use an auger to clear the branch drain line closest to any stopped-up fixtures. Branch drain lines may be serviced through the cleanout fittings located at the end of the branch. Because waste water may be backed up in the drain lines, always open a cleanout with caution. Place a bucket and rags under the opening to catch waste water. Never position yourself directly under a cleanout opening while unscrewing the plug or cover.

If using an auger on the branch line does not solve the problem, then the clog may be located in a main waste-vent stack. To clear the stack, run an auger cable down through the roof vent. Make sure that the cable of your auger is long enough to reach down the entire length of the stack. If it is not, you may want to rent or borrow another auger. Always use extreme caution when working on a ladder or on a roof.

If no clog is present in the main stack, the problem may be located in the sewer service line. Locate the main cleanout, usually a Y-shaped fitting at the bottom of the main waste-vent stack. Remove the plug and push the cable of a hand auger into the opening.

Some sewer service lines in older homes have a house trap. The house trap is a U-shaped fitting located at the point where the sewer line exits the house. Most of the fitting will be beneath the floor

surface, but it can be identified by its two openings. Use a hand auger to clean a house trap.

If the auger meets solid resistance in the sewer line, retrieve the cable and inspect the bit. Fine, hair-like roots on the bit indicate the line is clogged with tree roots. Dirt on the bit indicates a collapsed line.

Use a power auger to clear sewer service lines that are clogged with tree roots. Power augers (page 248 to 249) are available at rental centers. However, a power auger is a large, heavy piece of equipment. Before renting, consider the cost of rental and the level of your do-it-yourself skills versus the price of a professional sewer cleaning service. If you rent a power auger, ask the rental dealer for complete instructions on how to operate the equipment.

Always consult a professional sewer cleaning service if you suspect a collapsed line.

Tools & Materials ▶

Adjustable wrench or pipe wrench	Penetrating oil
Hand auger	Cleanout plug (if needed)
Cold chisel	Pipe joint compound
Ball-peen hammer	Electrical drum auger
Bucket	Gloves
Ladder	Teflon Tape
Phillips screwdriver	
Rags	

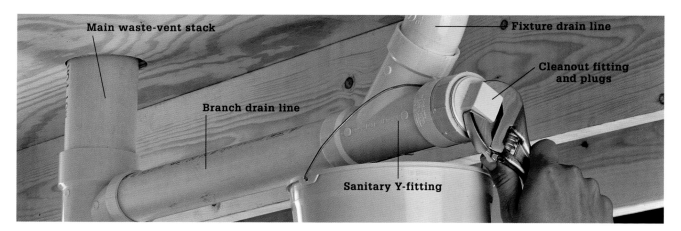

Main waste-vent stack
Fixture drain line
Cleanout fitting and plugs
Branch drain line
Sanitary Y-fitting

Clear a branch drain line by locating the cleanout fitting at the end of the line. Place a bucket underneath the opening to catch waste water, then slowly unscrew the cleanout plug with an adjustable wrench. Clear clogs in the branch drain line with a hand auger.

How to Clear a Branch Drain Line

Clear the main waste and vent stack by running the cable of a hand auger down through the roof vent. Always use extreme caution while working on a ladder or roof.

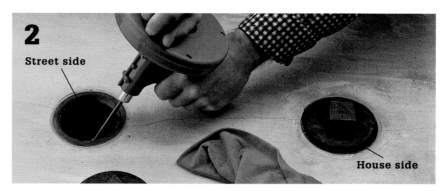

Clear the house trap in a sewer service line using a hand auger. Slowly remove only the plug on the "street side" of the trap. If water seeps out the opening as the plug is removed, the clog is in the sewer line beyond the trap. If no water seeps out, auger the trap. If no clog is present in the trap, replace the street-side plug and remove the house-side plug. Use the auger to clear clogs located between the house trap and main stack.

How to Replace a Main Drain Cleanout Plug

Remove the cleanout plug, using a large wrench. If the plug does not turn out, apply penetrating oil around the edge of the plug, wait 10 minutes, and try again. Place rags and a bucket under fitting opening to catch any water that may be backed up in the line.

Remove stubborn plugs by placing the cutting edge of a cold chisel on the edge of the plug. Strike the chisel with a ball-peen hammer to move plug counterclockwise. If the plug does not turn out, break it into pieces with the chisel and hammer. Remove all broken pieces.

Replace the old plug with a new plug. Apply pipe joint compound to the threads of the replacement plug and screw into the cleanout fitting.

Alternate: Replace the old plug with an expandable rubber plug. A wing nut squeezes the rubber core between two metal plates. The rubber bulges slightly to create a watertight seal.

How to Power-Auger a Floor Drain

Remove the cover from the floor drain using a slotted or Phillips screwdriver. On one wall of the drain bowl you'll see a cleanout plug. Remove the cleanout plug from the drain bowl with your largest channel-type pliers. This cleanout allows you to bypass the trap. If it's stuck, apply penetrating oil to the threads and let it sit a half an hour before trying to free it again. If the wrench won't free it, rent a large pipe wrench from your home center or hardware store. You can also auger through the trap if you have to.

Power Auger Large Lines ▸

If you choose to auger a larger line, you may find yourself opening a cleanout with 10 or 20 vertical feet of waste water behind it. Be careful. The cap may unexpectedly burst open when it's loose enough, spewing noxious waste water uncontrollably over anything in its path, including you! Here are some precautions:

Whenever possible, remove a trap or cleanout close to the top of the backed-up water level. Run your auger through this. Make sure the auger and its electric connections will not get wet should waste water spew forcefully from the cleanout opening.

Use the spear tool on the power auger first, to let the water drain out through a smaller hole before widening it with a larger cutting tool. If you are augering through a 3 or 4" cleanout, use three bits: the spear, a small cutter, and then a larger cutter to do the best job.

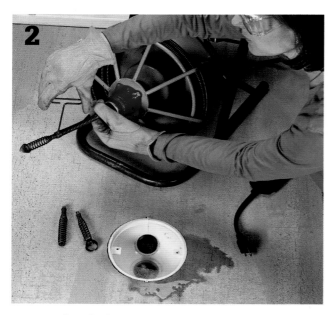

Rent an electric drum auger with at least 50 feet of ½-inch cable. The rental company should provide a properly sized, grounded extension cord, heavy leather gloves, and eye protection. The auger should come with a spear tool, cutter tool, and possibly a spring tool suitable for a 2-inch drainline. Attach the spearhead first (with the machine unplugged).

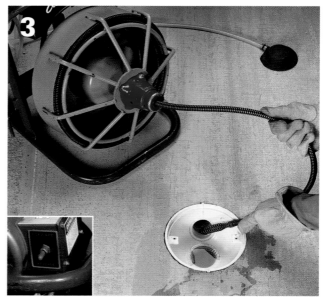

Wear close-fitting clothing and contain long hair. Place the power auger machine in a dry location within 3 ft. of the drain opening. Plug the tool into a grounded, GFI-protected circuit. Wear eye protection and gloves. Position the footswitch where it is easy to actuate. Make sure the FOR/REV switch is in the Forward position (inset photo). Hand feed the cleaning tool and some cable into the drain or cleanout before turning the machine on.

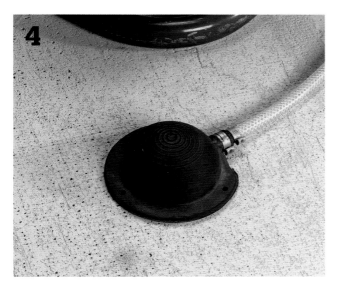

Stationary power augers (as opposed to pistol-grip types) are controlled by a foot pedal called an actuator so you can turn the power on and off hands-free.

With both gloved hands on the cable, depress the foot actuator to start the machine. Gradually push the rotating cable into the drain opening. If the rotation slows or you cannot feed more cable into the drain, pull back on the cable before pushing it forward again. Don't force it. The cable needs to be rotating whenever the motor is running or it can kink and buckle. If the cleaning tool becomes stuck, reverse it, back the tool off the obstruction, and switch back to Forward.

Gradually work through the clog by pulling back on the cable whenever the machine starts to bog down and push it forward again when it gains new momentum. Never let the cable stop turning when the motor is running. When you have broken through the clog or snagged an object, withdraw the cable from the line. Manually pull the cable from the drain line while continuing to run the drum Forward. When the cleaning tool is close to the drain opening, release the foot actuator and let the cable come to a stop before feeding the last 2 or 3 ft. of cable into the drum by hand.

After clearing the drain pipe, run the auger through the trap. Finish cleaning the auger. Wrap Teflon tape clockwise onto the plug threads and replace the plug. Run hot water through a hose from the laundry sink or use a bucket to flush remaining debris through the trap and down the line.

Branch Drains & Vents

In our demonstration project, we will replace branch drains for a bathtub and vanity sink. The tub drain will run down into the basement before connecting to the main waste-vent stack, while the vanity drain will run horizontally to connect directly to the stack.

A vent pipe for the bathtub runs up into the attic, where it will join the main waste-vent stack. The vanity sink, however, requires no secondary vent pipe, since its location falls within the critical distance of the new waste-vent stack.

Tools & Materials ▸

Reciprocating saw
 or jigsaw
Drain pipe
Riser clamps
Solvent glue
Marker

Metal Protector
 plates
Vent elbow

Remove old pipes only where they obstruct the planned route for the new pipes. You will probably have to remove drain and water supply pipes at each fixture location, but the remaining pipes usually can be left in place. A reciprocating saw with metal-cutting blade works well for this job.

How to Replace Branch Drains

Establish a route for vertical drain pipes running through wall cavities down into the basement. For our project, we cut away a section of the wall sole plate in order to run a 1½" bathtub drain pipe from the basement up to the bathroom.

From the basement, cut a hole in the bottom of the wall, below the opening you cut. Measure, cut, and insert a length of drain pipe up into the wall to the bathroom. A length of flexible CPVC pipe can be useful for guiding the drain pipe up into the wall. For very long pipe runs, you may need to join two or more lengths of pipe with couplings as you insert the run.

Secure the vertical drain pipe with a riser clamp supported on 2 × 4 blocks nailed between joists. Take care not to overtighten the clamps, which can damage the pipe.

Riser clamp

2 × 4 block

Install a horizontal pipe from the waste T-fitting on the waste-vent stack to the vertical drain pipe. Maintain a downward slope toward the stack of ¼" per ft., and use a Y-fitting with 45° elbow to form a cleanout where the horizontal and vertical drain pipes meet.

Cleanout

Solvent-glue a waste T-fitting to the top of the vertical drain pipe. For a bathtub drain, as shown here, the T-fitting must be well below floor level to allow for the bathtub drain trap. You may need to notch or cut a hole in floor joists to connect the drain trap to the waste-T.

From the attic, cut a hole into the top of the bathroom wet wall, directly above the bathtub drain pipe. Run a 1½" vent pipe down to the bathtub location, and solvent-glue it to the waste-T. Make sure the pipe extends at least 1 ft. into the attic.

(continued)

7

Remove wall surfaces as necessary to provide access for running horizontal drain pipes from fixtures to the new waste-vent stack. In our project, we ran 1½" drain pipe from a vanity sink to the stack. Mark the drain route on the exposed studs, maintaining a ¼" per ft. downward slope toward the stack. Use a reciprocating saw or jigsaw to notch out the studs.

8

Riser clamp

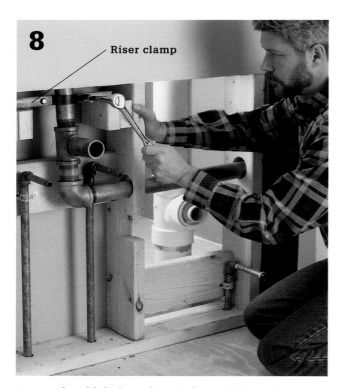

Secure the old drain and vent pipes with riser clamps supported by blocking attached between the studs.

9

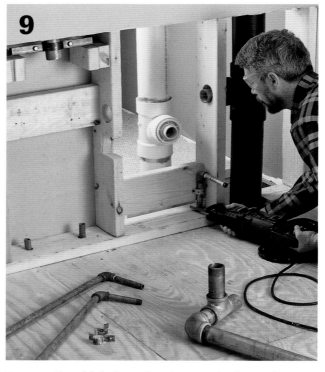

Remove the old drain and water supply pipes, where necessary, to provide space for running the new drain pipes.

Using a sweep elbow and straight length of pipe, assemble a drain pipe to run from the drain stubout location to the waste T-fitting on the new waste-vent stack. Use a 90° elbow and a short length of pipe to create a stubout extending at least 2" out from the wall. Secure the stubout to a ¾" backer board attached between studs.

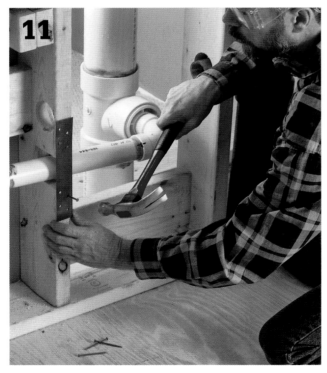

Protect the drain pipes by attaching metal protector plates over the notches in the studs. Protector plates prevent drain pipes from being punctured when wall surfaces are replaced.

In the attic, use a vent elbow and straight length of pipe to connect the vertical vent pipe from the tub to the new waste-vent stack.

Main Stacks

Although a main waste-vent stack rarely rusts through entirely, it can be nearly impossible to join new branch drains and vents to an old cast-iron stack. For this reason, plumbing contractors sometimes recommend replacing the iron stack with plastic pipe during a plumbing renovation project.

Be aware that replacing a main waste-vent stack is not an easy job. You will be cutting away heavy sections of cast iron, so working with a helper is essential. Before beginning work, make sure you have a complete plan for your plumbing system and have designed a stack that includes all the fittings you will need to connect branch drains and vent pipes. While work is in progress, none of your plumbing fixtures will be usable. To speed up the project and minimize inconvenience, do as much of the demolition and preliminary construction work as you can before starting work on the stack.

Because main waste-vent stacks may be as large as 4" in diameter, running a new stack through existing walls can be troublesome. To solve this problem, our project employs a common solution: framing a chase in the corner of a room to provide the necessary space for running the new stack from the basement to the attic. When the installation is completed, the chase will be finished with wallboard to match the room.

Tools & Materials ▸

Riser clamps
Cast-iron snapcutter
Reciprocating saw
Rag
Plumb bob
PVC plastic pipe
Waste-vent pipe
Solvent glue
Ladder
Vent T
Pry bar
Roofing cement

Rubber gasket
flashing nails

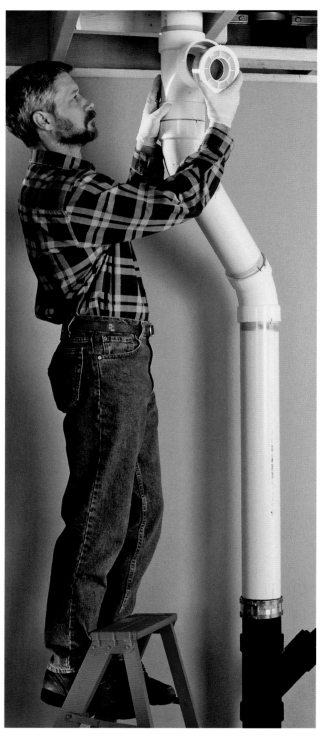

A new main waste-vent stack is best installed near the location of the old stack. In this way, the new stack can be connected to the basement floor cleanout fitting used by the old cast-iron stack.

How to Replace a Main Waste-Vent Stack

Secure the cast-iron waste-vent stack near the ceiling of your basement, using a riser clamp installed between the floor joists. Use wood blocks attached to the joists with 3" wallboard screws to support the clamp. Also clamp the stack in the attic, at the point where the stack passes down into the wall cavity. *Warning: A cast-iron stack running from basement to attic can weigh several hundred pounds. Never cut into a cast-iron stack before securing it with riser clamps above the cut.*

Use a cast-iron snap cutter (page 268) or a reciprocating saw to sever the stack near the floor of the basement, about 8" above the cleanout, and near the ceiling, flush with the bottom of the joists. Have a helper hold the stack while you are cutting out the section. *Note: After cutting into the main stack, plug the open end of the pipe with a cloth to prevent sewer gases from rising into your home.*

Nail blocking against the bottom of the joists across the severed stack. Then, cut a 6"-diameter hole in the basement ceiling where the new waste-vent stack will run, using a reciprocating saw. Suspend a plumb bob at the centerpoint of the opening as a guide for aligning the new stack.

(continued)

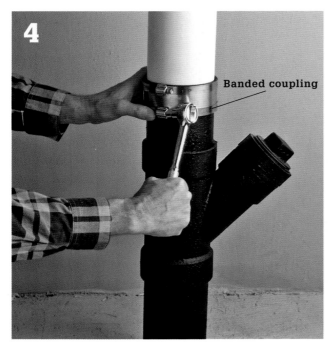

4

Banded coupling

Attach a 5-ft. segment of PVC plastic pipe the same diameter as the old waste-vent stack to the exposed end of the cast-iron cleanout fitting, using a banded coupling with neoprene sleeve.

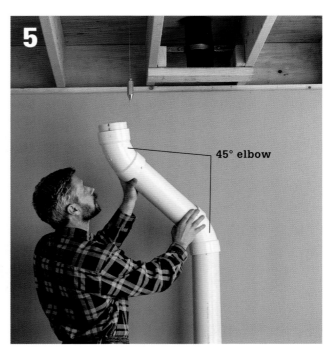

5

45° elbow

Dry-fit 45° elbows and straight lengths of plastic pipe to offset the new stack, lining it up with the plumb bob centered on the ceiling opening.

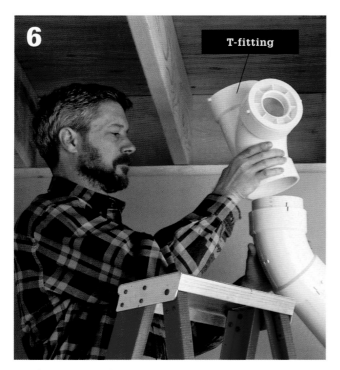

6

T-fitting

Dry-fit a waste T-fitting on the stack, with the inlets necessary for any branch drains that will be connected in the basement. Make sure the fitting is positioned at a height that will allow the branch drains to have the correct ¼" per ft. downward slope toward the stack.

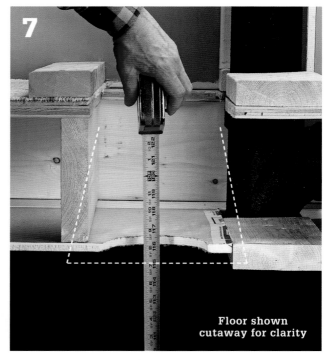

7

Floor shown cutaway for clarity

Determine the length for the next piece of waste-vent pipe by measuring from the basement T-fitting to the next planned fitting in the vertical run. In our project, we installed a T-fitting between floor joists, where the toilet drain was connected.

Cut a PVC plastic pipe to length, raise it into the opening, and dry-fit it to the T-fitting. *Note: For very long pipe runs, you may need to construct this vertical run by solvent-gluing two or more segments of pipe together with couplings.*

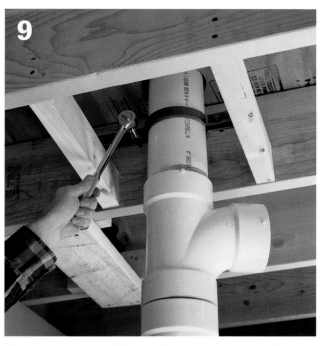

Check the length of the stack, then solvent-glue all fittings together. Support the new stack with a riser clamp resting on blocks attached between basement ceiling joists.

Bathroom

Sole plate for framed chase

Attach the next waste T-fitting to the stack. In our demonstration project, the waste-T lay between floor joists and was used to connect the toilet drain. Make sure the waste-T is positioned at a height that will allow for the correct ¼" per ft. downward slope for the toilet drain.

Add additional lengths of pipe, with waste T-fittings installed where other fixtures will drain into the stack. In our example, a waste-T with a 1½" bushing insert was installed where the vanity sink drain was attached to the stack. Make sure the T-fittings are positioned to allow for the correct downward pitch of the branch drains.

(continued)

12

Cut a hole in the ceiling where the waste-vent stack will extend into the attic, then measure, cut, and solvent-glue the next length of pipe in place. The pipe should extend at least 1 ft. up into the attic.

13

Remove the roof flashing from around the old waste-vent stack. You may need to remove shingles in order to accomplish this. *Note: Always use caution when working on a roof. If you are unsure of your ability to do this work, hire a roof repair specialist to remove the old flashing and install new flashing around the new vent pipe.*

14

In the attic, remove old vent pipes, where necessary, then sever the cast-iron soil stack with a cast-iron cutter, and lower the stack down from the roof opening with the aid of a helper. Support the old stack with a riser clamp installed between joists.

Solvent-glue a vent T with a 1½" bushing in the side inlet to the top of the new waste-vent stack. The side inlet should point toward the nearest auxiliary vent pipe extending up from below.

Finish the waste-vent stack installation by using 45° elbows and straight lengths of pipe to extend the stack through the existing roof opening. The new stack should extend at least 1 ft. through the roof, but no more than 2 ft.

How to Flash a Waste-Vent Stack

Loosen the shingles directly above the new vent stack, and remove any nails, using a flat pry bar. When installed, the metal vent flashing will lie flat on the shingles surrounding the vent pipe. Apply roofing cement to the underside of the flashing.

Slide the flashing over the vent pipe, and carefully tuck the base of the flashing up under the shingles. Press the flange firmly against the roof deck to spread the roofing cement, then anchor it with rubber gasket flashing nails. Reattach loose shingles as necessary.

Supply Pipes

When replacing old water supply pipes, we recommend that you use Type M rigid copper or PEX. Use ¾" pipe for the main distribution pipes and ½" pipes for the branch lines running to individual fixtures.

For convenience, run hot and cold water pipes parallel to one another, between 3" and 6" apart. Use the straightest, most direct routes possible when planning the layout, because too many bends in the pipe runs can cause significant resistance and reduce water pressure.

It is a good idea to remove old supply pipes that are exposed, but pipes hidden in walls can be left in place unless they interfere with the installation of the new supply pipes.

Tools & Materials ▸

Male-threaded adapter
Full-bone control valve
Copper pipes
T-fittings

Support copper supply pipes at least every 10 ft. along vertical runs and 6 ft. along horizontal runs (check local codes). Always use copper or plastic support materials with copper; never use steel, which can interact with copper and cause corrosion.

How to Replace Water Supply Pipes

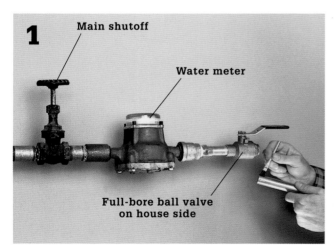

Shut off the water on the street side of the water meter, then disconnect and remove the old water pipes from the house side. Solder a ¾" male-threaded adapter and full-bore control valve to a short length of ¾" copper pipe, then attach this assembly to the house side of the water meter. Extend the ¾" cold-water distribution pipe toward the nearest fixture, which is usually the water heater.

At the water heater, install a ¾" T-fitting in the cold-water distribution pipe. Use two lengths of ¾" copper pipe and a full-bore control valve to run a branch pipe to the water heater. From the outlet opening on the water heater, extend a ¾" hot water distribution pipe. Continue the hot and cold supply lines on parallel routes toward the next group of fixtures in your house.

Establish routes for branch supply lines by drilling holes located in stud cavities. Install T-fittings, then begin the branch lines by installing brass control valves. Branch lines should be made with ¾" pipe if they are supplying more than one fixture; ½" if they are supplying only one fixture.

Full brass control valves

Extend the branch lines to the fixtures. In our project, we ran ¾" vertical branch lines up through the framed chase to the bathroom. Route pipes around obstacles, such as a main waste-vent stack, by using 45° and 90° elbows and short lengths of pipe.

Where branch lines run through studs or floor joists, drill holes or cut notches in the framing members, then insert the pipes. For long runs of pipe, you may need to join two or more shorter lengths of pipe, using couplings as you create the runs.

Install ¾" to ½" reducing T-fittings and elbows to extend the branch lines to individual fixtures. In our bathroom, we installed a hot and cold stubout for the bathtub and sink, and a cold-water stubout for the toilet. Cap each stubout until your work has been inspected and the wall surfaces have been completed.

Burst Pipes

If a water pipe freezes and breaks, your first priority may be getting it working again—whatever it takes. There are a number of temporary fix products out there, some involving clamps and sleeves, others, epoxy putties and fiberglass tape. These repairs usually can get you through a weekend okay. We also show you how to apply full slip repair couplings, a more permanent fix. Whatever repair approach you take, please, please, please, don't leave for the store without first determining a) the diameter of your pipe and b) the material of your pipe.

Tools & Materials ▸

Metal file
Repair clamps
Marker
Tubing cutter
Adjustable wrench
Pliers

Water supply pipes can burst for many reasons, but the most common cause is water freezing and expanding inside the pipe. First turn off the water, then apply a fix.

How to Patch Pipes with Repair Clamps

Dry off the damaged area of the pipe and file down any sharp edges with a metal file. Place the rubber sleeve that comes with the repair clamp around the ruptured area. The seam should be on the opposite side of the pipe from the damage.

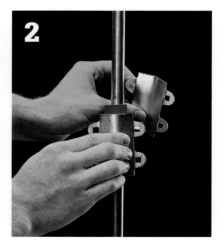

Position the two halves of the repair clamp so the rubber sleeve is sandwiched between the repair clamps.

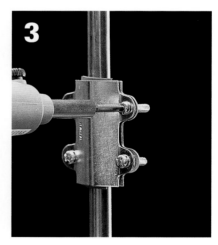

Insert bolts through the bolt holes in the repair clamp and thread nuts onto the ends. Tighten the bolts until the pressure from the clamp seals the damages area. *Note: This is a temporary repair only. Replace the damaged pipe as soon as possible.*

How to Install a Repair Coupling

1

Full slip repair coupling

For a longer lasting (not permanent) repair, use a compression-fit, full-slip repair coupling. These come with parts to make a compression union—you can also buy a slip coupling that's just a piece of copper tubing with an inside diameter equal to the outside diameter of the tubing being repaired, but these require soldering. Turn off water at the nearest control valve. Mark the boundaries of the pipe section to be replaced.

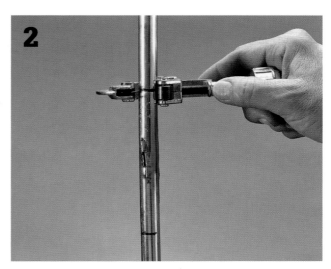

2

Cut out the damaged pipe section with a tubing cutter. Both wheels of the cutter should rest evenly on the pipe. Rotate the cutter around the pipe. The line it cuts should make a perfect ring, not a spiral. Tighten the cutter a little with each rotation until the pipe snaps. Repeat at your other mark.

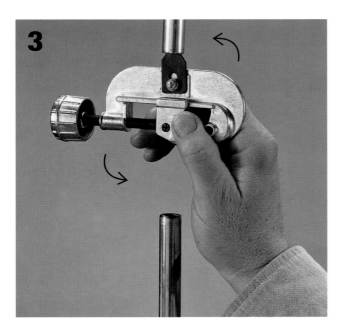

3

Deburr the insides of the pipes with the triangular blade on the tubing cutter.

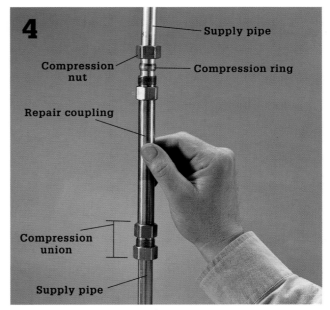

4

Supply pipe

Compression nut

Compression ring

Repair coupling

Compression union

Supply pipe

Slip the compression nuts and rings supplied with the repair coupling onto the cut ends of the pipe being repaired and then slip the repair coupling over one end. Slide the coupling farther onto the pipe and then slide it back the other way so it fits over the other pipe section and the repair area is centered inside the coupling. Tighten each compression nut with pliers while stabilizing the coupling with an adjustable wrench.

Noisy Pipes

Pipes can make a loud banging noise when faucets are turned off or when valves on washing machines (or other automatic appliances) shut abruptly. The sudden stop of flowing water traps air and creates a shock wave, called water hammer, that slams through the water supply system. Some pipes may knock against wall studs or joists, creating additional noise.

Water hammer can be more than an annoyance. The shockwave can cause damage and eventually failure in pipes and fittings. If a pressure-relief valve on your water heater leaks, it may not be a faulty valve, but a pressure surge in the supply system.

You can eliminate water hammer by installing a simple device called a water hammer arrester in the supply line. Inexpensive point-of-use arresters are small enough to be installed easily near the noisy valve or appliance (the closer the better). They can be positioned horizontally or vertically or at an angle without any change in effectiveness. Unlike with old-style air chambers, water cannot fill a water hammer arrester, so they should be effective for the life of the system.

Pipes that bang against studs or joists can be quieted by cushioning them with pieces of pipe insulation. Make sure pipe hangers are snug and that pipes are well supported.

Tools & Materials ▸

Reciprocating saw
  or hacksaw
Propane torch (for
  sweating copper)
Pipe wrenches (for
  galvanized iron)
Adjustable wrench

Foam rubber
  pipe insulation
Pipe and fittings,
  as needed
Utility knife
Teflon tape

Clattering pipes can be a major annoyance, but they also should alert you of a problem with the supply system.

Loose pipes may bang or rub against joist hangers, creating noise. Use pieces of foam rubber pipe insulation to cushion pipes.

How to Install a Water Hammer Arrester

Shut off the water supply and drain the pipes. Measure and cut out a section of horizontal pipe for a T-fitting.

Install a T-fitting as close to the valve as possible. Use techniques described on pages.

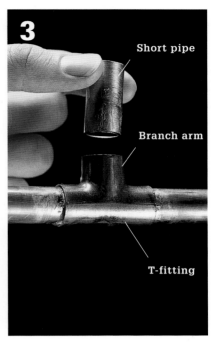

Install a short piece of pipe in the branch arm of the T-fitting. This short pipe will be used to attach a threaded fitting.

Install a threaded fitting. Use a fitting recommended by the manufacturer of your arrester.

Wrap the threads of the arrester in Teflon tape. Thread the arrester onto the fitting by hand. Tighten by holding the fitting with one adjustable wrench and turning the arrester with the other. Do not overtighten. Turn the water on and check for leaks.

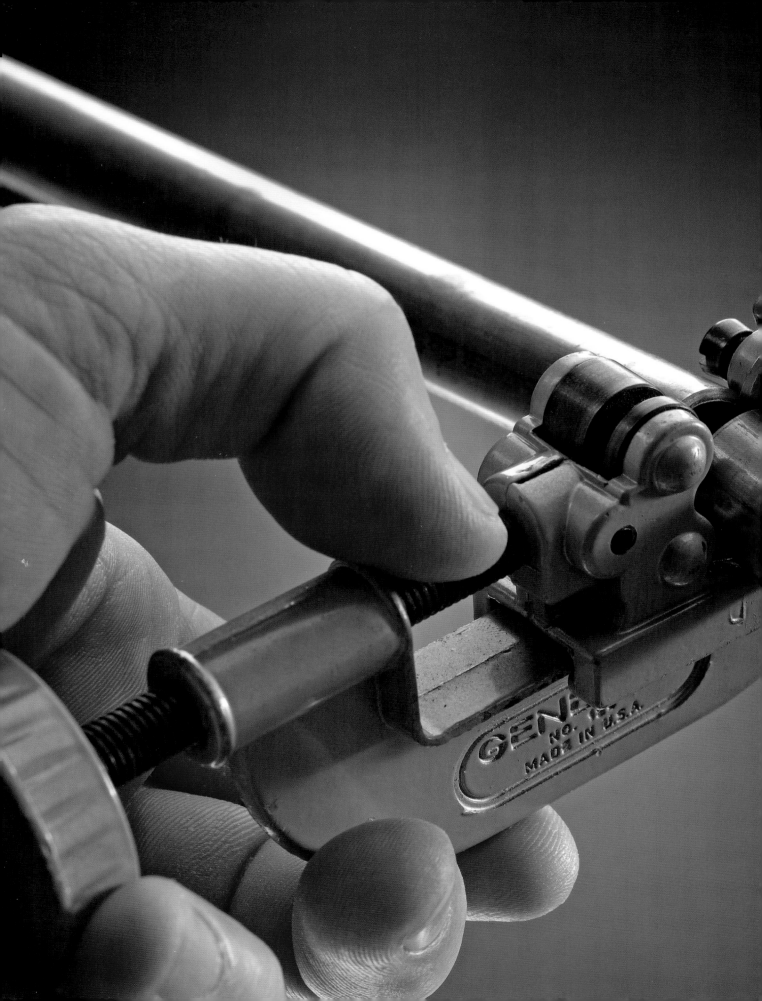

Plumbing Tools, Materials & Skills

Home plumbing does not require many expensive specialty tools. A good pair of channel-type pliers will carry much of the load by themselves. But occasions will arise where having a spud wrench or a basin wrench may well be worth the small investment required for these plumbing tools. Larger, more expensive tools such as an electric drain auger can be rented. As with any home improvement pursuit, plumbing simply demands that you choose the correct tool for the job. This chapter will help you make these choices.

The type of plumbing material you employ has a profound effect on how you do the job. Plastic pipes are joined by solvent weld, while copper sweated and pieces of PEX are joined with crimping rings. Each type of material carries with it a small army of fittings and adapters and handling tools. Here, you'll see how to match the parts correctly.

Finally, good work comes down to good technique and patience. We can't teach you patience, but here we show you the techniques you'll need to become an accomplished home plumber.

In this chapter:

- Plumbing Tools
- Plumbing Materials
- Copper
- Rigid Plastic Pipe
- Outdoor Flexible Plastic Pipe
- Cross-Linked Plyethylene (PEX)
- Galvanized Iron
- Cast Iron
- Pipe Fittings
- Shutoff Valves
- Valves & Hose Bibs
- Compression Fittings
- Flare Fittings
- Gas Pipe Fittings

Plumbing Tools

Many plumbing projects and repairs can be completed with basic hand tools you probably already own. Adding a few simple plumbing tools will prepare you for all the projects in this book. Specialty tools, such as a snap cutter or appliance dolly, are available at rental centers. When buying tools, invest in quality products.

Always care for tools properly. Clean tools after using them, wiping them free of dirt and dust with a soft rag. Prevent rust on metal tools by wiping them with a rag dipped in household oil. If a metal tool gets wet, dry it immediately, and then wipe it with an oiled rag. Keep toolboxes and cabinets organized. Make sure all tools are stored securely.

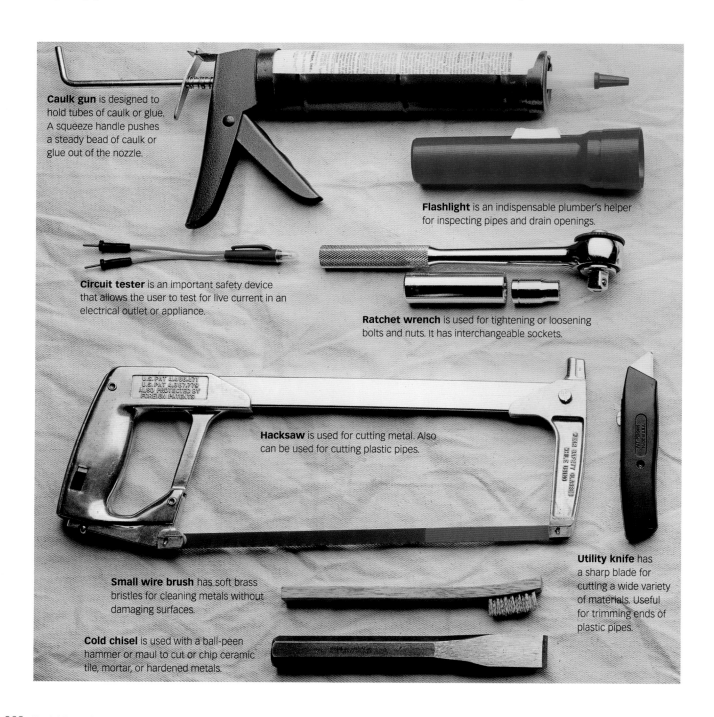

Caulk gun is designed to hold tubes of caulk or glue. A squeeze handle pushes a steady bead of caulk or glue out of the nozzle.

Flashlight is an indispensable plumber's helper for inspecting pipes and drain openings.

Circuit tester is an important safety device that allows the user to test for live current in an electrical outlet or appliance.

Ratchet wrench is used for tightening or loosening bolts and nuts. It has interchangeable sockets.

Hacksaw is used for cutting metal. Also can be used for cutting plastic pipes.

Utility knife has a sharp blade for cutting a wide variety of materials. Useful for trimming ends of plastic pipes.

Small wire brush has soft brass bristles for cleaning metals without damaging surfaces.

Cold chisel is used with a ball-peen hammer or maul to cut or chip ceramic tile, mortar, or hardened metals.

Files are used to smooth the edges of metal, wood, or plastic. The round file (top) can be used to remove burrs from the insides of pipes. The flat file is used for all general smoothing tasks.

Ball-peen hammer is made for striking metallic tools, like a cold chisel.

Screwdrivers include the two most common types: the slotted (top), and the Phillips.

A basin wrench fits into the tight area behind a sink to tighten and loosen the nut on the faucet tailpieces

Adjustable wrench has a movable jaw that permits the wrench to fit a wide variety of bolt heads or nuts.

Channel-type pliers have a movable handle that allows the jaws to be adjusted for maximum gripping strength. The insides of the jaws are serrated to prevent slipping.

Needlenose pliers have thin jaws for gripping small objects or for reaching into confined areas.

Putty knife is helpful for scraping putty or caulk from appliances and fixtures.

Tape measure should have a retractable steel blade at least 16 feet long.

Level is used for setting new appliances and checking slope.

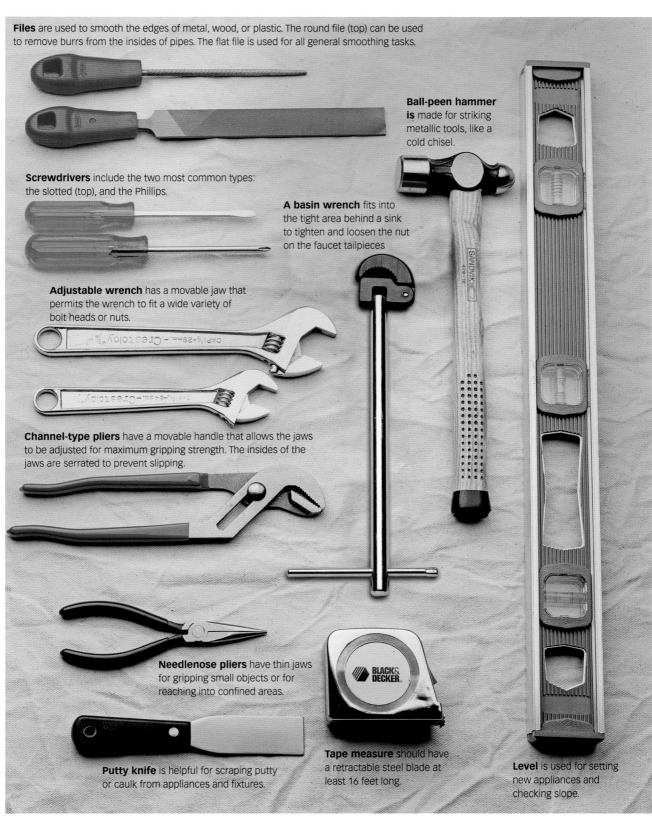

(continued)

Tubing cutter makes straight, smooth cuts in plastic and copper pipe. A tubing cutter usually has a triangular blade for removing burrs from the insides of pipes.

Closet auger is used to clear toilet clogs. It is a slender tube with a crank handle on one end of a flexible auger cable. A special bend in the tube allows the auger to be positioned in the bottom of the toilet bowl. The bend is usually protected with a rubber sleeve to prevent scratching the toilet.

Plastic tubing cutter works like a gardener's pruners to cut flexible plastic pipes quickly.

Spud wrench is specially designed for removing or tightening large nuts that are 2 to 4" in diameter. Hooks on the ends of the wrench grab onto the lugs of large nuts for increased leverage.

Plunger clears drain clogs with water and air pressure. The force cup (shown) is used for toilet bowls. The flange usually can be folded up into the cup for use as a standard plunger.

Hand auger, sometimes called a snake, is used to clear clogs in drain lines. A long, flexible steel cable is stored in the disk-shaped crank. A pistol-grip handle allows the user to apply steady pressure on the cable.

Blow bag, sometimes called an expansion nozzle, is used to clear drains. It attaches to a garden hose and removes clogs with powerful spurts of water. The blow bag is best used on floor drains.

Propane torch (left) is used for soldering fittings to copper pipes. Light the torch quickly and safely using a spark lighter (above).

Pipe wrench has a movable jaw that adjusts to fit a variety of pipe diameters. Pipe wrench is used for tightening and loosening pipes, pipe fittings, and large nuts. Two pipe wrenches often are used together to prevent damage to pipes and fittings.

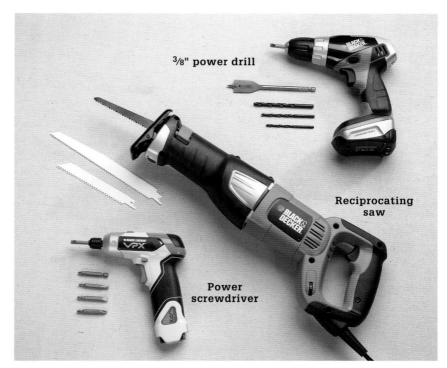

³⁄₈" power drill

Reciprocating saw

Power screwdriver

Power hand tools can make any job faster, easier, and safer. Cordless power tools offer added convenience. Use a cordless ³⁄₈" power drill for virtually any drilling task.

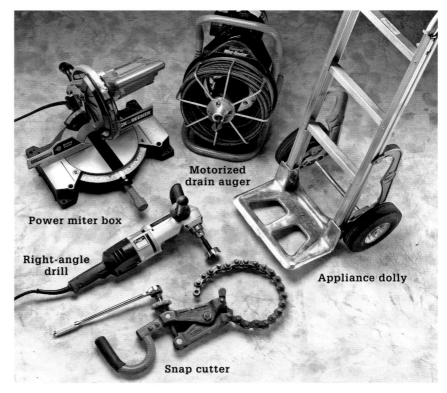

Motorized drain auger

Power miter box

Right-angle drill

Appliance dolly

Snap cutter

Rental tools may be needed for large jobs and special situations. A power miter saw makes fast, accurate cuts in a wide variety of materials, including plastic pipes. A motorized drain auger clears tree roots from sewer service lines. Use an appliance dolly to move heavy objects like water heaters. A snap cutter is designed to cut tough cast-iron pipes. The right-angle drill is useful for drilling holes in hard-to-reach areas.

Plumbing Materials

Common Pipe & Tube Types ▸

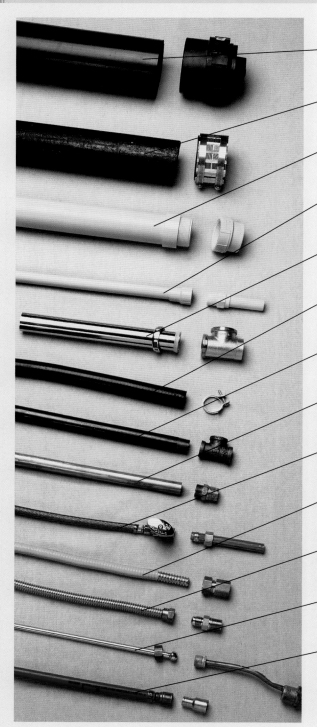

Benefits & Characteristics

ABS (acrylonitrile butadiene styrene) was once approved for use in DWV systems. Most local codes now prohibit ABS for new installations, but in some cases it can be added to pre-existing ABS DWV systems.

Cast iron is strong but hard to work with. Repairs should be made with plastic pipe, if allowed.

PVC (polyvinyl chloride) is rigid plastic that resists heat and chemicals. Lightweight tubes and heavier Schedule 40.

CPVC (chlorinated polyvinyl chloride) rigid plastic is inexpensive and withstands high temperature and pressure.

Chromed brass has an attractive shiny surface and is used for drain traps where appearance is important.

PE (polyethylene) plastic is a black or bluish flexible pipe sometimes used for main water service lines as well as irrigation systems.

Black pipe (iron pipe) generally is threaded at the ends to accept female-threaded fittings. Not for potable water.

Rigid copper is used for water supply pipes. It resists corrosion and has smooth surfaces for good water flow.

Braided metal is used for water supply tubes that connect shutoff valves to fixtures.

Flexible stainless steel (protective coated) connectors are used to attach gas appliances to supply stopcocks.

Flexible stainless steel (uncoated) connectors are used to attach gas appliances to supply stopcocks

Chromed copper supply tube is used in areas where appearance is important. Easy to bend and fit.

PEX (cross-linked polyethylene) is flexible and is approved by major building codes for water supply.

Flexible copper tubing (not shown) bends easily and requires fewer couplings than rigid copper.

Common Uses	Lengths	Diameters	Fitting Methods	Tools Used for Cutting
Pipes; drain traps	Sold by linear ft.	2", 3", 4"	Glue and plastic	Miter box or hacksaw
Main drain- waste-vent stack	5 ft., 10 ft.	3", 4"	Banded neoprene couplings	Snap cutter or hacksaw
Drain & vent pipes; drain traps	10 ft., 20 ft.; or sold by linear ft.	$1\frac{1}{4}$", $1\frac{1}{2}$", 2", 3", 4"	Solvent glue and/or plastic fittings	Tubing cutter, miter box, or hacksaw
Hot & cold water supply pipes	10 ft.	$\frac{3}{8}$", $\frac{1}{2}$", $\frac{3}{4}$", 1"	Solvent glue and plastic fittings, or with compression fittings	Tubing cutter, miter box, or hacksaw
Valves & shutoffs; drain traps, supply risers	Lengths vary	$1\frac{1}{4}$", $\frac{1}{2}$", $\frac{3}{4}$", $1\frac{1}{4}$", $1\frac{1}{2}$"	Compression fittings, or with metal solder	Tubing cutter, hacksaw, or reciprocating saw
Outdoor cold water supply pipes	Sold in coils of 25 to hundreds of ft.	$\frac{1}{4}$" to 1"	Rigid PVC fittings and stainless steel hose	Ratchet-style plastic pipe cutter or miter saw
Gas supply pipe	Sold in lengths up to 10 ft.	$\frac{3}{4}$", 1"	Threaded connectors	Hacksaw, power cutoff saw or reciprocating saw with bi-metal blade
Hot & cold water supply pipes	10 ft., 20 ft.; or sold by linear ft.	$\frac{3}{8}$", $\frac{1}{2}$", $\frac{3}{4}$", 1"	Metal solder or compression fittings	Tubing cutter, hacksaw, or jig saw
Supply tubes	12" or 20"	$\frac{3}{8}$"	Compression coupling or compression fittings	Do not cut
Gas ranges, dryers, water heaters	36" or 48"	$\frac{5}{8}$", $\frac{1}{2}$" (OD)	Compression coupling	Do not cut
Gas ranges, dryers, water heaters	36" or 48"	$\frac{5}{8}$", $\frac{1}{2}$" (OD)	Compression coupling	Do not cut
Supply tubing	12", 20", 30"	$\frac{3}{8}$"	Brass compression fittings	Tubing cutter or hacksaw
Water supply, tubing for radiant floors	Sold in coils of 25 ft. to hundreds of ft.	$\frac{1}{4}$" to 1"	Crimp fittings	Tubing cutter
Gas supply; hot & cold water supply	30-ft., 60-ft. coils; or by ft.	$\frac{1}{4}$", $\frac{3}{8}$", $\frac{1}{2}$", $\frac{3}{4}$", 1"	Brass flare fittings, solder, compression fittings,	Tubing cutter or hacksaw

Copper

Copper is the ideal material for water supply pipes. It resists corrosion and has smooth surfaces that provide good water flow. Copper pipes are available in several diameters (page 314), but most home water supply systems use ½" or ¾" pipe. Copper pipe is manufactured in rigid and flexible forms.

Rigid copper, sometimes called hard copper, is approved for home water supply systems by all local codes. It comes in three wall-thickness grades: Types M, L, and K. Type M is the thinnest, the least expensive, and a good choice for do-it-yourself home plumbing.

Rigid Type L usually is required by code for commercial plumbing systems. Because it is strong and solders easily, Type L may be preferred by some professional plumbers and do-it-yourselfers for home use. Type K has the heaviest wall thickness and is used most often for underground water service lines.

Flexible copper, also called soft copper, comes in two wall-thickness grades: Types L and K. Both are approved for most home water supply systems, although flexible Type L copper is used primarily for gas service lines. Because it is bendable and will resist a mild frost, Type L may be installed as part of a water supply system in unheated indoor areas, like crawl spaces. Type K is used for underground water service lines.

A third form of copper, called DWV, is used for drain systems. Because most codes now allow low-cost plastic pipes for drain systems, DWV copper is seldom used.

Copper pipes are connected with soldered, compression, or flare fittings (see chart below). Always follow your local code for the correct types of pipes and fittings allowed in your area.

Soldered fittings, also called sweat fittings, often are used to join copper pipes. Correctly soldered fittings (pages 278 to 280) are strong and trouble-free. Copper pipe can also be joined with compression fittings (pages 312 to 313) or flare fittings (page 317). See chart below.

Copper Pipe & Fitting Chart ▸

| | Rigid Copper | | | Flexible Copper | | |
Fitting Method	Type M	Type L	Type K	Type L	Type K	General Comments
Soldered	yes	yes	yes	yes	yes	Inexpensive, strong, and trouble-free fitting method. Requires some skill.
Compression	yes		not	no	no	Makes repairs and replacement easy. More expensive than solder. Best used on flexible copper.
Flare	no	no	yes	yes	yes	Use only with flexible copper pipes. Usually used as a gas-line fitting. Requires some skill.

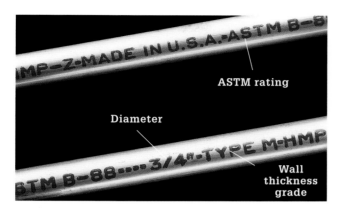

Grade stamp information includes the pipe diameter, the wall-thickness grade, and a stamp of approval from the ASTM (American Society for Testing and Materials). Type M pipe is identified by red lettering, Type L by blue lettering.

Bend flexible copper pipe with a coil-spring tubing bender to avoid kinks. Select a bender that matches the outside diameter of the pipe. Slip bender over pipe using a twisting motion. Bend pipe slowly until it reaches the correct angle, but not more than 90º.

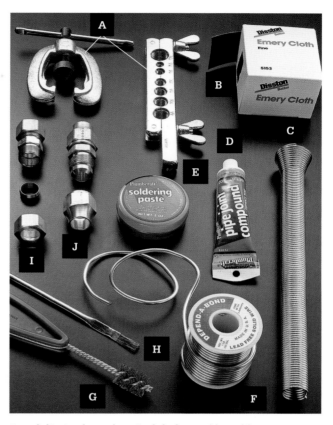

Specialty tools and materials for working with copper include: flaring tools (A), emery cloth (B), coil-spring tubing bender (C), pipe joint compound (D), soldering paste (flux) (E), lead-free solder (F), wire brush (G), flux brush (H), compression fitting (I), flare fitting (J).

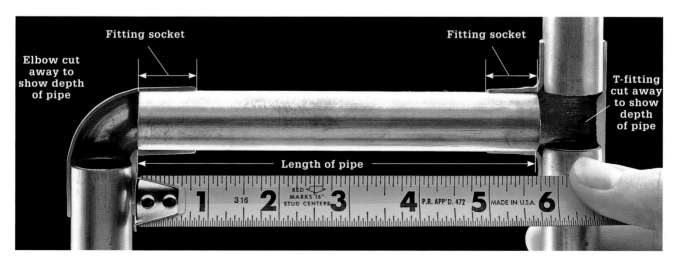

Find the length of copper pipe needed by measuring between the bottom of the copper fitting sockets (fittings shown in cutaway). Mark the length on the pipe with a felt-tipped pen.

Cutting & Soldering Copper

The best way to cut rigid and flexible copper pipe is with a tubing cutter. A tubing cutter makes a smooth, straight cut, an important first step toward making a watertight joint. Remove any metal burrs on the cut edges with a reaming tool or round file.

Copper can be cut with a hacksaw. A hacksaw is useful in tight areas where a tubing cutter will not fit. Take care to make a smooth, straight cut when cutting with a hacksaw.

A soldered pipe joint, also called a sweated joint, is made by heating a copper or brass fitting with a propane torch until the fitting is just hot enough to melt metal solder. The heat draws the solder into the gap between the fitting and pipe to form a watertight seal. A fitting that is overheated or unevenly heated will not draw in solder. Copper pipes and fittings must be clean and dry to form a watertight seal.

Tools & Materials ▸

Tubing cutter with
   reaming tip
   (or hacksaw
   and round file)
Wire brush
Flux brush
Propane torch
Spark lighter
   (or matches).
Round file

Cloth
Adjustable wrench
Channel-type pliers
Copper pipe
Copper fittings
Emery cloth
Soldering paste (flux)
Sheet metal
Lead-free solder
Rag

Protect wood from the heat of the torch flame while soldering, using a double layer (two 18" × 18" pieces) of 26-gauge sheet metal. Buy sheet metal at hardware stores or building supply centers and keep it to use with all soldering projects.

Soldering Tips ▸

Use caution when soldering copper. Pipes and fittings become very hot and must be allowed to cool before handling.

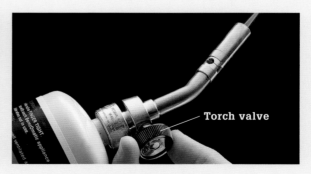

Torch valve

Prevent accidents by shutting off propane torch immediately after use. Make sure valve is closed completely.

How to Cut Rigid & Flexible Copper Pipe

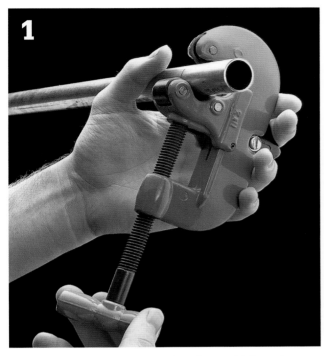

Place the tubing cutter over the pipe and tighten the handle so that the pipe rests on both rollers, and the cutting wheel is on the marked line.

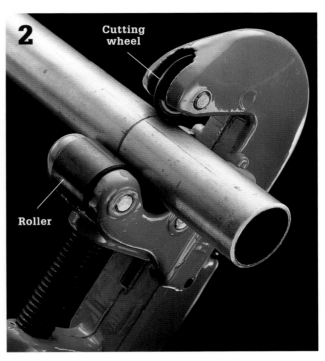

Turn the tubing cutter one rotation so that the cutting wheel scores a continuous straight line around the pipe.

Rotate the cutter in the opposite direction, tightening the handle slightly after every two rotations, until the cut is complete.

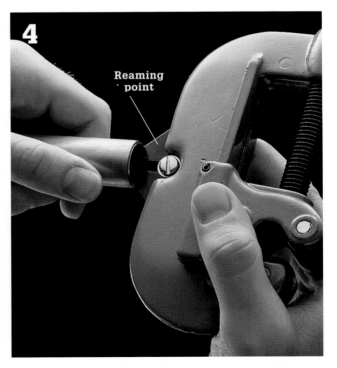

Remove sharp metal burrs from the inside edge of the cut pipe, using the reaming point on the tubing cutter, or a round file.

How to Solder Copper Pipes & Fittings

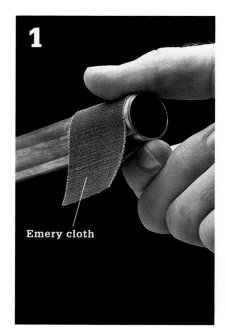

Clean the end of each pipe by sanding with emery cloth. Ends must be free of dirt and grease to ensure that the solder forms a good seal.

Clean the inside of each fitting by scouring with a wire brush or emery cloth.

Apply a thin layer of soldering paste (flux) to end of each pipe, using a flux brush. Soldering paste should cover about 1" of pipe end.

Apply a thin layer of flux to the inside of the fitting.

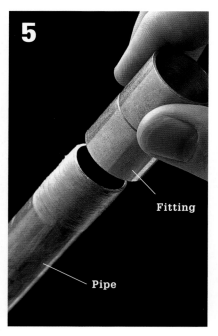

Assemble each joint by inserting the pipe into the fitting so it is tight against the bottom of the fitting sockets. Twist each fitting slightly to spread soldering paste.

Use a clean dry cloth to remove excess flux before soldering the assembled fitting.

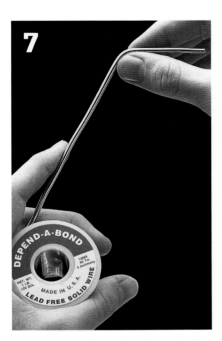

Prepare the wire solder by unwinding 8" to 10" of wire from spool. Bend the first 2" of the wire to a 90° angle.

Open the gas valve and trigger the spark lighter to ignite the torch.

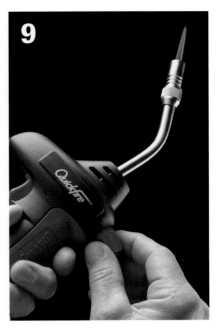

Adjust the torch valve until the inner portion of the flame is 1" to 2" long.

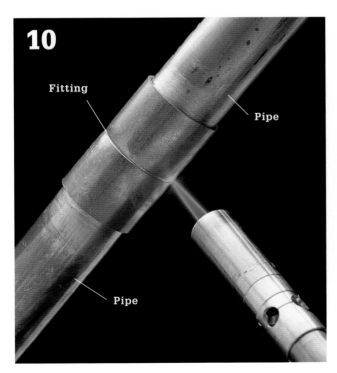

Fitting

Pipe

Pipe

Move the torch flame back and forth and around the pipe and the fitting to heat the area evenly.

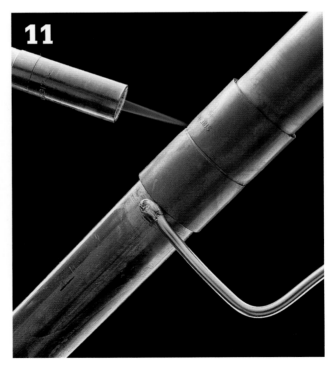

Heat the other side of the copper fitting to ensure that heat is distributed evenly. Touch solder to pipe. Solder will melt when the pipe is at the right temperature.

(continued)

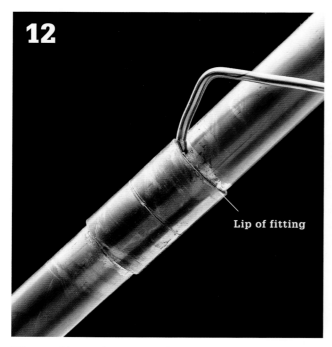

When solder melts, remove the torch and quickly push ½" to ¾" of solder into each joint. Capillary action fills the joint with liquid solder. A correctly soldered joint should show a thin bead of solder around the lips of the fitting.

Lip of fitting

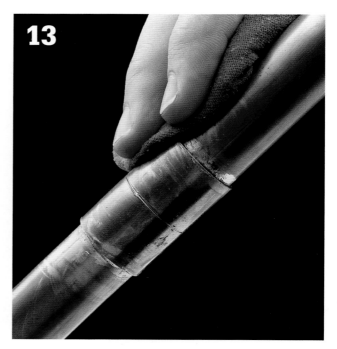

Allow the joint to cool briefly, then wipe away excess solder with a dry rag. *Caution: Pipes will be hot. If joints leak after water is turned on, disassemble and resolder.*

How to Solder Brass Valves

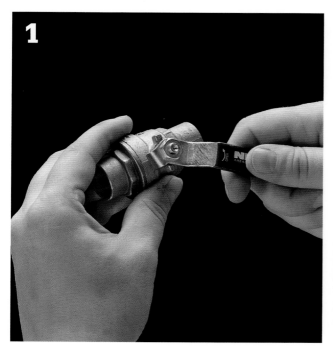

Valves should be fully open during all stages of the soldering process.

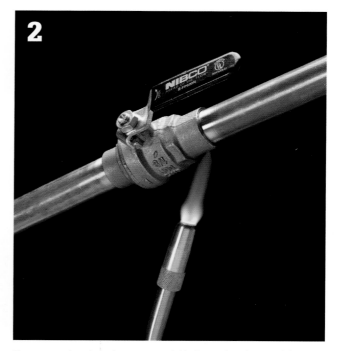

To prevent valve damage, quickly heat the pipe and the flanges of the valve, not the valve body. After soldering, cool the valve by spraying with water.

How to Take Apart Soldered Joints

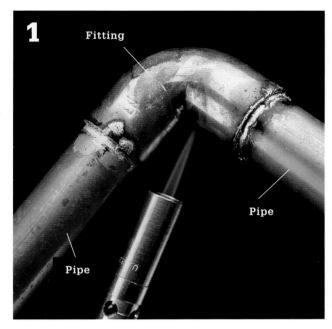

Turn off the water and drain the pipes by opening the highest and lowest faucets in the house. Light your torch. Hold the flame tip to the fitting until the solder becomes shiny and begins to melt.

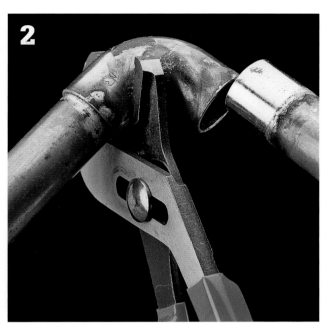

Use channel-type pliers to separate the pipes from the fitting.

Remove old solder by heating the ends of the pipe with your torch. Use a dry rag to wipe away melted solder quickly. *Caution: Pipes will be hot.*

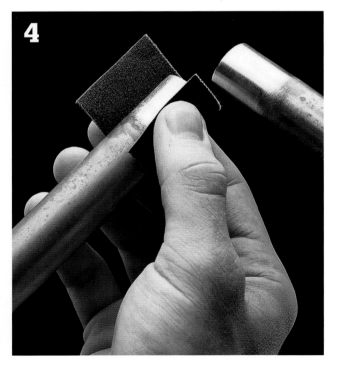

Use emery cloth to polish the ends of the pipe down to bare metal. Never reuse fittings.

Rigid Plastic Pipe

Cut rigid ABS, PVC, or CPVC plastic pipes with a tubing cutter or with any saw. Cuts must be straight to ensure watertight joints.

Rigid plastics are joined with plastic fittings and solvent glue. Use a solvent glue that is made for the type of plastic pipe you are installing. For example, do not use ABS solvent on PVC pipe. Some solvent glues, called "all-purpose" or "universal" solvents, are designed to be used on all types of plastic pipe, but are inferior to specific types.

Solvent glue hardens in about 30 seconds, so test-fit all plastic pipes and fittings before gluing the first joint. For best results, the surfaces of plastic pipes and fittings should be dulled with emery cloth and liquid primer before they are joined.

Liquid solvent glues and primers are toxic and flammable. Provide adequate ventilation when fitting plastics, and store them away from any source of heat.

Plastic grip fittings can be used to join rigid or flexible plastic pipes to copper plumbing pipes (page 274).

Solvent welding is a chemical bonding process used to permanently join PVC pipes and fittings.

Tools & Materials ▸

Tape measure	Plastic pipe
Felt-tipped pen	Fittings
Tubing cutter	Emery cloth
(or miter box	Plastic pipe primer
or hacksaw)	Solvent glue
Utility knife	Rag
Channel-type pliers	Petroleum jelly
Gloves	

Primer and solvent glue are specific to the plumbing material being used. Do not use all-purpose or multi-purpose products. Light to medium body glues are appropriate for DIYers as they allow the longest working time and are easiest to use. The products work best when fresh, so buy small containers and throw out any unused product after a few months.

How to Cut Rigid Plastic Pipe

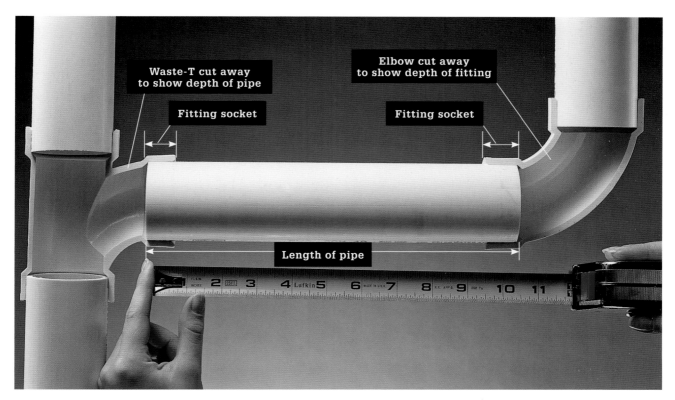

Find the length of plastic pipe needed by measuring between the bottoms of the fitting sockets (fittings shown in cutaway). Mark the length on the pipe with a felt-tipped pen.

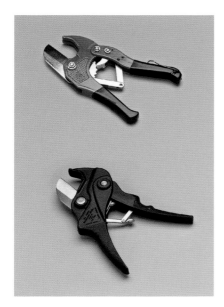

Plastic tubing cutters do a fast, neat job of cutting. You'll probably have to go to a professional plumbing supply store to find one, however. They are not interchangeable with metal tubing cutters.

The best cutting tool for plastic pipe is a power miter saw with a fine tooth woodworking blade or a plastic-specific blade.

A ratcheting plastic-pipe cutter can cut smaller diameter PVC and CPVC pipe in a real hurry. If you are plumbing a whole house you may want to consider investing in one. They also are sold only at plumbing supply stores.

How to Solvent-Glue Rigid Plastic Pipe

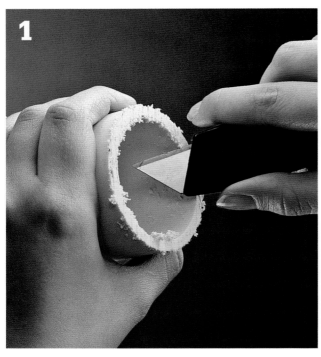

Remove rough burrs on cut ends of plastic pipe, using a utility knife.

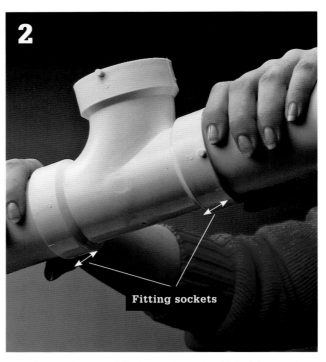

Test-fit all pipes and fittings. Pipes should fit tightly against the bottom of the fitting sockets.

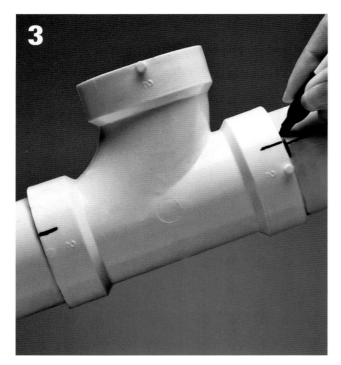

Mark the depth of the fitting sockets on the pipes. Take pipes apart. Clean the ends of the pipes and fitting sockets with emery cloth.

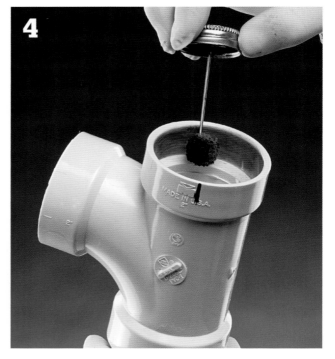

Apply a light coat of plastic pipe primer to the ends of the pipes and to the insides of the fitting sockets. Primer dulls glossy surfaces and ensures a good seal.

Solvent-glue each joint by applying a thick coat of solvent glue to the end of the pipe. Apply a thin coat of solvent glue to the inside surface of the fitting socket. Work quickly: solvent glue hardens in about 30 seconds.

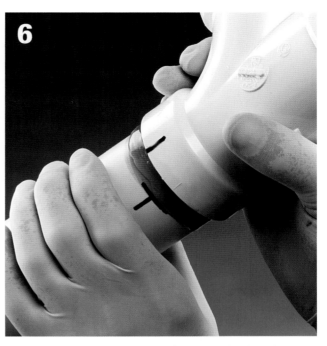

Quickly position the pipe and fitting so that the alignment marks are offset by about 2". Force the pipe into the fitting until the end fits flush against the bottom of the socket.

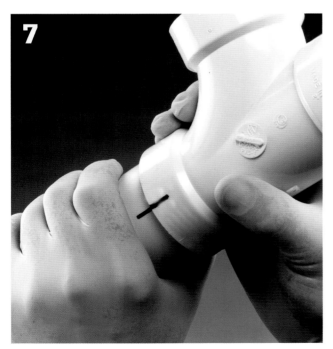

Spread solvent by twisting the pipe until the marks are aligned. Hold the pipe in place for about 20 seconds to prevent the joint from slipping.

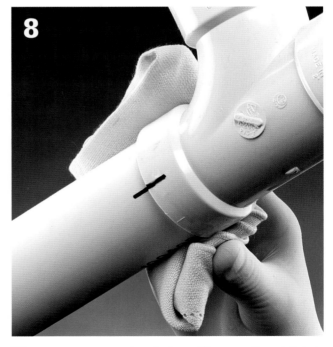

Wipe away excess solvent glue with a rag. Do not disturb the joint for 30 minutes after gluing.

Working with Outdoor Flexible Plastic Pipe

Flexible PE (polyethylene) pipe is used for underground cold water lines. Very inexpensive, PE pipe is commonly used for automatic lawn sprinkler systems and for extending cold water supply to utility sinks in detached garages and sheds.

Unlike other plastics, PE is not solvent-glued, but is joined using "barbed" rigid PVC fittings and stainless steel hose clamps. In cold climates, outdoor plumbing lines should be shut off and drained for winter.

Tools & Materials ▸

Tape measure
Tubing cutter
Screwdriver
    or wrench
Pipe joint compound
Flexible pipe
Fittings
Hose clamps
Utility knife

Connect lengths of PE pipe with a barbed PVC fitting. Secure the connection with stainless steel hose clamps.

Connect PE pipe to an existing cold water supply pipe by splicing in a T-fitting to the copper pipe and attaching a drain-and-waste shutoff valve and a female-threaded adapter. Screw a barbed PVC male-threaded adapter into the copper fitting, then attach the PE pipe. The drain-and-waste valve allows you to blow the PE line free of water when winterizing the system.

How to Cut & Join Outdoor Flexible Plastic Pipe

Cut flexible PE pipe with a plastic tubing cutter, or use a miter box or sharp knife. Remove any rough burrs with a utility knife.

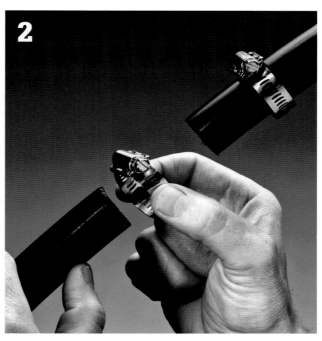

Fit stainless steel hose clamps over the ends of the flexible pipes being joined.

Option: To ensure a tighter fit, dab some pipe joint compound onto the barbs so they are easier to slide into the flexible plastic pipe. Apply pipe joint compound to the barbed ends of the T-fitting. Work each end of PE pipe over the barbed portions of the fitting and into position.

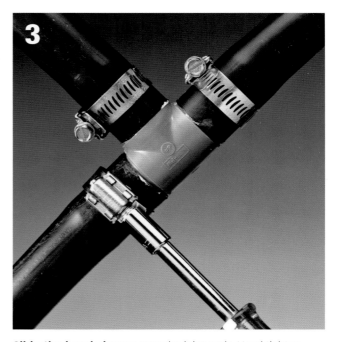

Slide the band clamps over the joint ends. Hand tighten each clamp with a screwdriver or wrench.

Cross-Linked Polyethylene (PEX)

Cross-linked polyethylene (PEX) is growing quickly in acceptance as a supply pipe for residential plumbing. It's not hard to understand why. Developed in the 1960s but relatively new to the United States, this supply pipe combines the ease of use of flexible tubing with the durability of rigid pipe. It can withstand a wide temperature range (from subfreezing to 180° F); it is inexpensive; and it's quieter than rigid supply pipe.

PEX is flexible plastic (polyethylene, or PE) tubing that's reinforced by a chemical reaction that creates long fibers to increase the strength of the material. It has been allowed by code in Europe and the southern United States for many years, but has won approval for residential supply use in most major plumbing codes only recently. It's frequently used in manufactured housing and recreational vehicles and in radiant heating systems. Because it is so flexible, PEX can easily be bent to follow corners and make other changes in direction. From the water main and heater, it is connected into manifold fittings that redistribute the water in much the same manner as a lawn irrigation system.

For standard residential installations, PEX can be joined with very simple fittings and tools. Unions are generally made with a crimping tool and a crimping ring. You simply insert the ends of the pipe you're joining into the ring, then clamp down on the ring with the crimping tool. PEX pipe, tools, and fittings can be purchased from most wholesale plumbing suppliers and at many home centers. Coils of PEX are sold in several diameters from ¼" to 1". PEX tubing and fittings from different manufacturers are not interchangeable. Any warranty coverage will be voided if products are mixed.

Tools & Materials ▸

Tape measure
Felt-tipped pen
Full-circle
  crimping tool
Go/no-go gauge
Tubing cutter
PEX pipe

Manifolds
Protector plates
PEX fittings
Utility knife
Plastic hangers
Crimp ring

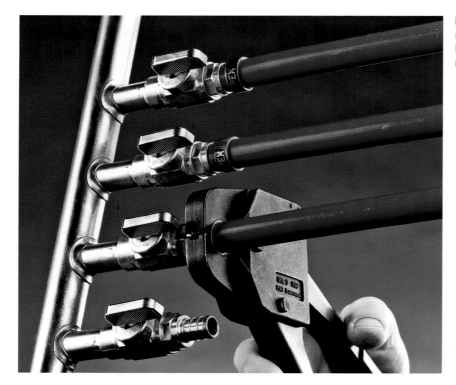

PEX pipe is a relatively new water supply material that's growing in popularity in part because it can be installed with simple mechanical connections.

PEX Tools & Materials

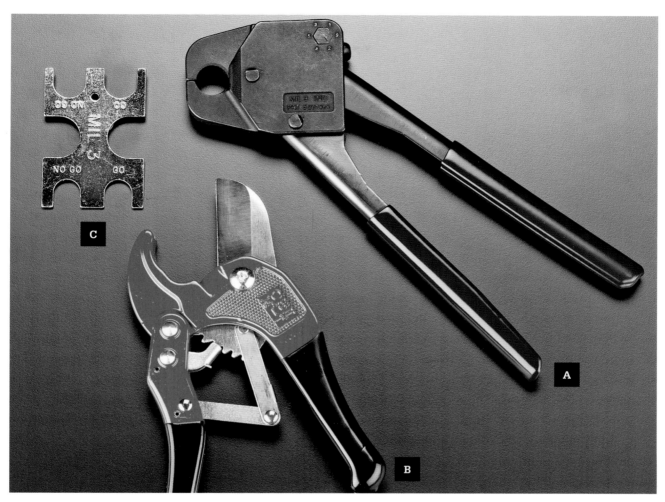

Specialty tools for installing PEX are available wherever PEX is sold. The basic set includes a full-circle crimping tool (A), a tubing cutter (B), and a go/no-go gauge (C) to test connections after they've been crimped.

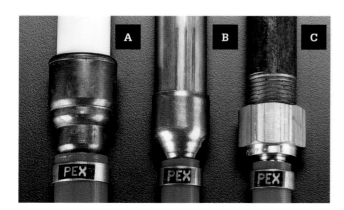

PEX is connected to other water supply materials with transition fittings, including CPVC-to-PEX (A), copper-to-PEX (B), and iron-to-PEX (C).

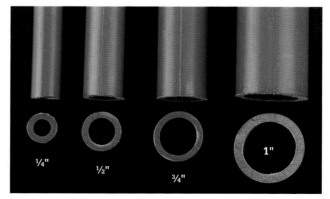

Generally, you should use the same diameter PEX as is specified for rigid supply tubing, but in some "home run" installations (see next page) you can use ⅜" PEX where ½" rigid copper would normally be used.

PEX Installation

Check with your local plumbing inspector to verify that PEX is allowed in your municipality. PEX has been endorsed by all major plumbing codes in North America, but your municipality may still be using an older set of codes. Follow the guidelines below when installing PEX:

- Do not install PEX in above-ground exterior applications because it degrades quickly from UV exposure.
- Do not use PEX for gas lines.
- Do not use plastic solvents or petroleum-based products with PEX (they can dissolve the plastic).
- Keep PEX at least 12" away from recessed light fixtures and other potential sources of high heat.

- Do not attach PEX directly to a water heater. Make connections at the heater with metallic tubing (either flexible water-heater connector tubing or rigid copper) at least 18" long; then join it to PEX with a transition fitting.
- Do not install PEX in areas where there is a possibility of mechanical damage or puncture. Always fasten protective plates to wall studs that house PEX.
- Always leave some slack in installed PEX lines to allow for contraction and in case you need to cut off a bad crimp.
- Use the same minimum branch and distribution supply-pipe dimensions for PEX that you'd use for copper or CPVC, according to your local plumbing codes.

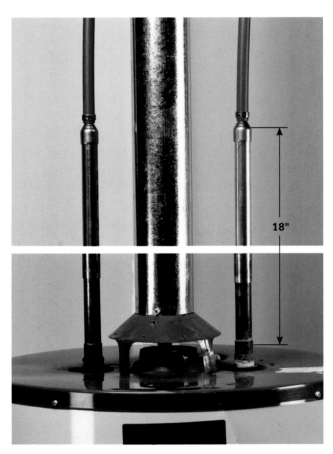

Do not connect PEX directly to a water heater. Use metal connector tubes. Solder the connector tubes to the water heater before attaching PEX. Never solder metal tubing that is already connected to PEX lines.

Bundle PEX together with plastic ties when running pipe through wall cavities. PEX can contract slightly, so leave some slack in the lines.

Buying PEX

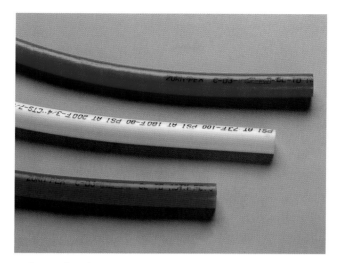

Color coding is a practice many PEX manufacturers have embraced to make identification easier. Because the material is identical except for the color, you can buy only one color (red is more common) and use it for both hot and cold supply lines.

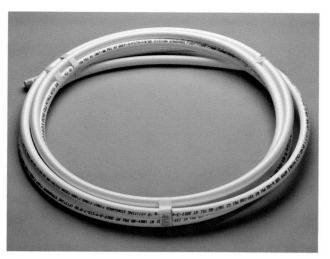

PEX combines the flexibility of plastic tubing with the durability of rigid supply pipe. It is sold in coils of common supply-pipe diameters.

The PEX Advantage ▶

PEX supply tubing offers a number of advantages over traditional rigid supply tubing:

- Easy to install. PEX does not require coupling joints for long runs or elbows and sweeps for turns. The mechanical connections do not require solvents or soldering.
- Easy to transport. Large coils are lightweight and much easier to move around than 10-ft. lengths of pipe.
- Good insulation. The PEX material has better thermal properties than copper for lessened heat loss.

- Quiet. PEX will not rattle or clang from trapped air or kinetic energy.
- Good for retrofit jobs. PEX is easier to snake through walls than rigid supply tubing and is compatible with copper, PVC, or iron supply systems if the correct transition fittings are used. If your metal supply tubes are used to ground your electrical system, you'll need to provide a jumper if PEX is installed in midrun. Check with a plumber or electrician.
- Freeze resistance. PEX retains some flexibility in sub-freezing conditions and is less likely to be damaged than rigid pipe, but it is not frostproof.

General Codes for PEX ▶

PEX has been endorsed for residential use by all major building codes, although some municipal codes may be more restrictive. The specific design standards may also vary, but here are some general rules:

- For PEX, maximum horizontal support spacing is 32" and maximum vertical support spacing is 10 ft.

- Maximum length of individual distribution lines is 60 ft.
- PEX is designed to withstand 210° F water for up to 48 hours. For ongoing use, most PEX is rated for 180 degree water up to 100 pounds per square inch of pressure.
- Directional changes of more than 90 degrees require a guide fitting (see page 307).

System Designs

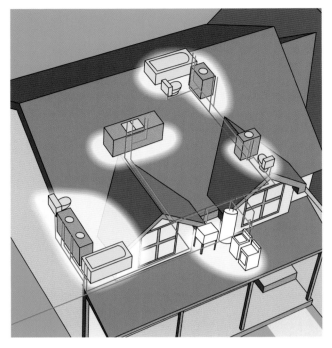

Trunk-and-branch systems are configured in much the same way as a traditional rigid copper or PVC supply systems. A main supply line (the trunk line) carries water to all of the outlets via smaller branch lines that tie into the trunk and serve a few outlets in a common location.

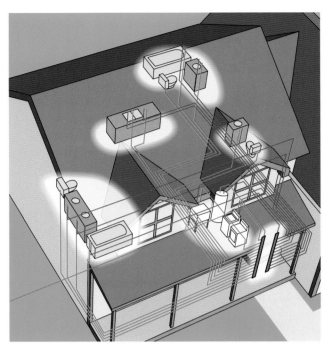

Home run systems rely on one or two central manifolds to distribute the hot and cold water very efficiently. Eliminating the branch fittings allows you to use thinner supply pipe in some situations.

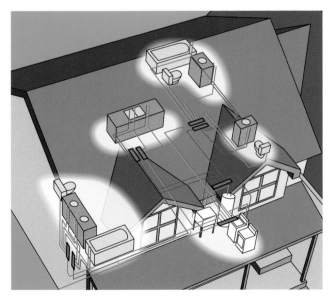

Remote manifold systems are a hybrid between traditional trunk-and-branch systems and home run systems. Instead of relying on just one or two manifolds, they employ several smaller manifolds downline from a larger manifold. Each smaller manifold services a group of fixtures, as in a bathroom or kitchen.

Choosing a PEX system ▸

- For maximum single-fixture water pressure: Trunk and branch
- For economy of materials: Trunk and branch or remote manifold
- For minimal wait times for hot water (single fixture): Home run
- For minimal wait times for hot water (multiple fixtures used at same approximate time): Trunk and branch or remote manifold
- For ease of shutoff control: Home run
- For lowest number of fittings and joints: Home run

How to Make PEX Connections

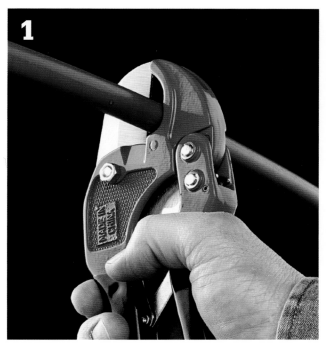

Cut the pipe to length, making sure to leave enough extra material so the line will have a small amount of slack once the connections are made. A straight, clean cut is very important. For best results, use a tubing cutter.

Inspect the cut end to make sure it is clean and smooth. If necessary, deburr the end of the pipe with a sharp utility knife. Slip a crimp ring over the end.

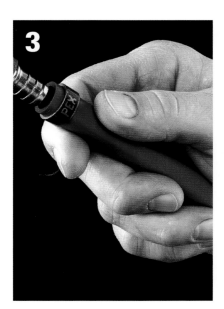

Insert the barbed end of the fitting into the pipe until it is snug against the cut edges.Position the crimp ring so it is ⅛" to ¼" from the end of the pipe, covering the barbed end of the fitting. Pinch the fitting to hold it in place.

Align the jaws of a full-circle crimping tool over the crimp ring and squeeze the handles together to apply strong, even pressure to the ring.

Test the connection to make sure it is mechanically acceptable, using a go/no-go gauge. If the ring does not fit into the gauge properly, cut the pipe near the connection and try again.

How to Plumb a PEX Water-Supply System

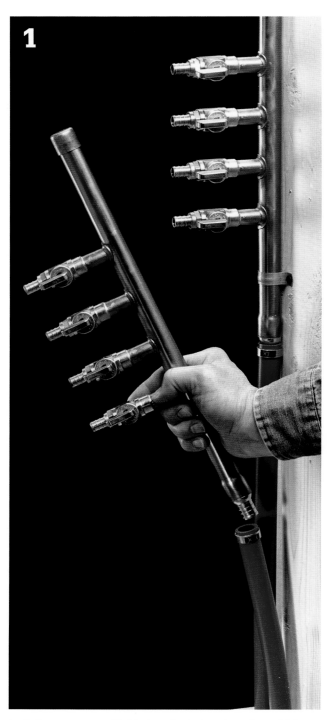

Install copper manifolds (one for hot and one for cold) in an accessible location central to the fixtures. The manifold should have one outlet for each supply line it will support (fixtures that require hot and cold supply will need a separate outlet for each). Run supply lines from the water heater and water main to the copper manifolds. Connect the supply pipes to the manifolds with crimp fittings.

A manifold may be attached vertically or horizontally, but it must be anchored with correctly sized hangers screwed to the framing members.

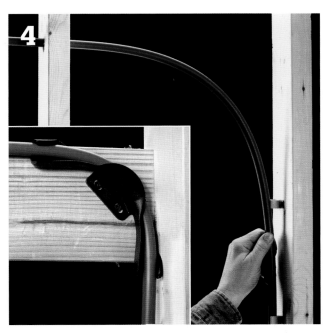

Starting at each fixture (and leaving at least 12" of extra pipe exposed), run appropriately sized PEX through holes in the framing to the manifolds. Pipes may be bundled together loosely with plastic ties. Protect the line with a nailing plate at each stud location. Be sure to leave some slack in the supply lines.

Support the pipe with a plastic hanger near every floor or ceiling and midway up vertical runs. Also use hangers to guide pipe near the beginnings and ends of curves and near fittings. Use a plastic guide for sharp curves (inset). Do not bend PEX so sharply that it kinks.

Cut each branch supply line to length (leave some extra in case you need to recrimp). Install shutoff valves for each outlet (most manifolds come with preattached valves). Connect the PEX branch supply lines to the shutoff valves. Label each pipe. Use a short length of PEX and a plug to seal any unused outlets (inset).

Galvanized Iron

Galvanized iron pipe often is found in older homes, where it is used for water supply and small drain lines. It can be identified by the zinc coating that gives it a silver color and by the threaded fittings used to connect pipes.

Galvanized iron pipes and fittings will corrode with age and eventually must be replaced. Low water pressure may be a sign that the insides of galvanized pipes have a buildup of rust. Blockage usually occurs in elbow fittings. Never try to clean the insides of galvanized iron pipes. Instead, remove and replace them as soon as possible.

Galvanized iron pipe and fittings are available at hardware stores and home improvement centers. Always specify the interior diameter (I.D.) when purchasing galvanized pipes and fittings. Pre-threaded pipes, called nipples, are available in lengths from 1" to 1 ft. If you need a longer length, have the store cut and thread the pipe to your dimensions.

Old galvanized iron can be difficult to repair. Fittings are often rusted in place, and what seems like a small job may become a large project. For example, cutting apart a section of pipe to replace a leaky fitting may reveal that adjacent pipes are also in need of replacement. If your job takes an unexpected amount of time, you can cap off any open lines and restore water to the rest of your house. Before you begin a repair, have on hand nipples and end caps that match your pipes.

Taking apart a system of galvanized iron pipes and fittings is time-consuming. Disassembly must start at the end of a pipe run, and each piece must be unscrewed before the next piece can be removed. Reaching the middle of a run to replace a section of pipe can be a long and tedious job. Instead, use a special three-piece fitting called a union. A union makes it possible to remove a section of pipe or a fitting without having to take the entire system apart.

Note: Galvanized iron is sometimes confused with "black iron." Both types have similar sizes and fittings. Black iron is used only for gas lines.

Tools & Materials ▸

Tape measure	Nipples
Reciprocating saw	End caps
with metal-cutting	Union fitting
blade or a hacksaw	Pipe joint compound
Pipe wrenches	Replacement fittings
Propane torch	(if needed)
Wire brush	

Galvanized pipe was installed in homes for both gas and water supply pipes until the middle part of the last century. Although it is not used for new installations today, it can still be repaired easily using simple tools and techniques.

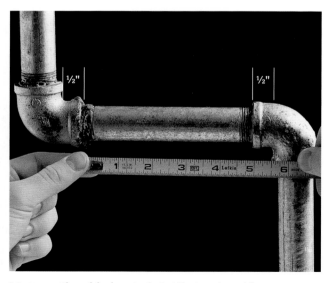

Measure the old pipe. Include ½" at each end for the threaded portion of the pipe inside fitting. Bring overall measurement to the store when shopping for replacement parts.

How to Remove & Replace a Galvanized Iron Pipe

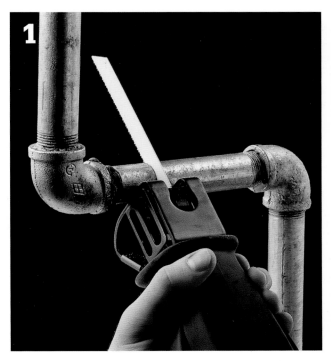

Cut through galvanized iron pipe with a reciprocating saw and a metal-cutting blade or with a hacksaw.

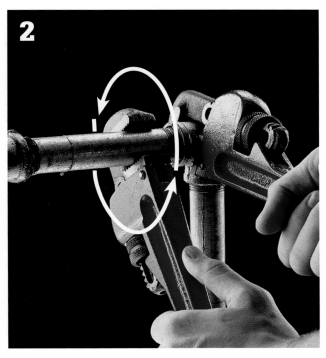

Hold the fitting with one pipe wrench, and use another wrench to remove the old pipe. The jaws of the wrenches should face opposite directions. Always move the wrench handle toward the jaw opening.

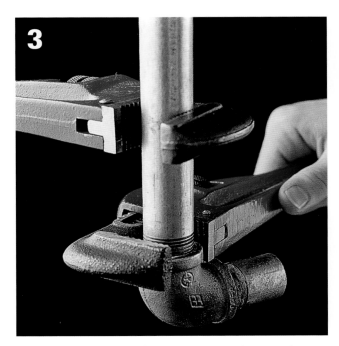

Remove any corroded fittings using two pipe wrenches. With the jaws facing in opposite directions, use one wrench to turn fitting and the other to hold the pipe. Clean the pipe threads with a wire brush.

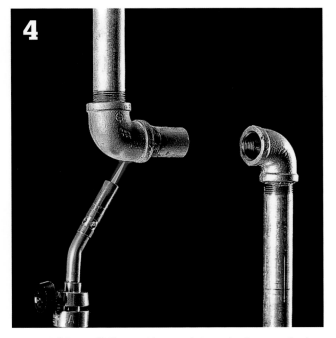

Heat stubborn fittings with a torch to make them easier to remove. Apply flame for 5 to 10 seconds. Protect wood and other flammable materials from heat, using a double layer of sheet metal.

(continued)

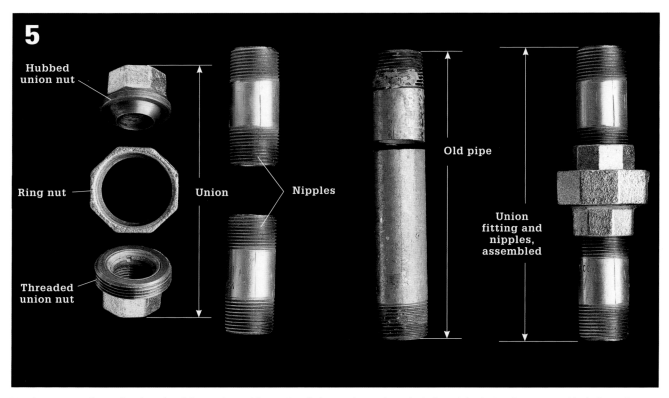

5

Hubbed union nut

Ring nut

Threaded union nut

Union

Nipples

Old pipe

Union fitting and nipples, assembled

Replace a section of galvanized iron pipe with a union fitting and two threaded pipes (nipples). When assembled, the union and nipples must equal the length of the pipe that is being replaced.

6

Pipe joint compound

Apply a bead of pipe joint compound around the threaded ends of all pipes and nipples. Spread the compound evenly over the threads with your fingertip.

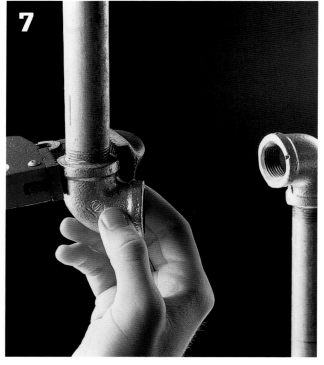

7

Screw new fittings onto pipe threads. Tighten fittings with two pipe wrenches, leaving them about one-eighth turn out of alignment to allow assembly of the union.

Screw the first nipple into the fitting, and tighten with a pipe wrench.

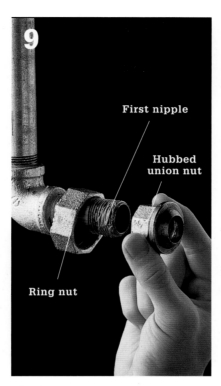

Slide a ring nut onto the installed nipple, then screw the hubbed union nut onto the nipple and tighten with a pipe wrench.

First nipple

Hubbed union nut

Ring nut

Screw the second nipple onto the other fitting. Tighten with a pipe wrench.

Second nipple

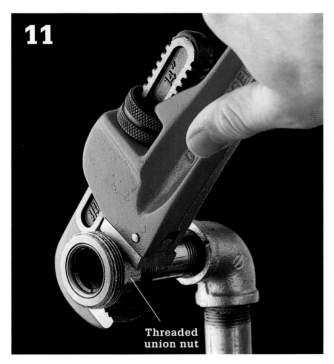

Threaded union nut

Screw the threaded union nut onto the second nipple. Tighten with a pipe wrench. Turn pipes into alignment, so that the lip of the hubbed union nut fits inside the threaded union nut.

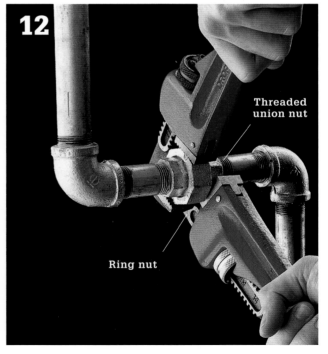

Threaded union nut

Ring nut

Complete the connection by screwing the ring nut onto the threaded union nut. Tighten the ring nut with pipe wrenches.

Cast Iron

Cast iron pipe often is found in older homes, where it is used for large DWV pipes, especially the main stack and sewer service lines. It can be identified by its dark color, rough surface, and large size. Cast-iron pipes in home drains usually are 3" or more in diameter.

Cast-iron pipes may rust through or hubbed fittings (below) may leak. If your house is more than 30 years old, you may find it necessary to replace a cast-iron pipe or joint.

Cast iron is heavy and difficult to cut and fit. For this reason, leaky cast-iron pipe usually is replaced with PVC of the same diameter. PVC can be joined to cast iron easily, using a banded coupling (below).

Snap cutters are the traditional tool of choice for cutting cast iron (see page 307), but today's variable-speed reciprocating saws do the job easily and safely. Use a long metal-cutting blade and set the saw at low speed. Wear eye and ear protection when cutting cast iron pipe.

Tools & Materials ▸

Tape measure
Chalk
Adjustable wrenches
Reciprocating
   saw (or rented
   snap cutter)
Ratchet wrench
Screwdriver

Riser clamps or
   strap hangers
Two wood blocks
2½" wallboard screws
Banded couplings
Plastic
   replacement pipe

Cast-iron pipe was used almost exclusively for drain systems until the introduction of heavy-duty PVC drain pipes. It is tough to work with and in most cases replacing it makes sense.

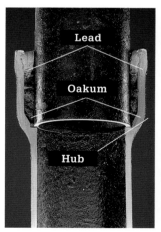

Hubbed fittings (shown cutaway, left) were used to join cast-iron pipe. Hubbed pipe has a straight end and a flared end. The straight end of one pipe fits inside the hub of the next pipe. In the old days, joints were sealed with packing material (oakum) and lead. Repair leaky joints by cutting out the entire hubbed fitting and replacing with plastic pipe.

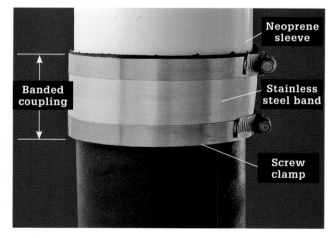

Banded couplings may be used to replace leaky cast iron with a PVC or ABS plastic pipe. The new plastic pipe is connected to the remaining cast-iron pipe with a banded coupling. Banded coupling has a neoprene sleeve that seals the joint. Pipes are held together with stainless steel bands and screw clamps.

Cutting Cast-Iron Pipe

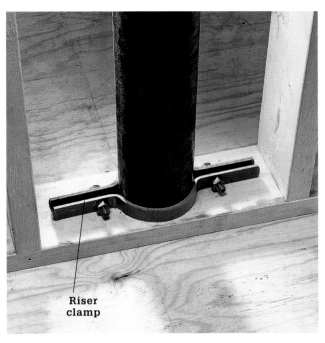

Before cutting a horizontal run of cast-iron drain pipe, make sure it is supported with strap hangers every 5 ft. and at every joint connection.

Before cutting a vertical run of cast-iron pipe, make sure it is supported at every floor level with a riser clamp. Never cut through pipe that is not supported.

How to Remove & Replace a Section of Cast-Iron Pipe

Use chalk to mark cut lines on the cast-iron pipe. If replacing a leaky hub, mark at least 6" on each side of hub.

Support lower section of pipe by installing a riser clamp flush against the bottom plate or floor.

Support the upper section of pipe by installing a riser clamp 6" above the pipe section to be replaced. Attach wood blocks to the studs with 2½" deck screws, so that the riser clamp rests on tops of blocks.

(continued)

Wrap the chain of the snap cutter around the pipe, so that the cutting wheels are against the chalkline.

Tighten the chain and snap the pipe according to the tool manufacturer's directions.

Repeat cutting at the other chalkline. Remove cut section of pipe.

Cut a length of PVC plastic pipe to be ½" shorter than the section of cast-iron pipe that has been cut away.

Screw clamp

Banded clamp

Neoprene sleeve

Slip a banded coupling and a neoprene sleeve onto each end of the cast-iron pipe.

Make sure the cast-iron pipe is seated snugly against the rubber separator ring molded into the interior of the sleeve.

Fold back the end of each neoprene sleeve, until the molded separator ring on the inside of the sleeve is visible.

Position the new plastic pipe so it is aligned with the cast-iron pipes.

Roll the ends of the neoprene sleeves over the ends of the new plastic pipe.

Slide stainless steel bands and clamps over the neoprene sleeves.

Tighten the screw clamps with a ratchet wrench or screwdriver.

Pipe Fittings

Use the photos on these pages to identify the plumbing fittings specified in the project how-to directions found in this book. Each fitting shown is available in a variety of sizes to match your needs. Always use fittings made from the same material as your pipes.

Pipe fittings come in a variety of shapes to serve different functions within the plumbing system. DWV fittings include:

Vents: In general, the fittings used to connect vent pipes have very sharp bends with no sweep. Vent fittings include the vent T and vent 90° elbow. Standard drain pipe fittings can also be used to join vent pipes.

Horizontal-to-vertical drains: To change directions in a drain pipe from the horizontal to the vertical, use fittings with a noticeable sweep. Standard fittings for this use include waste T-fittings and 90° elbows. Y-fittings and 45° and 22½° elbows can also be used for this purpose.

Vertical-to-horizontal drains: To change directions from the vertical to the horizontal, use fittings with a very pronounced, gradual sweep. Common fittings for this purpose include the long-radius T-Y-fitting and some Y-fittings with 45° elbows.

Horizontal offsets in drains: Y-fittings, 45° elbows, 22½° elbows, and long sweep 90° elbows are used when changing directions in horizontal pipe runs. Whenever possible, horizontal drain pipes should use gradual, sweeping bends rather than sharp turns.

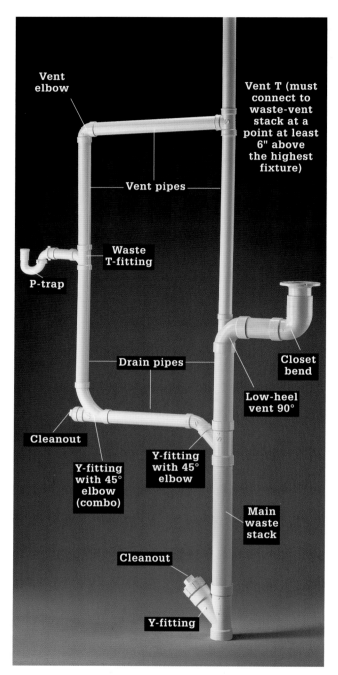

Basic DWV tree shows the correct orientation of drain and vent fittings in a plumbing system. Bends in the vent pipes can be very sharp, but drain pipes should use fittings with a noticeable sweep. Fittings used to direct falling waste water from a vertical to a horizontal pipe should have bends that are even more sweeping. Your local plumbing code may require that you install cleanout fittings where vertical drain pipes meet horizontal runs.

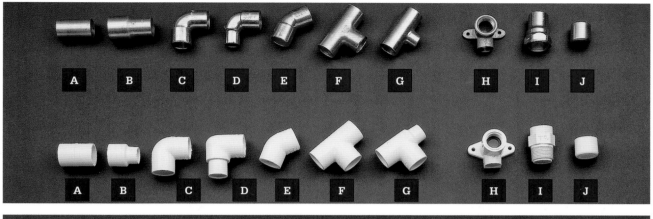

Water supply fittings are available for copper (top), CPVC plastic (center), and PEX (bottom). Fittings for CPVC and copper are available in many shapes, including: unions (A), reducers (B), 90° elbows (C), reducing elbows (D), 45° elbows (E), T-fittings (F), reducing T-fittings (G), drop-ear elbows (H), threaded adapters (I), and caps (J). Common PEX fittings (bottom) include unions (K), PEX-to-copper unions (L), 90° elbows (M), T-fittings (N), plugs (O), drop-ear elbows (P), and threaded adapters (Q).

Water supply valves are available in brass or plastic and in a variety of styles, including: drain-and-waste valves (A), gate valve (B), full-bore ball valves (C), fixture shutoff valve (D), vacuum breaker (E), and hose bib (F).

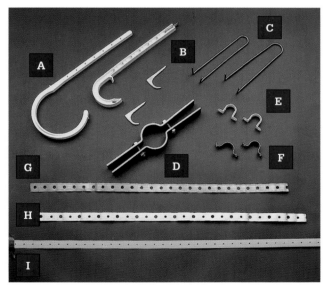

Support materials for pipes include: plastic pipe hangers (A), copper J-hooks (B), copper wire hangers (C), riser clamp (D), plastic pipe straps (E), copper pipe straps (F), flexible copper, steel, and plastic pipe strapping (G, H, I). Do not mix metal types when supporting metal pipes; use copper support materials for copper pipe, and steel for steel and cast-iron pipes.

T-fittings

Low-heel vent 90°

Waste-T

Vent T

Waste-T with additional side inlet

Waste cross

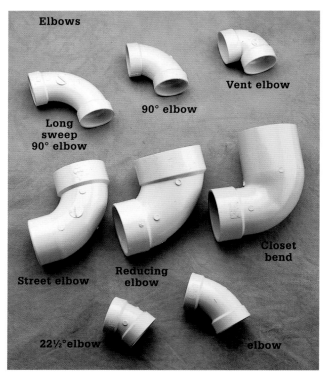

Elbows

Vent elbow

90° elbow

Long sweep 90° elbow

Closet bend

Street elbow

Reducing elbow

22½° elbow

elbow

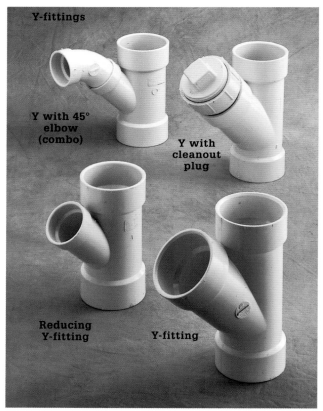

Y-fittings

Y with 45° elbow (combo)

Y with cleanout plug

Reducing Y-fitting

Y-fitting

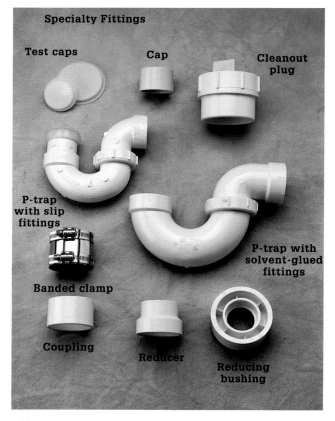

Specialty Fittings

Test caps

Cap

Cleanout plug

P-trap with slip fittings

P-trap with solvent-glued fittings

Banded clamp

Coupling

Reducer

Reducing bushing

Fittings for DWV pipes are available in many configurations, with openings ranging from 1¼" to 4" in diameter. When planning your project, buy plentiful numbers of DWV and water supply fittings from a reputable retailer with a good return policy. It is much more efficient to return leftover materials after you complete your project than it is to interrupt your work each time you need to shop for a missing fitting.

How to Use Transition Fittings

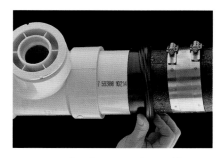

Connect plastic to cast iron with banded couplings. Rubber sleeves cover ends of pipes and ensure a watertight joint.

1-1/2"-to-1-1/4" reducing transition

3" no-hub neoprene coupling

Make transitions in DWV pipes with rubber couplings. The two products shown here (Mission-brand fittings, see Resources page 329) can be used to connect pipes of different materials, as well as same-material pipes that need a transition.

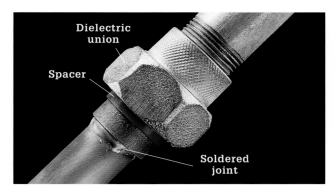

Dielectric union

Spacer

Soldered joint

Connect copper to galvanized iron with a dielectric union. A dielectric union is threaded onto iron pipe and is soldered to copper pipe. A dielectric union has a plastic spacer that prevents corrosion caused by an electrochemical reaction between dissimilar metals.

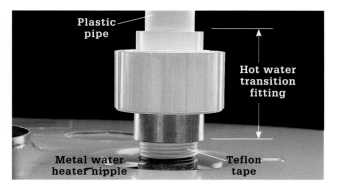

Plastic pipe

Hot water transition fitting

Metal water heater nipple

Teflon tape

Connect metal hot water pipe to plastic with a hot water transition fitting that prevents leaks caused by different expansion rates of materials. Metal pipe threads are wrapped with Teflon tape. Plastic pipe is solvent-glued to fitting.

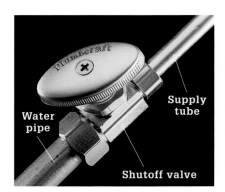

Water pipe

Supply tube

Shutoff valve

Connect a water pipe to any fixture supply tube, using a shutoff valve.

Fixture tailpiece

Coupling nut

Supply tube

Connect any supply tube to a fixture tailpiece with a coupling nut. The coupling nut compresses the bell-shaped end of the supply tube against the fixture tailpiece.

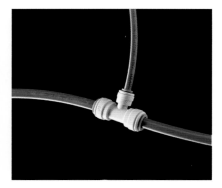

Specialty supply fittings can be used to supply portable water fixtures such as icemakers and hot water dispensers. The John-Guest Speed-Fit fitting shown here (see Resources, page 330) is designed to connect to clear tubing or the manufacturer's proprietary plastic supply tubing.

Shutoff Valves

Worn-out shutoff valves or supply tubes can cause water to leak underneath a sink or other fixture. First, try tightening the fittings with an adjustable wrench. If this does not fix the leak, replace the shutoff valves and supply tubes.

Shutoff valves are available in several fitting types. For copper pipes, valves with compression-type fittings (pages 212 to 213) are easiest to install. For plastic pipes, use grip-type valves. For galvanized iron pipes, use valves with female threads.

Older plumbing systems often were installed without fixture shutoff valves. When repairing or replacing plumbing fixtures, you may want to install shutoff valves if they are not already present.

Tools & Materials ▸

Hacksaw
Tubing cutter
Adjustable wrench
Tubing bender

Felt-tipped pen
Shutoff valves
Supply tubes
Pipe joint compound

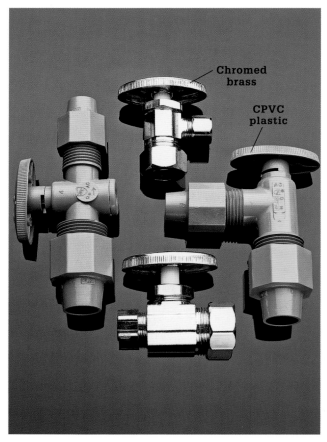

Shutoff valves allow you to shut off the water to an individual fixture so it can be repaired. They can be made from durable chromed brass or lightweight plastic. Shutoff valves come in ½" and ¾" diameters to match common water pipe sizes.

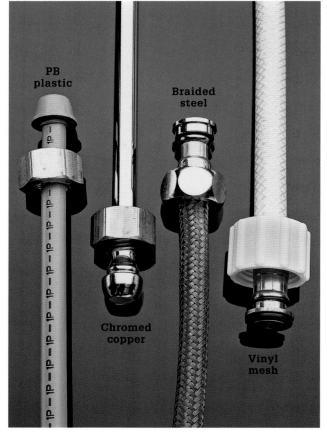

Supply tubes are used to connect water pipes to faucets, toilets, and other fixtures. They come in 12", 20", and 30" lengths. PB plastic and chromed copper tubes are inexpensive. Braided steel and vinyl mesh supply tubes are easy to install.

How to Install Shutoff Valves & Supply Tubes

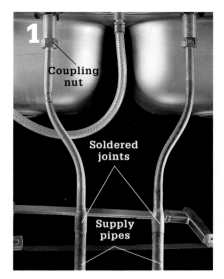

Turn off water at the main shutoff valve. Remove old supply pipes. If pipes are soldered copper, cut them off just below the soldered joint, using a hacksaw or tubing cutter. Make sure the cuts are straight. Unscrew the coupling nuts and discard the old pipes.

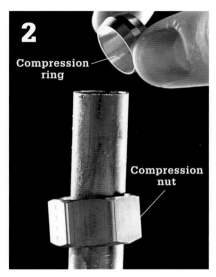

Slide a compression nut and a compression ring over the copper water pipe. Threads of the nut should face the end of the pipe.

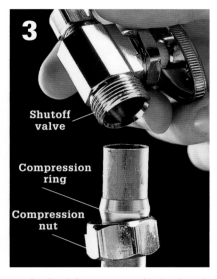

Apply pipe joint compound to the threads of the shutoff valve or compression nut. Screw the compression nut onto the shutoff valve and tighten with an adjustable wrench.

Bend chromed copper supply tube to reach from the tailpiece of the fixture to the shutoff valve, using a tubing bender. Bend the tube slowly to avoid kinking the metal.

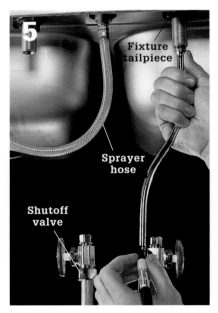

Position the supply tube between fixture tailpiece and the shutoff valve, and mark the tube to length. Cut the supply tube with a tubing cutter (page 270).

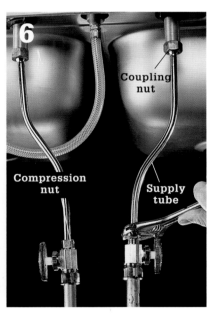

Attach the bell-shaped end of the supply tube to the fixture tailpiece with a coupling nut, then attach the other end to the shutoff valve with compression ring and nut. Tighten all fittings with an adjustable wrench.

Valves & Hose Bibs

Valves make it possible to shut off water at any point in the supply system. If a pipe breaks or a plumbing fixture begins to leak, you can shut off water to the damaged area so that it can be repaired. A hose bib is a faucet with a threaded spout, often used to connect rubber utility or appliance hoses.

Valves and hose bibs leak when washers or seals wear out. Replacement parts can be found in the same universal washer kits used to repair compression faucets. Coat replacement washers with heatproof grease to keep them soft and prevent cracking.

Remember to turn off the water before beginning work.

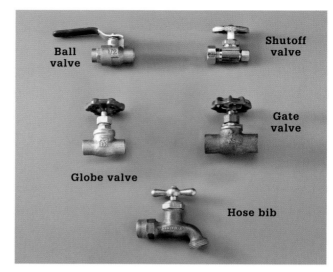

With the exception of chromed shutoff valves that are installed at individual fixtures (see previous pages), valves and hose bibs are heavy-duty fittings, usually with a brass body they are installed in-line to regulate water flow. Gate valves and globe valves are similar and are operated with a wheel-type handle that spins. Ball valves are operated with a handle much like a gas pipe stopcock and are considered by pros to be the most reliable. Hose bibs are spigots with a threaded end designed to accept a female hose coupling.

Tools & Materials ▸

Screwdriver
Adjustable wrench
Universal washer kit
Heatproof grease

How to Fix a Leaky Hose Bib

Remove the handle screw, and lift off the handle. Unscrew the packing nut with an adjustable wrench.

Unscrew the spindle from the valve body. Remove the stem screw and replace the stem washer. Replace the packing washer, and reassemble the valve.

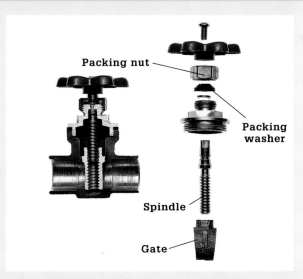

Gate valve has a movable brass wedge, or "gate," that screws up and down to control water flow. Gate valves may develop leaks around the handle. Repair leaks by replacing the packing washer or packing string found underneath the packing nut.

Globe valve has a curved chamber. Repair leaks around the handle by replacing the packing washer. If valve does not fully stop water flow when closed, replace the stem washer.

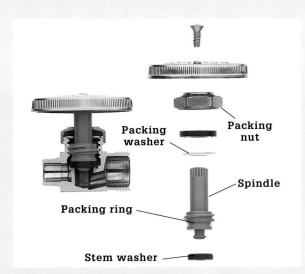

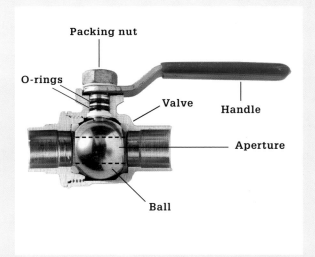

Shutoff valve controls water supply to one or more fixtures. A shutoff valve has a plastic spindle with a packing washer and a snap-on stem washer. Repair leaks around the handle by replacing the packing washer. If a valve does not fully stop water flow when closed, replace the stem washer. Shutoff valves with multiple outlets are available to supply several fixtures from a single supply.

Ball valve contains a metal ball with an aperture (or controlled hole) in the center. The ball is controlled by a handle. When the handle is turned the hole is positioned parallel to the valve (open) or perpendicular (closed).

Compression Fittings

Compression fittings are used to make connections that may need to be taken apart. Compression fittings are easy to disconnect and are often used to install supply tubes and fixture shutoff valves. Use compression fittings in places where it is unsafe or difficult to solder, such as in crawl spaces.

Compression fittings are used most often with flexible copper pipe. Flexible copper is soft enough to allow the compression ring to seat snugly, creating a watertight seal. Compression fittings also may be used to make connections with Type M rigid copper pipe.

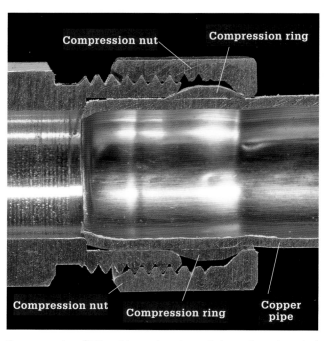

Compression fitting (shown in cutaway) shows how threaded compression nut forms seal by forcing the compression ring against the copper pipe. Compression ring is covered with pipe joint compound before assembling to ensure a perfect seal.

Tools & Materials ▸

Felt-tipped pen
Tubing cutter
   or hacksaw
Adjustable wrenches

Brass compression
   fittings
Pipe joint compound
   or Teflon tape

How to Attach Supply Tubes to Fixture Shutoff Valves with Compression Fittings

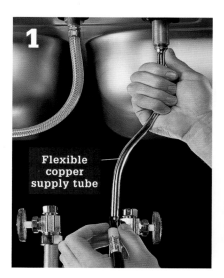

Bend flexible copper supply tube and mark to length. Include ½" for portion that will fit inside valve. Cut tube.

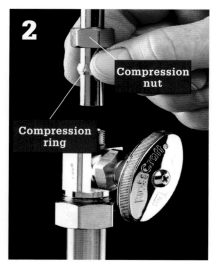

Slide the compression nut and then the compression ring over the end of the pipe. The threads of the nut should face the valve.

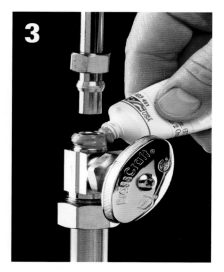

Apply a small amount of pipe joint compound to the threads. This lubricates the threads.

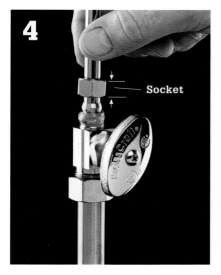

Insert the end of the pipe into the fitting so it fits flush against the bottom of the fitting socket.

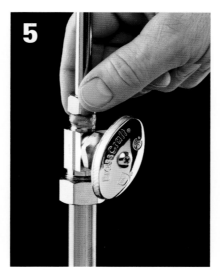

Slide the compression ring and nut against the threads of the valve. Hand tighten the nut onto the valve.

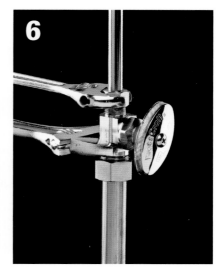

Tighten the compression nut with adjustable wrenches. Do not overtighten. Turn on the water and watch for leaks. If the fitting leaks, tighten the nut gently.

How to Join Two Copper Pipes with a Compression Union Fitting

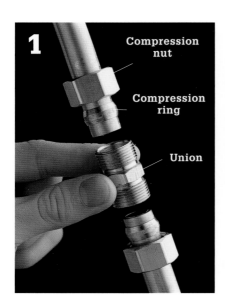

Slide compression nuts and rings over the ends of pipes. Place a threaded union between the pipes.

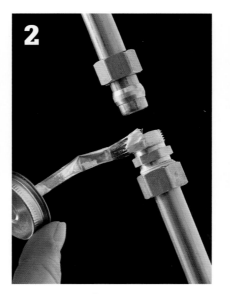

Apply a layer of pipe joint compound or Teflon tape to the union's threads, then screw compression nuts onto the union.

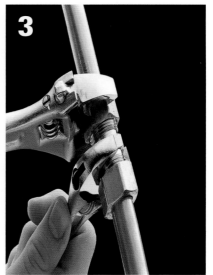

Hold the center of the union fitting with an adjustable wrench and use another wrench to tighten each compression nut one complete turn. Turn on the water. If the fitting leaks, tighten the nuts gently.

Gas Pipe Fittings

Few word combinations strike more fear into the hearts of liability lawyers than "do-it-yourself" and "gas." Of course there is good reason for this, as working with gas pipe and making gas hookups carry extremely high potential for catastrophe if errors are made. And that is why many municipalities insist that only licensed professionals may install or service gas lines and appliances. If your municipality is one of these, follow the law and keep your hands off the gas. It simply is not worth the risk of doing it yourself.

If your area allows ambitious homeowners to work on their own gas lines and appliances, you should still take some extra time considering whether you really ought to call a professional. If you do decide to proceed, follow all safety precautions to the letter and be very, very careful.

Technically, working with gas pipe is not too different from working with water supply tubing or DWV pipe. For home fuel, gas comes in two forms: natural gas, which is delivered via a pipeline, and liquefied petroleum gas (LP gas), which is stored in a refillable tank or "bottle" at the property. Appliances cannot use these gases interchangeably, though conversion kits are available. Make sure your appliance matches the type of gas you have available.

Tools & Materials ▸

Adjustable wrench
Gas pipe thread
    compound
Leak detector
    solution
Teflon tape

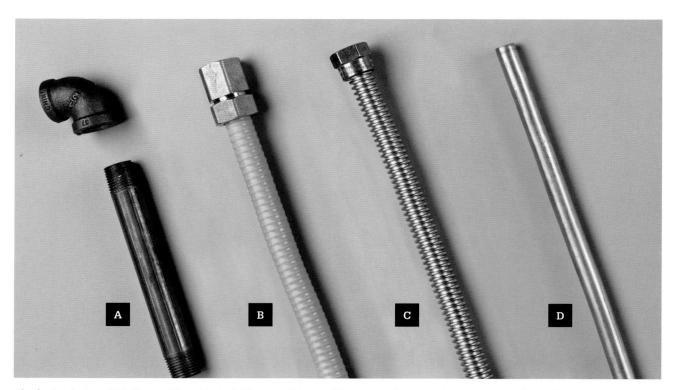

Black steel pipe (A) is the traditional material for gas piping and is acceptable everywhere. Corrugated stainless steel tubing is coated with PVC (B). Because it is flexible, fewer connections need to be made and the possibility for leaks is diminished. Some areas may not allow this piping. Flexible pipe (C) is often used for connecting appliances to supply lines. Soft copper (D) may be used for gas in some areas, but is not allowable for gas lines in other jurisdictions.

Parts of a Gas Delivery System

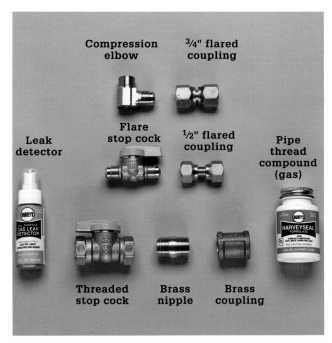

Gas valves and fittings may look similar to those used for water, but use only gas-rated valves and fittings for gas installations. Valves feature quarter-turn on to off and are available with threaded or flare connections. Fittings are available in many sizes measured by outside diameter (O.D.). Fittings can be either are threaded or flared and male or female. Thread compound and leak detector solution are important parts of the gas plumbing tool kit.

A natural gas meter has a pressure regulator and shut off valve. The shut off valve is activated with a special gas shut off wrench, or an adjustable wrench.

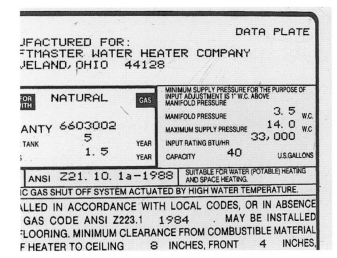

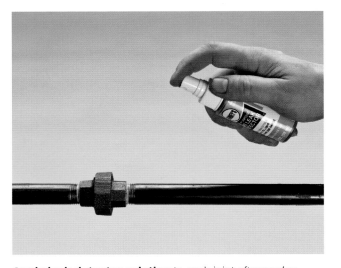

Pipe size requirements for gas line installation are determined by adding up the input BTUs necessary for each appliance, plus the distance from the supply line to the appliance. Input BTU requirements are listed on identification tags that are required to be attached to all gas appliances.

Apply leak detector solution to each joint after you've restored the gas flow to make sure there are no leaks. Leaking gas will cause bubbles in the solution. Do not use ordinary soap—it can lead to corrosion of the metal around the seal.

Working with Black Pipe

Working with black pipe is virtually the same as working with galvanized pipe (See pages 296 to 299). The pipe used must be new or, if reused, used previously only for gas fittings.

Black pipe threads are cut in a tapered manner referred to as National Pipe Taper (NPT). The diameter of the male-threaded pipe is smaller at the end. This is why it is easier to thread a fitting on initially, but gets more difficult with each turn. MPT and FPT refer to male and female threads cut to this standard.

All threads should have pipe joint compound applied before being fitted and all joints must be tested with leak detector solution once the installation is complete. Pipe compounds may be gray, thick paste, or white PTFE (Teflon) paste. You may also use yellow PTFE tape. White PTFE tape that's commonly used for waterlines and hookups is not acceptable for gas line use.

After completing an installation and turning the gas on, each connection must be checked for leaks. Use leak detecting solution sprayed around each joint. If gas is leaking, the solution will bubble and foam. Do not use detergent as a leak detector—it contains corrosive chemicals that may degrade the connection. Tightening the leaky joint will mean that all subsequent joints need to be tightened, not loosened, to accommodate the new alignment. Loosening will potentially create more leaks.

Black pipe is available in a wide variety of threaded lengths. Shorter lengths are referred to as nipples. If you can't make the standard lengths work for your application, most pipe retailers have thread cutting machines and will cut and thread pipe to length, usually for a fee.

Black pipe fittings include Ts, reducers, elbows with two female-threaded ends, street elbows with a male- and a female-threaded end, couplings, and caps.

Shut off the gas by turning the handle of the nearest in-line stopcock so it is perpendicular to the gas line.

Apply an approved gas pipe thread compound liberally all over the threads.

Hand tighten the fittings on to the threaded pipe as far as you can.

After hand tightening, turn the fitting or pipe at least one full turn to tighten. In order to achieve the proper alignment, you may tighten up to two full turns, but do not overtighten. Use one pipe wrench to stabilize the fixed pipe or fitting, while using the second wrench to tighten the movable pipe or fitting.

How to Make a Flared Fitting

Flared fittings are used to connect soft copper gas supply pipes to a threaded nipple: either on a gas appliance or another fitting. The key to success using a flared fitting is making a perfectly flared end in the tubing with a flaring tool. Flaring tools can be purchased at most hardware stores. Make sure the brass flared fitting you purchase matches the diameter of the soft copper tubing you are using. Handle the soft copper gently and avoid overtightening the flaring tool, which can cause the copper tube to crack

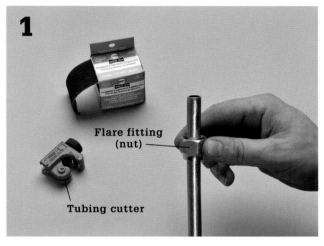

Cut the end of the soft copper tubing with a tubing cutter and deburr the ends. Slide the brass flare nut over the cut end, with the threaded female end facing out.

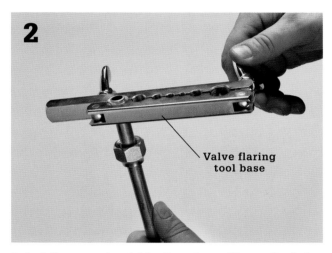

Select the correct outside diameter setting on the flaring tool base strip and then insert the tubing end into the opening. Clamp the base shut tightly.

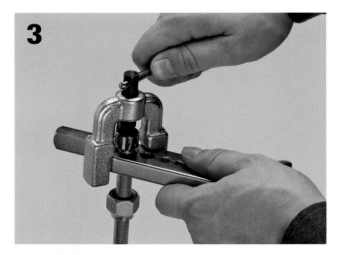

Orient the flaring cone in the reamer over the open end of the tubing and tighten the flaring tool until the cone is seated fully in the tubing end, causing it to flare out.

Remove the tool and inspect the flared tube end, making sure there are no cracks and the nut fits cleanly against the flared tube end. Attach the nut to the threaded nipple and tighten to make the joint. Test for leaks.

APPENDIX: Planning Your Project

Start planning by drawing maps. Mapping your home's plumbing system is a good way to familiarize yourself with the plumbing layout and can help you when planning plumbing renovation projects. With a good map, you can envision the best spots for new fixtures and plan new pipe routes more efficiently. Maps also help in emergencies, when you need to locate burst or leaking pipes quickly.

Draw a plumbing map for each floor on tracing paper, so you can overlay floors and still read the information below. Make your drawings to scale and have all plumbing fixtures marked. Fixture templates and tracing paper are available at drafting supply stores.

Snoop around your basement for clues about the locations of supply, drain, vent, and gas pipes in your walls.

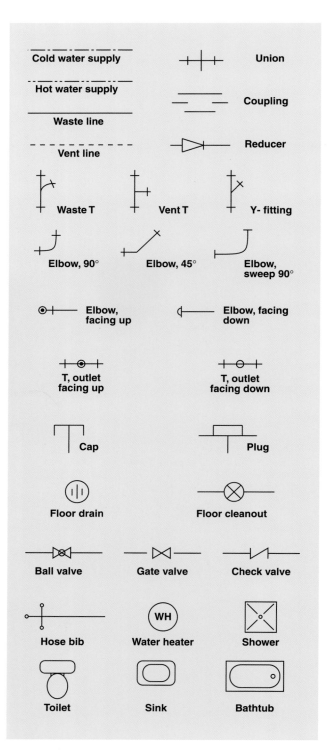

Cold water supply
Hot water supply
Waste line
Vent line
Waste T
Vent T
Y-fitting
Elbow, 90°
Elbow, 45°
Elbow, sweep 90°
Elbow, facing up
Elbow, facing down
T, outlet facing up
T, outlet facing down
Cap
Plug
Floor drain
Floor cleanout
Ball valve
Gate valve
Check valve
Hose bib
Water heater
Shower
Toilet
Sink
Bathtub

Union
Coupling
Reducer

Use standard plumbing symbols on your map to identify the components of your plumbing system. These symbols will help you and your building inspector follow connections and transitions more easily.

How to Map Your Plumbing System

Draw a floorplan for the basement. The drawing should be scaled, legible, and accurate. Note the plumbing features using the symbols on the previous page.

Draw the first floor on a separate piece of transparent drafting paper, using the same scale that you used for the basement. Draw separate floorplans for any additional floors.

Overlay upper-floor diagrams onto the first-floor map, and mark the location of pipes—generally they will extend directly up from fixtures below. If first-story and second-story fixtures are not closely aligned, the supply pipes follow an offset route in wall or floor cavities. By overlaying the maps, you can see the relation and distance between fixtures and accurately estimate pipe routes.

Option: Use floor plans of your house to create your plumbing map. Convert the general outlines for each story to tracing paper. The walls can be drawn larger than scale to fit all the plumbing symbols you will map, but keep overall room dimensions and plumbing fixtures to scale. Be sure to make diagrams for basements and attic spaces as well.

Understanding Plumbing Codes

The plumbing inspector is the final authority when it comes to evaluating your work. By visually examining and testing your new plumbing, the inspector ensures that your work is safe and functional.

The plumbing code is the set of regulations that building officials and inspectors use to evaluate your project plans and the quality of your work. Codes vary from region to region, but most are based on the National Uniform Plumbing Code, the authority we used in the development of this book.

Code books are available for reference at bookstores and government offices. However, they are highly technical, difficult-to-read manuals. More user-friendly for do-it-yourselfers are the variety of code handbooks available at bookstores and libraries. These handbooks are based on the National Uniform Plumbing Code but are easier to read and include many helpful diagrams and photos.

Plumbing code handbooks sometimes discuss three different plumbing "zones" in an effort to accommodate variations in regulations from state to state. The states included in each zone are listed below.

Zone 1: Washington, Oregon, California, Nevada, Idaho, Montana, Wyoming, North Dakota, South Dakota, Minnesota, Iowa, Nebraska, Kansas, Utah, Arizona, Colorado, New Mexico, Indiana, parts of Texas.

Zone 2: Alabama, Arkansas, Louisiana, Tennessee, North Carolina, Mississippi, Georgia, Florida, South Carolina, parts of Texas, parts of Maryland, parts of Delaware, parts of Oklahoma, parts of West Virginia.

Zone 3: Virginia, Kentucky, Missouri, Illinois, Michigan, Ohio, Pennsylvania, New York, Connecticut, Massachusetts, Vermont, New Hampshire, Rhode Island, New Jersey, parts of Delaware, parts of West Virginia, parts of Maine, parts of Maryland, parts of Oklahoma.

Remember that your local plumbing code always supersedes the national code. Local codes may be more restrictive than the national code. Your local building inspector is a valuable source of information and may provide you with a convenient summary sheet of the regulations that apply to your project.

GETTING A PERMIT

To ensure public safety, your community requires that you obtain a permit for most plumbing projects, including most of the projects demonstrated in this book.

When you visit your city building inspection office to apply for a permit, the building official will want to review three drawings of your plumbing project: a site plan, a water supply diagram, and a drain-waste-vent diagram. These drawings are described on this page. If the official is satisfied that your project meets code requirements, he or she will issue you a plumbing permit, which is your legal permission to begin work. The building official also will specify an inspection schedule for your project. As your project nears completion, you will be asked to arrange for an inspector to visit your home while the pipes are exposed to review the installation and ensure its safety.

Although do-it-yourselfers often complete complex plumbing projects without obtaining a permit or having the work inspected, we strongly urge you to comply with the legal requirements in your area. A flawed plumbing system can be dangerous, and it can potentially threaten the value of your home.

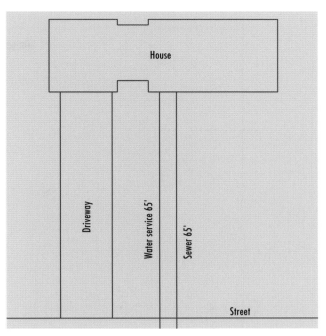

The site plan shows the location of the water main and sewer main with respect to your yard and home. The distances from your foundation to the water main and from the foundation to the main sewer should be indicated on the site plan.

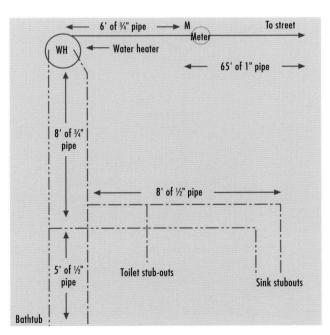

The supply riser diagram shows the length of the hot and cold water pipes and the relation of the fixtures to one another. The inspector will use this diagram to determine the proper size for the new water supply pipes in your system.

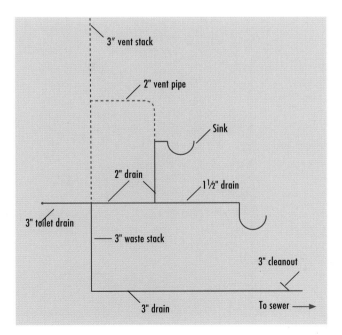

A DWV diagram shows the routing of drain and vent pipes in your system. Make sure to indicate the lengths of drain pipes and the distances between fixtures. The inspector will use this diagram to determine if you have properly sized the drain traps, drain pipes, and vent pipes in your project.

Sizing for Water Distribution Pipes

Fixture	Unit rating
Toilet	3
Vanity sink	1
Shower	2
Bathtub	2
Dishwasher	2
Kitchen sink	2
Clothes washer	2
Utility sink	2
Sillcock	3

Size of service pipe from street	Size of distribution pipe from water meter	Maximum length (ft.)— total fixture units					
		40	60	80	100	150	200
¾"	½"	9	8	7	6	5	4
¾"	¾"	27	23	19	17	14	11
¾"	1"	44	40	36	33	28	23
1"	1"	60	47	41	36	30	25
1"	1¼"	102	87	76	67	52	44

Water distribution pipes are the main pipes extending from the water meter throughout the house, supplying water to the branch pipes leading to individual fixtures. To determine the size of the distribution pipes, you must first calculate the total demand in "fixture units" (above, left) and the overall length of the water supply lines, from the street hookup through the water meter and to the most distant fixture in the house. Then, use the second table (above, right) to calculate the minimum size for the water distribution pipes. Note that the fixture unit capacity depends partly on the size of the street-side pipe that delivers water to your meter.

Sizes for Branch Pipes & Supply Tubes

Fixture	Min. branch pipe size	Min. supply tube size
Toilet	½"	⅜"
Vanity sink	½"	⅜"
Shower	½"	½"
Bathtub	½"	½"
Dishwasher	½"	½"
Kitchen sink	½"	½"
Clothes washer	½"	½"
Utility sink	½"	½"
Sillcock	¾"	N.A.
Water heater	¾"	N.A.

Branch pipes are the water supply lines that run from the distribution pipes toward the individual fixtures. Supply tubes are the vinyl, chromed copper, or braided tubes that carry water from the branch pipes to the fixtures. Use the chart above as a guide when sizing branch pipes and supply tubes.

Valve Requirements

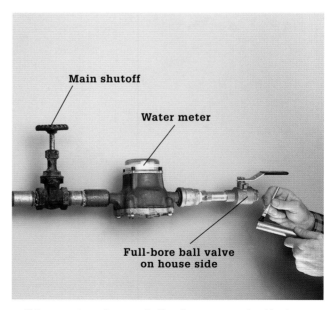

Main shutoff

Water meter

Full-bore ball valve on house side

Full-bore gate valves or ball valves are required in the following locations: on both the street side and house side of the water meter; on the inlet pipes for water heaters and heating system boilers. Individual fixtures should have accessible shutoff valves, but these need not be full-bore valves. All sillcocks must have individual control valves located inside the house.

Modifying Water Pressure

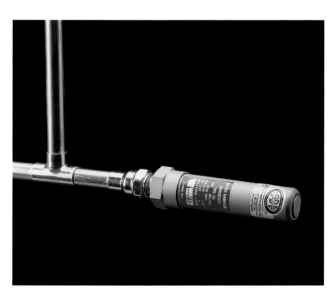

Pressure-reducing valve

Pressure-reducing valve (shown above) is required if the water pressure coming into your home is greater than 80 pounds per square inch (psi). The reducing valve should be installed near the point where the water service enters the building. A booster pump may be required if the water pressure in your home is below 40 psi.

Preventing Water Hammer

Water hammer arresters may be required by code. Water hammer is a problem that may occur when the fast-acting valves on washing machines or other appliances trap air and cause pipes to vibrate against framing members. The arrester works as a shock absorber and has a watertight diaphragm inside. It is mounted to a T-fitting installed near the appliance (see page 294).

Anti-Siphon Devices

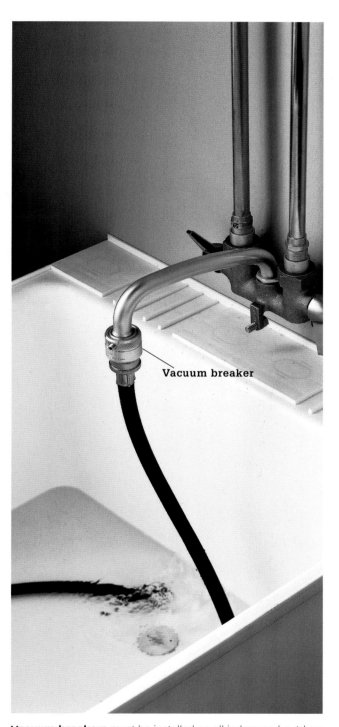

Vacuum breaker

Vacuum breakers must be installed on all indoor and outdoor hose bibs and any outdoor branch pipes that run underground (page 177, step 7). Vacuum breakers prevent contaminated water from being drawn into the water supply pipes in the event of a sudden drop in water pressure in the water main. When a drop in pressure produces a partial vacuum, the breaker prevents siphoning by allowing air to enter the pipes.

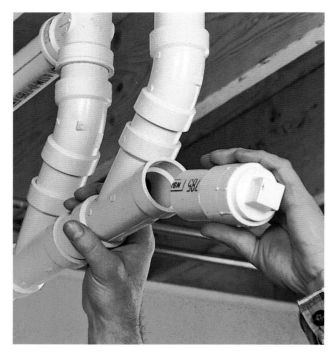

Drain cleanouts make your DWV system easier to service. In most areas, the plumbing code requires that you place cleanouts at the end of every horizontal drain run. Where horizontal runs are not accessible, removable drain traps will suffice as cleanouts.

Pipe Support Intervals

Type of pipe	Vertical-run support interval	Horizontal-run support interval
Copper	10 ft.	6 ft.
PEX	5 ft.	3 ft.
CPVC	10 ft.	3 ft.
PVC	10 ft.	4 ft.
Steel	12 ft.	10 ft.
Iron	15 ft.	5 ft.

Minimum intervals for supporting pipes are determined by the type of pipe and its orientation in the system. See page 40 for acceptable pipe support materials. Remember that the measurements shown above are minimum requirements; local code may require supports at closer intervals.

Fixture Units & Minimum Trap Size

Fixture	Fixture units	Min. trap size
Shower	2	2"
Vanity sink	1	1¼"
Bathtub	2	1½"
Dishwasher	2	1½"
Kitchen sink	2	1½"
Kitchen sink*	3	1½"
Clothes washer	2	1½"
Utility sink	2	1½"
Floor drain	1	2"

*Kitchen sink with attached food disposer

Minimum trap size for fixtures is determined by the drain fixture unit rating, a unit of measure assigned by the plumbing code. *Note: Kitchen sinks rate 3 units if they include an attached food disposer, 2 units otherwise.*

Sizes for Horizontal & Vertical Drain Pipes

Pipe size	Maximum fixture units for horizontal branch drain	Maximum fixture units for vertical drain stacks
1¼"	1	2
1½"	3	4
2"	6	10
2½"	12	20
3"	20	30
4"	160	240

Drain pipe sizes are determined by the load on the pipes, as measured by the total fixture units. Horizontal drain pipes less than 3" in diameter should slope ¼" per foot toward the main drain. Pipes 3" or more in diameter should slope ⅛" per foot. *Note: Horizontal or vertical drain pipes for a toilet must be 3" or larger.*

Vent Pipe Sizes, Critical Distances

Size of fixture drain	Minimum vent pipe size	Maximum critical distance
1¼"	1¼"	2½ ft.
1½"	1¼"	3½ ft.
2"	1½"	5 ft.
3"	2"	6 ft.
4"	3"	10 ft.

Vent pipes are usually one pipe size smaller than the drain pipes they serve. Code requires that the distance between the drain trap and the vent pipe fall within a maximum "critical distance," a measurement that is determined by the size of the fixture drain. Use this chart to determine both the minimum size for the vent pipe and the maximum critical distance.

Vent Pipe Orientation to Drain Pipe

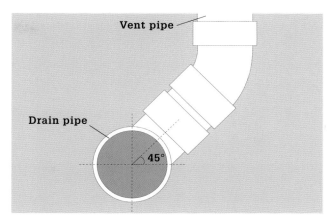

Vent pipes must extend in an upward direction from drains, no less than 45º from horizontal. This ensures that waste water cannot flow into the vent pipe and block it. At the opposite end, a new vent pipe should connect to an existing vent pipe or main waste-vent stack at a point at least 6" above the highest fixture draining into the system.

Wet Venting

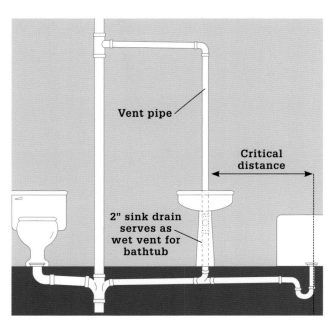

Wet vents are pipes that serve as a vent for one fixture and a drain for another. The sizing of a wet vent is based on the total fixture units it supports (opposite page): a 3" wet vent can serve up to 12 fixture units; a 2" wet vent is rated for 4 fixture units; a 1½" wet vent, for only 1 fixture unit. *Note: The distance between the wet-vented fixture and the wet vent itself must be no more than the maximum critical distance (chart above).*

Auxiliary Venting

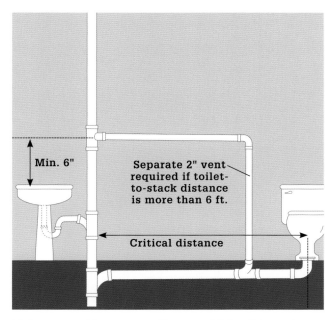

Fixtures must have an auxiliary vent if the distance to the main waste-vent stack exceeds the critical distance (chart above). A toilet, for example, should have a separate vent pipe if it is located more than 6 ft. from the main waste-vent stack. This secondary vent pipe should connect to the stack or an existing vent pipe at a point at least 6" above the highest fixture on the system.

Testing New Plumbing Pipes

When the building inspector comes to review your new plumbing, he or she may require that you perform a pressure test on the DWV and water supply lines as he or she watches. The inspection and test should be performed after the system is completed but before the new pipes are covered with wallboard. To ensure that the inspection goes smoothly, it is a good idea to perform your own pretest, so you can locate and repair any problems before the inspector visits.

The DWV system is tested by blocking off the new drain and vent pipes, then pressuring the system with air to see if it leaks. At the fixture stub-outs, the DWV pipes can be capped off or plugged with test balloons designed for this purpose. The air pump, pressure gauge, and test balloons required to test the DWV system can be obtained at tool rental centers.

Testing the water supply lines is a simple matter of turning on the water and examining the joints for leaks. If you find a leak, you will have to drain the pipes, then remake the faulty joints.

A pressure gauge and air pump are used to test DWV lines. The system is first blocked off at each fixture and at points near where the new drain and vent pipes connect to the main stack. Air is then pumped into the system to a pressure of 5 pounds per square inch (psi). To pass inspection, the system must hold this pressure for 15 minutes.

How to Test New DWV Pipes

Insert a test balloon into the test T-fittings at the top and bottom of the new DWV line, blocking the pipes entirely. *Note: Ordinary T-fittings installed near the bottom of the drain line and near the top of the vent line are generally used for test fittings.*

Block toilet drains with a test balloon designed for a closet bend. Large test balloons may have to be inflated with an air pump.

Cap off the remaining fixture drains by solvent-gluing test caps onto the stub-outs. After the system is tested, these caps are simply knocked loose with a hammer.

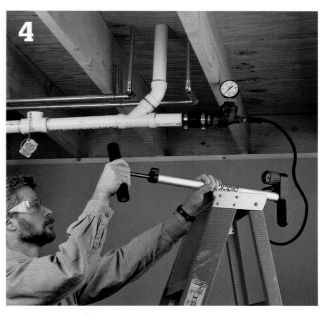

At a cleanout fitting, insert a weenie—a special test balloon with an air gauge and inflation valve. Attach an air pump to the valve on the weenie and pressurize the pipes to 5 psi. Watch the pressure gauge for 15 minutes to ensure that the system does not lose pressure.

If the DWV system loses air when pressurized, check each joint for leaks by rubbing soapy water over the fittings and looking for active bubbles. When you identify a problem joint, cut away the existing fitting and solvent-glue a new fitting in place, using couplings and short lengths of pipe.

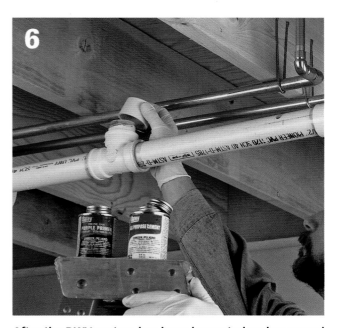

After the DWV system has been inspected and approved by a building official, remove the test balloons and close the test T-fittings by solvent-gluing caps onto the open inlets.

Glossary

Access panel — Opening in a wall or ceiling that provides access to the plumbing system

Air admittance valve — A valve that allows air into a drain line in order to facilitate proper draining. Often used where traditional vent pipe would be difficult to install.

Appliance — Powered device that uses water, such as a water heater, dishwasher, washing machine, whirlpool, or water softener

Auger — Flexible tool used for clearing obstructions in drain lines

Ballcock — Valve that controls the water supply entering a toilet tank

Blow bag — Expanding rubber device that attaches to a garden hose; used for clearing floor drains

Branch drain line — Pipe that connects additional lines to a drain system

Branch line — Pipe that connects additional lines to a water supply system

Cleanout — Cover in a waste pipe or trap that provides access for cleaning

Closet auger — Flexible rod used to clear obstructions in toilets

Closet bend — Curved fitting that fits between a closet flange and a toilet drain

Closet flange — Ring at the opening of a toilet drain, used as the base for a toilet

Coupling — Fitting that connects two pieces of pipe

DWV — Drain, waste, and vent; the system for removing water from a house

DWV stack — Pipe that connects house drain system to a sewer line at the bottom and vents air to outside of house at the top

Elbow — Angled fitting that changes the direction of a pipe

Fixture — Device that uses water, such as a sink, tub, shower, sillcock, or toilet

Flapper (tank ball) — Rubber seal that controls the flow of water from a toilet tank to a toilet bowl

Flux (soldering paste) — Paste applied to metal joints before soldering to increase joint strength

Hand auger (snake) — Hand tool with flexible shaft, used for clearing clogs in drain lines

Hose bib — Any faucet spout that is threaded to accept a hose

I.D. — Inside diameter; plumbing pipes are classified by I.D.

Loop vent — A special type of vent configuration used in kitchen sink island installations

Main shutoff valve — Valve that controls water supply to an entire house; usually next to the water meter

Motorized auger — Power tool with flexible shaft, used for clearing tree roots from sewer lines

Nipple — Pipe with threaded ends

O.D. — Outside diameter

Plumber's putty — A soft material used for sealing joints between fixtures and supply or drain parts

Reducer — A fitting that connects pipes of different sizes

Riser — Assembly of water supply fittings and pipes that distributes water upward

Run — Assembly of pipes that extends from water supply to fixture, or from drain to stack

Saddle valve — Fitting clamped to copper supply pipe, with hollow spike that punctures the pipe to divert water to another device, usually a dishwasher or refrigerator icemaker

Sanitary fitting — Fitting that joins DWV pipes; allows solid material to pass through without clogging

Shutoff valve — Valve that controls the water supply for one fixture or appliance

Sillcock — Compression faucet used on the outside of a house

Soil stack — Main vertical drain line, which carries waste from all branch drains to a sewer line

Solder — Metal alloy used for permanently joining metal (usually copper) pipes

T-fitting — Fitting shaped like the letter T used for creating or joining branch lines

Trap — Curved section of drain, filled with standing water, that prevents sewer gases from entering a house

Union — Fitting that joins two sections of pipe but can be disconnected without cutting

Vacuum breaker — Attachment for outdoor and below-ground fixtures that prevents waste water from entering supply lines if water supply pressure drops

Wet vent — Pipe that serves as a drain for one fixture and as a vent for another

Y-fitting — Fitting shaped like the letter Y used for creating or joining branch lines

Metric Conversion Chart

Lumber Dimensions

Nominal - U.S.	Actual - U.S. (in inches)	Metric	Nominal - U.S.	Actual - U.S. (in inches)	Metric
1 × 2	¾ × 1½	19 × 38 mm	1½ × 4	1¼ × 3½	32 × 89 mm
1 × 3	¾ × 2½	19 × 64 mm	1½ × 6	1¼ × 5½	32 × 140 mm
1 × 4	¾ × 3½	19 × 89 mm	1½ × 8	1¼ × 7¼	32 × 184 mm
1 × 5	¾ × 4½	19 × 114 mm	1½ × 10	1¼ × 9¼	32 × 235 mm
1 × 6	¾ × 5½	19 × 140 mm	1½ × 12	1¼ × 11¼	32 × 286 mm
1 × 7	¾ × 6¼	19 × 159 mm	2 × 4	1½ × 3½	38 × 89 mm
1 × 8	¾ × 7¼	19 × 184 mm	2 × 6	1½ × 5½	38 × 140 mm
1 × 10	¾ × 9¼	19 × 235 mm	2 × 8	1½ × 7¼	38 × 184 mm
1 × 12	¾ × 11¼	19 × 286 mm	2 × 10	1½ × 9¼	38 × 235 mm
1¼ × 4	1 × 3½	25 × 89 mm	2 × 12	1½ × 11¼	38 × 286 mm
1¼ × 6	1 × 5½	25 × 140 mm	3 × 6	2½ × 5½	64 × 140 mm
1¼ × 8	1 × 7¼	25 × 184 mm	4 × 4	3½ × 3½	89 × 89 mm
1¼ × 10	1 × 9¼	25 × 235 mm	4 × 6	3½ × 5½	89 × 140 mm
1¼ × 12	1 × 11¼	25 × 286 mm			

Metric Conversions

To Convert:	To:	Multiply by:	To Convert:	To:	Multiply by:
Inches	Millimeters	25.4	Millimeters	Inches	0.039
Inches	Centimeters	2.54	Centimeters	Inches	0.394
Feet	Meters	0.305	Meters	Feet	3.28
Yards	Meters	0.914	Meters	Yards	1.09
Square inches	Square centimeters	6.45	Square centimeters	Square inches	0.155
Square feet	Square meters	0.093	Square meters	Square feet	10.8
Square yards	Square meters	0.836	Square meters	Square yards	1.2
Ounces	Milliliters	30.0	Milliliters	Ounces	.033
Pints (U.S.)	Liters	0.473 (Imp. 0.568)	Liters	Pints (U.S.)	2.114 (Imp. 1.76)
Quarts (U.S.)	Liters	0.946 (Imp. 1.136)	Liters	Quarts (U.S.)	1.057 (Imp. 0.88)
Gallons (U.S.)	Liters	3.785 (Imp. 4.546)	Liters	Gallons (U.S.)	0.264 (Imp. 0.22)
Ounces	Grams	28.4	Grams	Ounces	0.035
Pounds	Kilograms	0.454	Kilograms	Pounds	2.2

Counterbore, Shank, & Pilot Hole Diameters

Screw Size	Counterbore Diameter for Screw Head (in inches)	Clearance Hole for Screw Shank (in inches)	Pilot Hole Diameter	
			Hard Wood (in inches)	Soft Wood (in inches)
#1	.146 (⁹⁄₆₄)	⁵⁄₆₄	³⁄₆₄	¹⁄₃₂
#2	¼	³⁄₃₂	³⁄₆₄	¹⁄₃₂
#3	¼	⁷⁄₆₄	¹⁄₁₆	³⁄₆₄
#4	¼	⅛	¹⁄₁₆	³⁄₆₄
#5	¼	⅛	⁵⁄₆₄	¹⁄₁₆
#6	⁵⁄₁₆	⁹⁄₆₄	³⁄₃₂	⁵⁄₆₄
#7	⁵⁄₁₆	⁵⁄₃₂	³⁄₃₂	⁵⁄₆₄
#8	⅜	¹¹⁄₆₄	⅛	³⁄₃₂
#9	⅜	¹¹⁄₆₄	⅛	³⁄₃₂
#10	⅜	³⁄₁₆	⅛	⁷⁄₆₄
#11	½	³⁄₁₆	⁵⁄₃₂	⁹⁄₆₄
#12	½	⁷⁄₃₂	⁹⁄₆₄	⅛

Resources

American Standard
800 442 1902
www.americanstandard-us.com

General Electric
www.ge.com

Hakatai
888 667 2429
www.hakatai.com
Featured on page 112, 114, 125

International Assoc. of Plumbing & Mechanical Officials
909 472 4100
www.iapmo.org

International Code Council
800 284 4406
www.iccsafe.org

John Guest Co.
Speedfit push-in fittings
www.johnguest.com

Kleer Drain
www.kleerdrain.com

Kleve Inc.
952 941 4211
www.kleveheating.com

Kohler
800 4 KOHLER
www.kohlerco.com

National Kitchen & Bathroom Assoc. (NKBA)
800 843 6522
www.nkba.com

Plumbing and Drainage Institute
978 557 0720
www.pdionline.org

Price Pfister
800 624 2120
Www.pricepfister.com

Swanstone
800 325 7008
Www.swanstone.com

Toto
800 350 8686
www.totousa.com

World Plumbing Council
+44 17 08 47 27 91
email: secretariat@worldplumbing.org
www.worldplumbing.org

Credits

p. 13 photo Terry J Alcorn / www.istock.com
p. 18 photo courtesy of Kohler
p. 19 photos courtesy of Price Pfister
p. 29 photo courtesy of GE
P. 48 photos courtesy of Price Pfister
p. 64 photo courtesy of Ceramic Tiles of Italy
p. 71 photos courtesy of Ceramic Tiles of Italy
p. 72 photo courtesy of American Standard
p. 73 photo (top left) courtesy of Kohler
p. 80 photo courtesy of Kohler
p. 96 bidet courtesy of Kohler
p. 97 photo courtesy of Toto
p. 100 urinal courtesy of Kohler

p. 101 (top left & right) photos courtesy of Kohler
p. 101 (lower left) photo Auke Holwerda / www.istock.com
p. 101 (lower right) photo courtesy of Kohler
p. 115 photo Jennifer Morgan / www.istock.com
p. 120 photo courtesy of Kohler
p. 122 photo courtesy of GE
p. 132 photo Nicola Gavin / www.istock.com
p. 137 (lower left & right) photos courtesy of Kohler
p. 137 (top right) photo courtesy of Ceramic Tiles of Italy
p. 140 (top) photo courtesy of Swanstone
p. 226 photo courtesy of Kohler
p. 315 photo Norman Pogson / www.istock.com

Index

Also From CREATIVE PUBLISHING international

ISBN 1-58923-355-7

ISBN 1-58923-356-5

Creative Publishing
international

400 First Avenue North • Suite 300 • Minneapolis, MN 55401 • www.creativepub.com

CREATIVE PUBLISHING international

Creative Publishing
international

400 First Avenue North • Suite 300 • Minneapolis, MN 55401 • 800-328-0590, opt 2 • www.creativepub.com